Acknowledgement

We acknowledge the
on which we work and
made – the Boon Wur
Kaurna, Kurnai, Larr
peoples. We pay our

The First People
storytellers, the first communities. Sovereignty has never been ceded; this land always was, and always will be, Aboriginal land.

'This book should be a seminal work in Australian letters.'

Nam Le

'*Against Disappearance* is hot with guts. Each startling essay complicates memory in this colony and beyond. When brought together, they present memory and presence as a conversation among those forced to the margins of power, rather than as a canon that any one of us can hold alone. Gracious but without flinching, these essayists interrogate just how we and they come to publicly remember and be remembered.'

Alison Whittaker

'This book gets to the very heart of witness, memory, archive and what it means to write. An incredible chorus of why multitudes matter. It is magnificent. I want to press *Against Disappearance* into the hands of everyone I know.'

Jazz Money

'Exciting, fresh, and profound. A diverse collection of First Nations and Writers of Colour, whose stories write underneath, between and above the mainstream to interrogate the nation. This collection will shift the way we think about and read creative nonfiction in the future.'

Jeanine Leane

'Not written for white readers or to industry specifications, uncompromising, non-pandering, filled with love, awash with talent, this collection of sovereign essays sets blisteringly high standards of integrity and originality.'

Maria Tumarkin

'This is truly an explosive anthology of exciting voices you will be hearing from years from now. Each essay is a marvel in itself, a microcosm of insight and inventiveness; and together they make up the brilliant future of new Australian writing.'

Alice Pung

AGAINST DISAPPEARANCE

ESSAYS on MEMORY

EDITED by
LEAH JING MCINTOSH
and ADOLFO ARANJUEZ

PANTERA
PRESS

Published in Australia in 2022
by Pantera Press

In partnership with *Liminal*
www.liminalmag.com

ISBN: 978-0-6489875-8-1 (Paperback)
ISBN: 978-0-6489875-9-8 (eBook)

A catalogue record for this book is available from the National Library of Australia

Cover photography by Thy Tran
Cover design and typesetting by Annie Luo
Proofreading by Jamali Bowden, Farzeen Imtiaz, Nadia Maunsell,
Jasmin McGaughey, Lucia Tường Vy Nguyễn, Marina Sano, Aditya Sud,
Kirsty van der Veer and Katherine Wong
Typeset in Whyte, by DINAMO, an independent foundry, and Williams Caslon Text

Printed and bound in Australia by McPherson's Printing Group

This book has been supported by the Pantera Press Foundation, with thanks to Writers Victoria for acting as an auspicing partner for this work.

The paper this book is printed on is certified against the Forest Stewardship Council® Standards. McPherson's Printing Group holds FSC® chain of custody certification SA-COC-005379. FSC® promotes environmentally responsible, socially beneficial and economically viable management of the world's forests

Archives

Opacities

Introduction

Leah Jing McIntosh

When we were making this book, I kept accidentally referring to it as '*After*' *Disappearance*. Each time I did, my wonderful co-editor, Adolfo Aranjuez, would gently correct me. It became a sort of joke between us, an inexplicable slippage. I have been thinking about the space between *after* and *against*. What happens after a disappearance? Loss opens into a clear blue horizon, darkening with all we do not know.

In so-called Australia, we seem to be citizens of an *after*. The enforced disappearance of cultures is often framed as natural or unavoidable, the way of things, when it is in fact the opposite: hegemonic power is as much about the stories it actively erases as those it tells. It suits the colony to mythologise a terra nullius, to declare Indigenous cultures non-existent and to work to make them so, rewriting cultures that have always been here into nothing. If nothing was here, then nothing could be murdered – or so the logic loops, bloodied hands wiped clean. It still suits the colony to continue this violence, overt or clandestine, always transforming, ever present. This racism builds its foundations atop a carceral state. At the time of writing, another all-white jury has decided that yet another white cop will go free after a murder charge. This racism takes the shape of the White Australia policy, of the state-sanctioned abduction of children and, even when official legislations are repealed, racism persists, so surreptitious and so unnoticed that to condemn it is to expose yourself to even more violence. Racism is 'an action and a rationale for action'[1] and so, in conjunction with physical violence, racism is insidious, found in the archives or in the commons, in the media or in the curriculum, each purposeful erasure or elision or refusal or revision or overturned murder charge infiltrating and warping and claiming collective memory.

In this context, *against* is a rallying cry: a commitment, a promise, an event. It requires work, and the work does not stop. Those who work *against* – against disappearance, against racism, against the colony – share in a commitment to praxis, to the small everyday actions that show us a way towards new futures, a way to oppose the lie that writing does not matter, that culture cannot have material repercussions, that it too disappears when faced with racism, genocide and colonisation. This book is another attempt at undoing erasure, whatever its antithesis may be, whatever presence we encounter from now. We know from history that change is not instantaneous, so we can only keep building.

▪

This book is a collection of the longlisted works from the *Liminal* & Pantera Press Nonfiction Prize, a national literary prize for First Nations writers and writers of colour. Our reasons for creating this prize, as well as this book, are complex. First, it challenges the historical whiteness of Australian literary prizes, and racism within the Australian literary landscape more broadly. The prize is an extension of *Liminal*, a project I have been working on for the past six years alongside friends and colleagues. At the heart of *Liminal* is the desire to intervene in the racist structures that shape this country's cultural industries, imaginary landscapes, collective memories. We work against this landscape that is hostile to the simple matter of our existence – not to mention our labour, our desires, our dreams.

'Much of the Australian white-settler canon reads for the first one-hundred and fifty years as a litany of othering,' writes Jeanine Leane. 'Beyond the First Australians, settler fictionists have depicted, almost, if not entirely carte-blanche, the representations of further diasporas arriving – "the yellow peril", for example.'[2] There are many components that continue to enable this 'litany of othering' in the contemporary literary ecosystem – curriculum at all levels of education, the publishing and media sectors, and government arts funding, to name a few. Literary prizes function as an endpoint to these systems. The Miles Franklin Literary Award touts itself as 'Australia's most prestigious literary prize, helping to support authors and to foster uniquely Australian literature'. It was founded in 1957, ten years before the 1967 Referendum that reversed the exclusion of Indigenous peoples from the laws and lawmaking of Australia, and sixteen years before the White Australia policy was fully repealed in 1973. Out of the sixty-five years the prize has been running, I can still count the number of winning Indigenous writers and writers of colour on one hand. Of course, the Miles Franklin is not alone in such disparities, but there is not enough space or time to name each prize that boasts excellence yet delivers a certain homogeneity year after year. In honesty, it is exhausting and telling that statistics are required to prove the reality of racism, which, as a racialised person, I cannot escape. Why are our accounts not enough? As Toni Morrison reminds us,

> the very serious function of racism [...] is distraction. It keeps you from doing your work. It keeps you explaining, over and over again, your reason for being. Somebody says you have no language, and so you spend 20 years proving that you do. Somebody says your head isn't shaped properly, so you have scientists working on the fact that it is. Somebody says that you have no art, so you dredge that up.[3]

So I am here to explain – as I have over and over again – that we *do* have art, and that we *do* have language. I am here to explain – as I have over and over again – that the structures and values of white supremacy are *not enough*. For a non-white person living in so-called Australia, to accept or adhere to the metrics that deem one *enough* seems futile. The yardstick is wielded as weapon; call it faux-meritocracy or a narrow vision of excellence or just good old-fashioned racism – such measures of 'value' were created with a white ontology in mind and never meant to serve us. This whiteness does not envision our presences, unless we make ourselves in its image. This is to say, this country's racist literary landscape does not dream for all of us.

But who is *us*? Because the *us* I am describing is a coalition created in reaction to racism, it is unavoidably complicated and imperfect. I am mindful of Eve Tuck and K. Wayne Yang's warning: 'There is a long and bumbled history of non-Indigenous peoples making moves to alleviate the impacts of colonization.'[4] In my work, I try to navigate my responsibility as a minoritised settler, working and living on the stolen lands of the Wurundjeri Woi Wurrung people. In thinking through what such a coalition might look like, I am reminded of the words of Audre Lorde: 'Without community there is no liberation, only the most vulnerable and temporary armistice between an individual and her oppression.' She continues, 'But community must not mean a shedding of our differences, nor the pathetic pretence that these differences do not exist.'[5] In acknowledging these differences, it is crucial to note that terms like 'people of colour' are inadequate precisely because of the differences they claim to *contain*, when such signifiers are always overflowing. When we describe these writers using such terms, it is with the vision to illuminate such thrilling difference; beneath its flimsy connotations, we find a way to reach for solidarity among difference in the hope of gradually leaving its umbrella and heading towards specificity. This book pits history, testimony and remembrance against the white colonial structures that continue to erase us, though these erasures and violences always unfold in ways that are different and unequally weighted.

Another reason for the prize, then, is my desire to create a mood of *possibility*. In our 2020 book *Collisions* (Pantera Press), a collection of fiction from our first literary prize, I quoted Samuel R. Delany's letter to an aspiring writer, which I will, for good measure, return to once more:

> The fact that you are writing, submitting, and winning awards means [...] you have already crashed through the greatest and most destructive hurdle racism sets in our way: the one that gives so many of us a self-image that says, 'Who am I to think I could ever write anything worth reading, that I have anything worth saying; or that anyone else might take joy in hearing it; how dare I think I have the right to speak, write, or be read.'[6]

It is *this* hurdle that we aim to smash through, by making spaces for racialised writers to do their work. We asked entrants to untangle the idea of the 'archive', for writing that troubled institutional accounts of history, for work that considered the politics of the personal archive, or what each of us chooses to remember, memorialise or forget. The essays are interested in memory: collective and personal, whispered or commanded, words smudged on paper or glowing on a screen. These writers trace memories buried, concealed in a suitcase, tucked away in a closet or under a bed; memories that rip through like a fire, burning long after it has been extinguished. They ask, *What of the memories we inherit, or the memories that were refused?* And then, too, of other inheritances: how trauma might be handed down through generations, and how easy it is to forget that one might be born with luck, obstinacy or a tendency for trouble. I have hope for what these entanglements with the past might mean for our shared future. Indeed, *hope* is a strand that runs through these essays – and how can it not? To put something down on paper carries a hope that someone else will pick it up.

▪

This book is organised into three parts. There are images and feelings and theorists that loop through; there are lines and moments and moods that pull together generations and geographies. The forms diverge and fracture, with a cacophony of endnotes and footnotes and Barthesian marginalia – a joyous refusal of referential coherence.

The first section, 'Inheritances', contains essays that trace lineages, considering what we possess, what was stolen and what is passed down. We begin with Mykaela Saunders' recollections of her Uncle Kev; against a history of violent settler-colonialism, she reflects on the colonial archive, interrupting her own narrative to tell us, 'I won't write any more about this because I don't want it in the archive.' In this refusal, Saunders asserts her right to opacity, a significant act of resistance. Similar acts are evident when writers reject linear accounts of the past. Lur Alghurabi pieces together a careful portrait of her mother, who 'doesn't write because she knows repeating memory cements it, and many of her memories are pain'. Kasumi Borczyk also thinks through maternal lines, presenting memory as footnoted strata, where your voice and the voices of your mother and your mother's mother can overlap, finishing one another's sentences across time.

Whereas some have sought to rethink the act of recollection, others hold the burden themselves. Ruby-Rose Pivet-Marsh recounts, 'I have been carrying those memories on my back and in my legs and along my arms for the both of us.' Hannah Wu's mother carries her memories of the Cultural Revolution in red notebooks tucked in a suitcase; she teaches Wu how to collect herself into words. Collection and collecting recur throughout this book, for to remember, it seems, is to assemble evidence of having lived. 'Every substance, item and creature,' suggests Jon Tjhia, 'is a gathering of its ancestors.' Echoing this gesture, Brandon K. Liew presents a genealogical account of Melbourne restaurant Shakahari, in an intimate layering of his life with the lives of his family.

The second section, 'Archives', circles around a provocation by Saidiya Hartman: 'Every historian of the multitude, the dispossessed, the subaltern, and the enslaved is forced to grapple with the power and authority of the archive,' Hartman posits, 'and the limits it sets on what can be known, whose perspective matters, and who is endowed with the gravity and authority of historical actor.'[7] These essays think through the violence of the state, of war, of displacement and dispossession. Veronica Gorrie exposes the cracks of the colonial archive – 'They hold many secrets the colonisers wished we never unravelled, but unravelling is all we do.' She gives voice to her great-aunt, Teresa, after finding only a single page about her in government archives. In researching Korean adoption, Ryan Gustaffson is faced with a similar lack, wondering how he might 'begin to assemble an archive when its materials are always elsewhere, where traces are to be excavated from between the lines'. When he looks and is faced with 'nothing', he turns to affect as a way to 'let it be the telling'.

André Dao wonders if the 'I remember' of individual testimony can ever overcome systematic destruction or organised forgetting. 'Erasing history is nothing new,' Elizabeth Flux reminds us. 'There are many reasons for wanting a blank slate, but most of the time it comes back to one thing: trying to control the story.' Along the lines of such forgetting, Barry Corr deems the settler archive 'unheimlich, uncanny, a fearful place'; he is left with no choice but to look at the archive aslant, 'beyond the reflections of that which has been left for us to see'. Yet, at the same time that we face these forcible cultural erasures, we encounter a growing misuse of personal data – Lucia Tường Vy Nguyễn examines the surveillance practices and panoptic measures of digital colonialism, which 'fuses the punitive with the pleasurable, much like how the Global North's imperialist ventures across the Global South have been connected by a genealogy of greed'. She cautions: 'Never forget how we mapped the world. Never forget how we drew the Web.'

The final section, 'Opacities', foregrounds the personal; perhaps because the self seems to come in fragments, this section contains some of the collection's most formally experimental pieces. Hassan Abul, the winner of the *Liminal* & Pantera Press Nonfiction Prize, documents his transition in 'Third Cowboy from the Sun'. As judges Brian Castro, Maddee Clark and Shakira Hussein note in their report:

> The vexed state of transitioning is mirrored with humour as well as irony: it is about being seen and about seeing, both of which require a distance, which works excellently as a technique of narrative expression. Creative, provocative and thoughtful, it is both a rare and courageous objectification of a self as well as a key analytic moment in one narrator's life and times.[8]

Abul admits that he does not 'keep records of my own changing form' – 'this whole thing has been too slippery, too experiential and dynamic, to fall easily into an archive. Any attempt would feel false.' Beyond gender, the body emerges as a home for memory elsewhere in this section. Of formative past moments, Lou Garcia-Dolnik writes, 'There is a history that sits within me. It is my history: I house it.' grace ugamay dulawan offers a similar proposition – 'Before I was civilised / names of generations stored in the flicking muscle of my tongue' – and evokes Morrison's aforementioned concerns around race and culture: 'Before I was civilised / I was artless.'

The collection's closing pieces ponder the relationship between person and place, and how this constrains what paths are available to us. Suneeta Peres da Costa worries that questions about home or identity might 'unearth something *in me* that couldn't be tamed or controlled'. Ouyang Yu tires of being framed as an 'angry Chinese poet', protesting, 'I have other qualities, such as humour and love.' And Hasib Hourani admits, 'i can't be anything but palestinian without the word "guilt" sinking down into me from the sky'; of visiting his homeland, he muses, 'i have written this landscape so many times, i don't have it in me to do it again. i just want to ask "what do we leave behind when we leave?"' The collection ends in the second person, moving from such intense interiority – the *I* or the *i* – to the invitational *you*. As though in response to Abul's concern over falsity, Frankey Chung-Kok-Lun offers: 'In writing this essay, you have made your own truth.'

A note on the book's cover; when I first saw this photograph in Thy Tran's *Cacher* (NB Books, 2018), it felt like a glimpse extended – the space between subject and viewer impossibly widening and closing. In French, *cacher* means 'to hide', and Tran's book is a documentation of a relationship across time, intimate moments collapsed into an archive. Tran places it as the very last image in *Cacher*. Following this mood, it seemed a fitting image with which to begin our book, one that is not intended to be a solution to the complexities or asymmetries or pains of disappearance. Instead, these essays widen and close; they trouble and disassemble; they collect and build. They are lyrical offerings in what it might mean to remember, or what it might mean to be opaque or intimate or generous, to be forgotten, or to forget. We are all, it seems, in the *after*. What might it mean to think through the past, through what hides or is hidden, to extend some hope? What could it mean to be *against*?

Leah Jing McIntosh
March 2022

1 Fields, Barbara J. and Fields, Karen E., *Racecraft: The Soul of Inequality in American Life*, Verso, London, 2012, p. 17.

2 Leane, Jeanine, 'Subjects of the Imagination: On Dropping the Settler Pen', *Overland*, 5 December 2018, https://overland.org.au/2018/12/subjects-of-the-imagination-on-dropping-the-settler-pen/

3 Morrison, Toni, 'A Humanistic View', public lecture, Black Studies Center, Portland State University, 30 May 1975.

4 Tuck, Eve and Yang, K. Wayne, 'Decolonization Is Not a Metaphor', *Decolonization: Indigeneity, Education & Society*, vol. 1, no. 1, 2012, p. 3.

5 Lorde, Audre, *The Master's Tools Will Never Dismantle the Master's House*, Penguin, London, 2017, p. 18.

6 Delany, Samuel R., *About Writing: Seven Essays, Four Letters, and Five Interviews*, Wesleyan University Press, Middletown, 2005, p. 199.

7 Hartman, Saidiya, *Wayward Lives, Beautiful Experiments: Intimate Histories of Riotous Black Girls, Troublesome Women and Queer Radicals*, Serpent's Tail, London, 2019, p. xiii.

8 The *Liminal* & Pantera Press Nonfiction Prize 2021 judges' report is available to read at https://www.liminalmag.com/prizes-fellowships/nonfiction-prize-winner

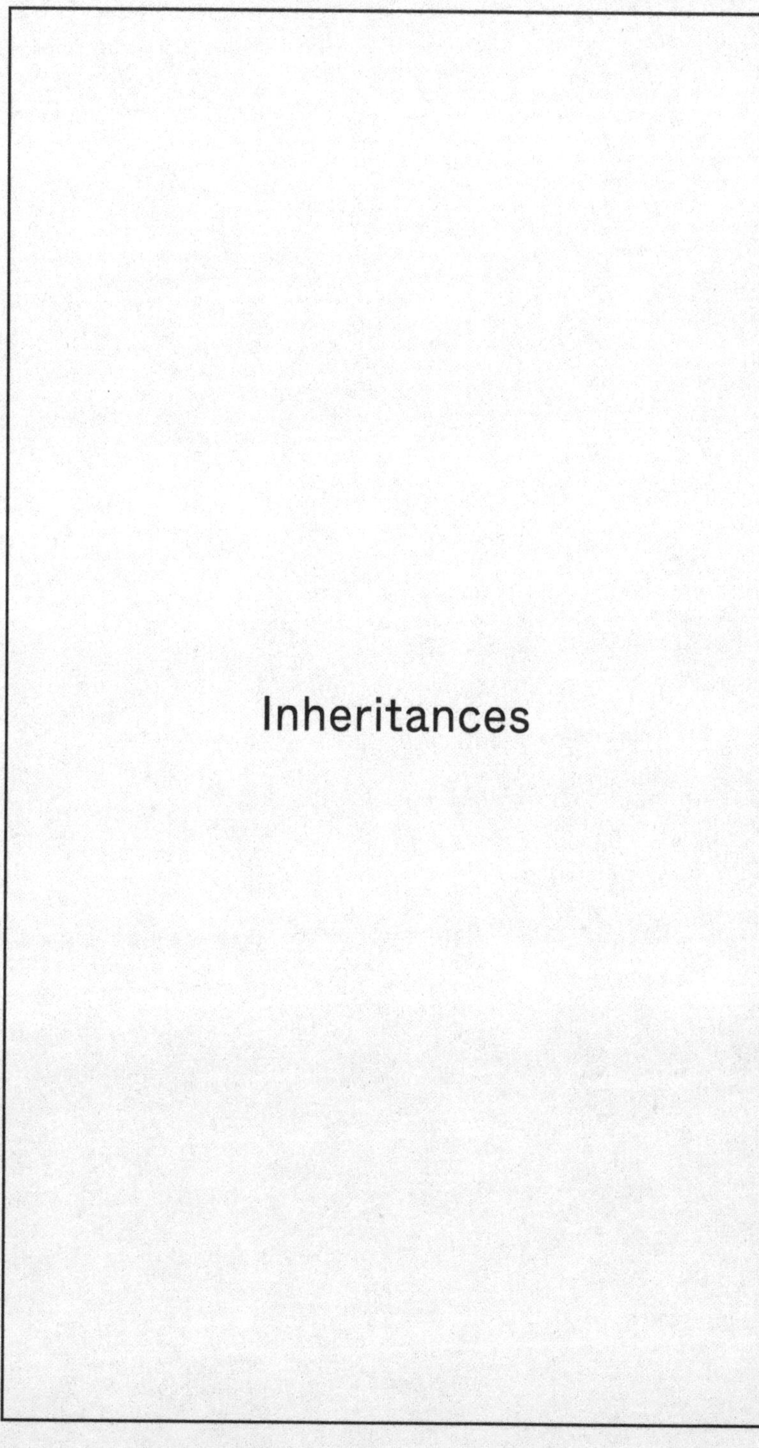

Inheritances

Communing with Uncle Kev Through the Archives, 1991–2021

Mykaela Saunders

I write to remember. I write to not forget.

I write to hear the voices of the people I miss inside my head because when I'm writing about them, they're yarning to me. Their voices are clear. And I eavesdrop and exhume their words so I can see, on the page, what I hear.

I am writing this essay to write about my Uncle Kev – to provide an account of our storytelling connections, a record of our ongoing haunting and jokes. I'm writing to archive our relationship and to enter our relationship into the archives. And I'm going to tell this story the way I see fit.

At the *Aborigines Making History* conference in Canberra in 1988, Yidinji activist and academic Henrietta Marrie (née Fourmile) presented a paper called 'Who Owns the Past? Aborigines as Captives of the Archives', wherein she said:

> To Aboriginal people, the key to our historical and cultural resources and therefore to our cultural and historical identities is firmly clasped in a white hand. Therefore [t]o be an Aborigine is having non-Aborigines control the documents from which other non-Aborigines write their version of our history.[1]

As my Uncle would say, *Fuck that for a joke!*

Look, I know how true this must have felt to Marrie (and every other blackfella) when she gave her paper on the bicentenary of British invasion on still-unceded Aboriginal land, and I know it's still true of most of our history post-1788, but I do not want this to be true anymore. I am a community-minded person, which means I'm forward-thinking – a futurist.

The archive is not neutral. My people know. The archive is a tool, a body of knowledge – created, curated, massaged and manipulated. Institutions have always lied to us and about us through falsification and omission of records, and they do love to get rid of any records that might incriminate them.

Our Old People told their own lies to wield power, too. They talked shit to nosy busybodies to hide our secrets; a lot of this nonsense ended up in the archive and is now presented as culture and fact.

This essay won't pretend to be neutral either. In the spirit of our protective Old People, I've chosen what stays in and what's left out. My cultural protocols inform my archival practice: I won't name living people or identify them relationally. I'll only refer to publicly available records and I'll only explicate my relationships to those who have passed away.

Now, let me take control of this narrative, my way. Let me tell the story of how I've communed with my Uncle through the archives over the last thirty years – which is also the story of me becoming a storyteller.

1991

I'm in primary school in Blacktown, and I love reading stories and I love listening to them. The storytellers I love the most are those who make me laugh and wonder and fear, all in the same story. I love listening to all my relations talk shit and serious when we visit each other.

But my favourite storyteller is Uncle Kev, hands down. He spins such a grouse yarn. He comes to live with us and he teaches us how to swear *(but only if you're at least four years old)* and I always pester him for stories.

Uncle Kev gives me a set of four cassette tapes, each a different bright-colour plastic: red, blue, yellow and green. The tapes play some old fella telling Dreamtime stories. I am obsessed with these tapes. I love the epic and magical nature of these stories. I love the old man's voice, his delivery.

He has a very old voice, musical and deep, and he sounds familiar but I can't place him. I love sitting in the lounge beside the tape player and entering whichever new world the old fella draws me into.

Also in this year, unbeknown to young me, the findings from the Royal Commission into Aboriginal Deaths in Custody (RCIADIC) are handed down, with life-saving recommendations – none of which have been implemented at the time of writing this essay. One of these recommendations is to keep Aboriginal people out of jail, to only use it as a last resort. Ha!

Also in 1991, the *Koori Mail* is established in Lismore, in Bundjalung Country, which will soon become our new home and community. The *Koori Mail* is Aboriginal-owned – firmly clasped in a black hand – and it'll go on keeping mob informed and connected for the next thirty years.

1994

Uncle Kev and his sibling meet their grandmother for the first time through Link-Up. She is the mother of Uncle Kev's mum, who I never got to meet as she died before I was born.

Uncle Kev's grandmother has advanced dementia, so he and his sibling don't learn much from her, but they are just grateful to be able to sit with her, to look at her face and hold her hand. Their grandmother dies soon after their meeting so I never get to meet her, but she leaves behind her own little archive: a shoebox containing returned letters and records from the welfare, from homes and other institutions. As with many Aboriginal families, the information we inherit is minimal yet precious to us, and the missing pieces tell a bigger story than what's there.

Through their grandmother's archive, the siblings find out that their mum has a brother, which means they have an Old Uncle. They find him. He is still alive!

We meet him. He's a beautiful old Koori man, gentle and kind, and he is rapt to have found some family after living his whole life an orphan and an only child. As toddlers, Old Uncle and his sister were separated from their mum and from each other; none of the three ever saw each other again and lived out their three congruent lifetimes of unloved living.

And as much as I would love to write more about this, I can't, because then it will be in the archive.

1997–1999

Uncle Kev comes to live with us in Tweed. He's always out on the balcony, either carving or playing yidaki with our Gomeroi neighbour, or he's listening to music and reading the *Koori Mail*, or he's drawing and scribbling in his notepad. He's always smoking, too. Through stories, through serious yarns and talking shit, he teaches me cultural and political and historical business (and also heaps of fucked-up jokes).

Then he moves up to Yirrkala, where he lives on and off for years.

2003

I want to study writing and I get accepted into uni, but my best mate takes his own life so I defer for a year. I start working at my old high school as a teacher's aide. I yarn with Uncle Kev about how shit suicide is, for everyone involved. He knows.

2004

I take up my deferred offer at uni but, a few months in, I'm assaulted and put in hospital. Then the panic attacks start and really push me around, showing me who's boss.

One bad day, once I get on top of the war in my head that I've battled out all day inside the toilet stall at uni, I call Uncle Kev. He hitches to uni and he drives home with me and we yarn about what is really important in life.

I quit uni, and he moves back to Yirrkala.

2006–2009

I'm back at uni – but this time I'm studying education, as I'm broke and getting older and I can't justify an arts degree. I study through block mode this time, so I can look after my three younger siblings who are in my care, and so I can still work at the school.

I get my diploma, then a bachelor's degree. I'm the first person in each line of my family to enter the record as a university graduate. Statistically, it's far more probable that my records would have been criminal. This is not a vindication of me, nor am I throwing my people under the bus. This is a condemnation of the injustice system, the welfare-to-prison pipeline, but I won't write any more about this because I don't want it in the archive.

2011

I move to London by myself to get away from things, for teaching work and to travel, but there's not enough of the first so there's not much of the latter.

A few months in, I get locked up for [redacted] and I'm treated like shit in there. When I get out, I yarn with Uncle Kev about it. We share stories about our experiences and it helps. I also start writing about my experiences, to process them.

Then Uncle Kev gets lung cancer so I move back home.

2012

It's Invasion Day and I'm at the hospital with my Uncle. He's been in a coma the last few weeks and I've been up here after work every night to stay with him. I yarn with him, talking shit and serious, hoping one or the other will convince him to wake up. But neither do.

I hold my beautiful Uncle's face and hand as he takes his last breath. Heavy metal is playing on the radio as he goes out. He leaves a few minutes after midnight, technically the day after the one we both hate. I can't and won't go to another Invasion Day rally for years.

We find out that our Old Uncle passed away on the same day as Uncle Kev.

When we go up to Uncle Kev's house to clean it everything is gone. Knowing he was going, my Uncle had carved yidaki furiously, to leave something behind for each of my brothers, cousins and nephews, and he had paintings made for me, my aunts, nieces and cousins. A whole body of work, an archive of culture, all gone. Hocked – and we know who by, but we ain't cop callers, and this must stay off the record.

I write my Uncle's eulogy. It's the hardest thing I've ever written and I don't ever want to write anything like that again.

A few weeks later, our old Gomeroi neighbour sees some of my Uncle's things in the hock shop. He recognises the yidaki as Uncle Kev's work because they used to play together years ago. Our neighbour yarns to the owner of the hock shop about the situation, and he returns the remaining things back to my family.

Uncle Kev's sibling takes his ashes up to Yirrkala on the community's request, where they lay him to rest in their way.

I move to Sydney for uni, and now that I'm learning how to research, I get the archive fever. I ask for great-grandmother's shoebox to find out what I can. It takes me years but I piece together a story and it's worse than we'd thought, and I have to end this story here.

2014

Aunty [redacted] says I am just like Uncle Kev because I'm living in my van and spending all my time in the mountains, in the bush and on the road.

But I'm living in my van because I can't afford rent because I'm studying full-time and I don't have the time to work the hours I need to earn enough to afford Sydney's rent. One happy side effect of working less is that I finish my studies quickly, and now I have time to just be, to think, and to write.

I start a blog called *Defender of the Faith*.[2] I review gigs and albums, and go on silly little rants and nice journeys through my mind using words. This blog is an archive of me finding my voice through talking shit and serious into a void, anonymously.

One day I'm camped up at the beach in my van. A piece of writing comes through me, whole. I write it by hand then type it into my phone and post it to my blog. This piece is called 'But You Don't Look Aboriginal' and it's mostly about my grandmother, my Uncle's mum, the stolen one I never knew because she passed away before I was born. I only know her through her absence and through her presence in the archive of my family's memory. I've grown up with other people's stories of her so most of my third-hand memories were originally hers. I think about her a lot so I know she's always with me; all my life I've had this relationship with her.

My blog post goes viral; at the dissolution of my blog two years later, the post has over 9000 shares and god knows how many more views. People from all over the world comment on my post. This piece teaches me terrifying responsibility as I learn the impact my words can have, how far my voice can project. All this attention gives me the confidence to write more creatively and I start experimenting in my journal.

2017

I want to learn how to write fiction, and I know how to be poor, so I move back into my van and go back to uni.

God, I love learning to write. I write my first short story, then my second. My Uncle talks to me as I write and he sneaks his way into my stories as characters, as dialogue, as voice and experience, and attitude: cheeky, and a little bit cooked.

Natalie Harkin is the University of Sydney's visiting writer, and I attend her lecture on 'Archival-Poetics'. I'm electrified by what she's done with her own family's archive.[3] I chew over whether I could do something similar with my family's horror stories, but I know I couldn't be so candid.

I scribble notes through Harkin's lecture, riffing on her brilliance. These notes will eventually become my first poems.

2018

I'm paid for my first bit of writing when AustLit republishes 'But You Don't Look Aboriginal' in its *Growing Up Indigenous in Australia* anthology.[4] I'm given an AustLit login and password as a perk, and I go digging through BlackWords, the most thorough, incredible archive of Indigenous literature.

I'm now immersed in study. I'm writing fiction and critique, and every day, I summon the will and the imagination to write our people into the future, something that many writers have refused us. But there are things I need to say in ways that aren't overwrought enough for long forms, and so I begin shaping bits of poetry after a lifetime of never understanding it.

A submission opportunity comes up with *Cordite Poetry Review*, with Harkin as guest editor. The theme is 'Domestic'. I submit a poem about my grandmother and the menial work she did, whose story is the throughline of 'But You Don't Look Aboriginal'.

On Christmas Eve, I'm eating dumplings with my partner when I get *Cordite*'s email that my poem's been chosen by Harkin, whose lecture inspired the poem.

I'm overwhelmed and I promise to read the poem out to my Uncle, but the busyness of the season eclipses my pride at being published. I don't even have time to scratch my arse, let alone talk to my Uncle who is a ghost about a poem I wrote about his mum who was an even bigger ghost for him and who has been nothing but a ghost to me.

I've been flown into New York City to take part in a performance exploring Black Deaths in Custody, and the effects that flow on through these abject horrors. The metronome of the performance is timed by some 147 flashes, one for each person who has died in custody over the last decade, though many more have died since the RCIADIC recommendations were handed down in 1991.

I don't feel good about being here but I can't put my finger on why until afterwards. Throughout the performance, I think about all that I and my family have been through, and are still going through, and I'm so sad, but I feel my Uncle with me, so I am comforted too.

After it's done, as those of us responsible for the work talk about our experiences, I learn that none of the others have been locked up or lost people to state murder, nor are any of their people in prison. Nobody has done any activism or advocacy for abolition. I am upset that none of the families of the people who are represented by this work were consulted, and none of the money generated from this performance will go to them. I am ashamed that I didn't do my due diligence and find all this out beforehand.

I need time alone. It was a huge job, and the lead-up was intense and busy and social so I need solitude to recentre myself. I don't have anyone to debrief with properly, anyway. My family is still directly oppressed by carceral systems – whose effects I've lived and breathed and researched and taught – and nobody here really understands that so there's not much to say. I feel alone, like a tourist among other tourists.

It is now two days after the performance. I'm having a big cry in the shower and I want to go home. I'm vulnerable and open, and present with the past, and all the big and heavy feelings that are swirling around inside me. I've been crying all day – big ugly crying, sick and sore and rundown crying, laid low and overwhelmed with all the study and personal stuff I've neglected the last few weeks to do this job. This is the crying that comes when you've been holding it in because everyone around you wants to be held, but nobody wants to hold you even though you need to be held most of all.

And as I do when I'm feeling sad and sore, instead of wishing I could talk with my Uncle, I just do. I have a yarn with Uncle Kev about everything – all the big feelings bubbling up around my failings, which feeds into talk about my writing (because I feel like a fucking failure at it), and then,

I remember my poem that's about to be published. I start to big-note a little about it, bigging myself up after feeling so sad. I tell my Uncle that this will be the first published poem in our family.

Ya big fucken liar, he whispers to me. *I did it first*.

And then I remember (or rather, he's reminded me) that he wrote a poem and had it published in the *Koori Mail* back in the day.

I piss-bolt from the shower to my room and computer, and search Uncle Kev's name + 'Koori Mail', and an entry comes up in the Australian Institute of Aboriginal and Torres Strait Islander Studies (AIATSIS) archive of the paper!

I enter the site but get lost inside. There's far too many issues. I select to search the editions from 1997 to 1999, those years he lived with us. I pick an issue from 1999 at random.

There, my Uncle's poem is in it! I bawl my eyes out reading it, this poem about his mum, my grandmother ghost, who I wrote about in my poem that's soon to be published.

But my Uncle doesn't let me rest because I then get the feeling that he might have written more poems, but I'm not sure how many, so lucky for me then I remember that I have access to the AustLit database, because my article was republished there last year – the piece about my grandmother and about our family's history of being thieved from each other, which is what my Uncle wrote about too.

I search Uncle Kev's name on the AustLit database. There are twelve poems, all published in the *Koori Mail* from 1997 to 1999. A whole body of work, an archive of culture, all in front of me. This is an immense gift and blessing to find these poems twenty years after he wrote them, and all those years after I started missing him, and now we are both in the AustLit archive together.

My Uncle's work is recorded for all to see in black and white, replete with issues and page numbers. Some are published under a nom de plume, but the angels at BlackWords have catalogued with care, and I find all the issues of the *Koori Mail* with his work in them and download each paper.

More crying as I read his words and hear his voice. I transcribe each poem. I decide that one day I'll engage with my Uncle's work through my own poetry, to write reflections on his poems, responses to them – a new medium for the still-flowing dialogue between us.

I also decide I want to write about this whole story, too, at some stage, but I don't know how yet. Through fiction? Or essay? A mixture of both? How to write this story without oversharing? How to tell my story without intruding on the stories of others? I just don't know yet, but I do know I don't want this read and judged by people who will read my worldview and beliefs as myth and superstition. I'll write this when the right opportunity comes up, when it can be read by people who'll treat my story with care. I trust that, one day, the right way to enter this into the archive will show itself to me.

In the meantime, I read my Uncle's poems over and over. I study his subjects and tones and techniques. I trace the evolution of his style over the two years he wrote them: they go from deep grief and lament about everything our family has lost to government interference, to fiery and wild, almost hip-hop delivery, to imaginative journeys of revenge, transcendence and Dreaming.

I'm obsessed with these twelve poems as individual pieces, and as a body of work. I am a beginner poet, as my Uncle was when he started, too. And I begin to learn about poetry experientially, the way he did, by writing more and reading more and feeling out what looks and sounds right.

Soon, my first piece of poetry is published in *Cordite*[5] – but it's not the first published poem in my family, as I've been reminded.

Then, my first short story is longlisted for a prize. This story draws on my Uncle's last months, and the lives of family members after prison.[6] I am ecstatic for about two hours, until I find out my brother has taken his own life.

I write my brother's eulogy. It's the hardest thing I've ever written and I don't ever want to write anything like that again.

The day after my brother's funeral, my story moves up to the shortlist. It's very hard to know what to feel about either of these things for a very long time.

2020

I am so fucking broke. I'm a postgrad in a pandemic, without a scholarship or institutional support. I enter every writing prize I am eligible for; I slam a hat down inside every ring I see.

I win a prize for poetry and another for a story, so I'm not so broke anymore, then my novel is shortlisted for another award. My Uncle is in all of these stories. More of my work is published, and I feel like a real writer now.

My Uncle's words about relational thinking come to me as I write an essay about cli-fi. I cite him, so his words are entered into the archive.

Then I give a lecture in which I talk about my journey as a writer, so of course I talk about how my Uncle and brother shaped my love of stories. I also vow that

> I'll never be one to write straight memoir. I dislike the spotlight too much to wanna stand under it naked in public [...] and I just don't have many stories that are solely mine. Most of my good stories I share with others, which makes these stories not just mine to tell [...] and I have too much respect for the people in my life to spread their secrets across a page for the attention of strangers, or for money or accolades.[7]

My talk is broadcast, recorded and uploaded to the internet, and now my own relational thoughts and ethical affirmations are in the archive, forever.

Throughout everything, my family attempt to break the welfare-to-prison pipeline's relentless stranglehold on us; we fight to keep our young people out of one institution, and we fight to keep our older people out of another one.

2021

I do not have time to write this essay. The deadline's the day after my thesis is due, but here we are! It's hard not to steal a little time to add to it most days, because it is a joy to archive my relationship with my Uncle, within which is threaded my journey into writing.

I write this to remember my Uncle Kev and to remind myself that, when I submit this thesis and this essay, I'll have time to myself again, time I can spend with my Uncle's precious poems, to sit with them and study them, and maybe write my own poems in dialogue with his, to keep on communing with the old fella through a brand-new archive – one growing from the rotting corpse of state control, and stretching into liberation, love, integrity and our own sovereign imaginings.

I write to remember that an archive is a culture of memory.

And I write to remember to keep tending my own memories, and my relationships with loved ones who have passed, who are all still with me whether I talk to them or not. And I write to remember that it's good to talk and it's good to write but it's important to be open and listen, too, because there's still so much that our dearly departed want us to remember.

1 Marrie was improvising on a definition of 'Indianness' by American historian W. T. Hagan – who, in turn, was responding to Winnebago tribal leader Reuben Snake's definitions. See Fourmile, Henrietta, 'Who Owns the Past?: Aborigines as Captives of the Archives', *Aboriginal History*, vol. 13, no. 1, 1989, p. 7.

2 Named for the 1984 Judas Priest album *Defenders of the Faith*, which my Uncle, my brother and I all love/d.

3 For more on this process and on Archival-Poetics, see Harkin, Natalie, 'Weaving Blankets of Story and Hearts of Gold: An Archival-Poetics Praxis', *Cordite Poetry Review*, no. 101, 2021, http://cordite.org.au/essays/weaving-blankets-hearts-of-gold/

4 Kilner, Kerry (ed.), *Growing Up Indigenous in Australia*, AustLit, St Lucia, 2018.

5 Saunders, Mykaela, 'Grandmother Ghosts', *Cordite Poetry Review*, no. 89, 2019, http://cordite.org.au/poetry/domestic/grandmother-ghosts/

6 This story was read by those family members and published with their blessings.

7 *Piss and Vinegar, an Autotheory*, Writing & Concepts Lecture Series, Linden Gallery, 2020, https://vimeo.com/481179873

All my gratitude to the Koori Mail *for being for us and about us for so long – you've meant so much to mob everywhere. And to the archivist angels at AIATSIS and at BlackWords – it was your careful work that delivered my beloved Uncle's poems to me, and I can't thank you enough for this precious gift.*

You Either Die a Refugee or Live Long Enough to See Yourself Become the Diaspora Writer

Lur Alghurabi

Silence [...] is a practice of confrontation, a 'counter-discourse'. It can function as a variation in the eternal repetition of discourses by causing a rupture in language, a subversion that turns language against itself. It is not just that one is silenced and thereby rendered invisible; rather, one can strategically choose to be silent by boycotting discourses, by refusing to participate in them.

— Nikita Dhawan[1]

Have I ever told you that my mother only speaks about the things she loves? The only things she will tell you about, all you will ever know about her, are the times when she wore a beautiful dress, or made a beautiful dress, or put a beautiful dress on one of us. She used to use a worn-out, beautiful dress to wipe the individual leaves of her ivy. When she made a wedding dress for her sister-in-law and embroidered flowers onto the kosha, everything was so beautiful they danced until the morning prayers. She made me a beautiful dress from Swiss embroidered fabric that her father sent as a gift all the way from exile. I wore it to my sister's third-grade graduation. My sister wore pistachio ballerina flats embroidered with chiffon gardenias, and my mother had made those, too.

My mother doesn't talk about anything she doesn't love. The Gulf War, in my mother's eyes, never happened. Food for oil? Never heard of it. The Sha'ban Uprising? We don't know what you're talking about. The Halabja massacre? You must have the wrong number. ISIS in Camp Speicher? I don't know her.

My mother doesn't talk about anything she doesn't love. My mother only talks about the things she loves. My mother is a manipulator of truth. My mother has had little peace.

My mother tells me about her lemon tree. The young blossoms need to be removed constantly so that the tree can keep its nutrients, so that, in a year or two, it can support fruit. It asks for patience, care and attention, and my mother delivers.

When my father laughs at his identification papers almost getting him shot, she says what a bad story that is. Has she told you, instead, about the time she made a red off-the-shoulder dress identical to Suad Hosni's in *Amiret Hobbi Ana* (*The Princess of My Love*) and got sent home from university for it? That was a great dress. She says she'll make me one for my honeymoon.

My mother doesn't say much about why her father was exiled. Something to do with the government, something to do with them shooting the dog. I don't know the details, but I know everything about the French make-up he sent her, expensive eyeliner she saved for birthdays and weddings, lipstick pencils she gave me once she had used them all up so I could play pretend with the empty tubes. Expensive silk scarves she wrapped her hair in every time she visited my father's family. She never told them about all the layers she took off as soon as she left their home. She tells me that's the reason they liked her, that they didn't need to know everything. She tells me a happy life is found once we stop talking too much, once we stop taking things so seriously. So what if she threw on a hijab for them on weekend trips? So what if she took it off once they weren't looking? Stop talking so much, she says, stop talking so much about everything. It's not important. Instead, let her tell you about the time she sewed 5000 purple sequins onto velvet fabric for her engagement dress, all the women who envied her, all the men who wished they had proposed first.

In every piece of writing, I construct a memory she will never acknowledge.

My mother doesn't believe in memoir. My mother has boycotted the discourse.

I think of all the times people I loved demanded silence, the way they were demanding peace. When I saw my best friend after ten years, and she told me she was in love with a Baathist, I said, Have you forgotten what they've done to us? To me? To you! To your mother! She said, 'Silence.'

Twenty years after leaving Iraq, we've finally gained Australian passports. For the first time, we are able to enter Iraq without being arrested at the airport. We stay for two weeks. The first thing we visit straight from the airport is the cemetery, where my mother's most important people wait for her.

Returning home, it was the first time I saw a photo of my mother as a child. One of her sisters went through old albums and put it on the dinner table. In the photo, my mother stands almost outside the circle they had created to fit in the frame. Her sisters in short dresses and white tights and fresh blow-dries, she in the far corner with a loose ponytail, a halo of frizz and a dotted shirt with sleeves that ended right above her elbow, the least flattering cut, and it's old, it's someone else's old shirt. Her smile is wide, but, when she sees the photo after thirty years, it's not wide. My mother cries. She remembers that she was not loved.

I show the photo to my friend. I pull it up on my phone and put it in front of him. I zoom in on my mother and I tap my nail against her hair, and I say, That's her, that's Mama, and then I zoom out and say, Now look at all her sisters and her uncles and her dad. Look how they're all standing so far away from her. Look how she looks like she's not one of them, like the nanny whose name no-one remembers. Look how she's dressed, and look how everyone else is dressed. Look at how the other girls are being hugged, look at how she's leaning against a rock. Look at her. Look at my mother, look at how she wasn't loved. I can handle my own pain, I can handle it just fine. What do I do when it's the pain of someone else? Like when they don't kill you, but they take your loved one hostage, and then you wish that they had killed you, because your personal pain is a paradise compared to tolerating the pain of your loved ones, knowing they are hurting, watching their smile disappear and their mouth and face wrinkle as soon as they see a photo, and you put your arm around their shoulder as they cry about something that's not even over, but there's nothing you can do. They still don't love her. They still treat her badly. When their kids get married, she gifts them the most expensive thing they need: the refrigerator for their new home, or the air conditioner, or the freezer, or the Kashan rugs, or the entire kitchen. She calls and they don't pick up, they only call when they want gossip. How are your daughters? Have they gone away? For university? Not safe. You should bring them back and find them husbands.

You might wonder why my mother was not loved, why I discovered it so late. I wish I could tell you. But perhaps you'd like to know that this confusion is like a parasite feasting on my insides. Maybe today I can just share it with you. Why was my mother not loved?

Here is a map: my mother was born with six siblings, and, in order of importance, they are: Safa, everyone else. Safa was her much-beloved brother and the only person she shared books with, because he was the only one who liked to read. My mother's father died when she was fourteen. Safa became the man of the house, and, in many senses, her father too. When my mother fell in love with my father, Safa's blessing was the only one she asked for. When my father took her out to buy her a gold dowry, Safa was the only person she took with her. When Safa got married to Saba, Saba became my mother's best friend and only sister, even though my mother already had five sisters. When, in 2007, my mother got a phone call that Safa was killed in an explosion outside his ice-cream shop, she cried for three months. She smiled, sometimes, when I told her about the boy I liked, or when my sister came back from school with a funny story, or when my father said he would make dinner that night (that made her smile the hardest), and sometimes, when my father asked her what spice went into a tepsi, she would cry, because Safa used to really love tepsi and, out of all her recipes, tepsi is the only one she has taught me.

My mother was heartbroken because, other than Safa, my mother was not loved. Does this make sense? No, it doesn't. Why was my mother not loved? This map is useless.

Can I write about Iraqi breakfast cream, a thick block like ice-cream but it doesn't give your teeth a migraine from the cold, from the woman in the town centre – she buys it from the factory in the country then resells it to city folk, her shop a blanket laid out on the side of the road. Little profit, but my father tips: he says it's not right, the woman came such a long way to sell. He gives the cream to me and says, This will break your vegan fast. I break my forty-day fast on the thirty-sixth day: buffalo cream on good bread, still warm from the baker, covered in Iraqi flour. It's different. It is soft and it is earthy. It's a brave thing, to be able to admit you're in pain. I'm in pain. I don't know how to write about the cream. What am I supposed to tell you? That milk in my country is better, because the cows are more resilient? That even a hint of buffalo milk in a block of cream makes all the difference, because it's fattier, and that hits a spot for me? That when my mother bites into it, she bursts into tears, and an even harder silence comes where she cries and says nothing, and this is so much worse than just silence? That my uncle, before he was killed, used to make our ice-cream with buffalo milk? That this is why it was the best in the markets? I want to take a photo of how it tastes. I feel love in the graveyard when my mother visits him, and when she pours the cold, clean water on his tombstone, is that like ice-cream to him, maybe? My mother. He showed her love. Not many people did.

I used to think that writing about trauma was healing, but then I heard someone say that healing implies a cure is possible, and then I stopped believing anything. My mother says forgetting is the greatest blessing from god, without it we'd be confined to a life of misery. Imagine if she thought of her brother every day, if she missed him every day. She says the reason she can laugh is that she doesn't think of his body shredded to pieces outside his shop, his blood and flesh mixed with melted pistachio ice-cream, waffle cones like dust. The whole family is wailing, and the explosion is on the news for only a few hours before another happens. It was July, and they couldn't let his body in the coffin visit all the houses before he was buried, just two or three, or his corpse would start to smell like one, so he died at 10 am and they buried him at noon. No, no, she doesn't think about that every day. She hardly wants to think about it at all. And unless there's a letter, unless someone shows a photo, she's fine, she's not thinking about it, she's fine if no-one mentions it, she's fine all the time because we never, ever mention it. And she's happy until something bad happens.

▪

We're a family of survivors. That's the price of staying alive. We have lived to tell the tale or lived to live through another one. We lived to see how much candy we could fit into our mouths, each piece growing stiff and hard like rocks until the insides of our cheeks erupted with blood. We have lost feeling, but not enough to forget that we are grieving. What emptiness.

I used to have a friend named Nancy. We met at a first-year anthropology course in university. She approached me to compliment the colours of my hijab, saying Muslim women are so much better dressed than white women, pointing to herself as an exhibit of the latter. She touched my scarf and asked where I bought my clothes. I said Zara and witnessed the glimmer in her eye fade to a dull disappointment.

At the beginning of our friendship, Nancy took me to a slam-poetry night. An internationally acclaimed poet was doing a reading about his extremely difficult journey as a refugee from Sudan, having fled after being threatened for criticising the government. Next to me, Nancy nodded furiously. She nodded and clapped each time he paused to take a breath, even when she was in tears. She couldn't believe just how much 'sad stuff' he'd had to go through. 'I'm ashamed to be Australian,' she said once he left the stage. 'Can you believe the way we treat refugees in this country? I'm so sorry,' she said to me, even though she didn't yet know I was a refugee, or where I was from. Then, like she'd had a sudden, important realisation, she tilted her head towards the poet and said, 'Hey, you could do that, too.'

To erase refugeeship, we take on profitless careers that require us to examine our pain in a way that is against the refugee's basic instinct for survival (examining pain, without professional supervision, without the right tools, can be fatal). My mother doesn't write because she knows repeating memory cements it, and many of her memories are pain. I look at the Sudanese poet and see that he has arrived: he can speak. Before, he could not speak, and now he can speak. His past journey has ended and so, now, I see him as free, standing in the centre of the room surrounded by admirers and friends, his past pains now a triumph. The ability to write means we are not refugees anymore. To be a writer is to depart from the silent community: to say, I am not one of you. I am not from you. I've made it. You leave me alone now. It doesn't matter if this is true or completely made up in my head. I believe it. Its impact is true. If I speak about this, then I have risen above it. I want to wash myself of refugeeship and its biggest danger: silence.

We look at the monsters in our suitcases. We unpack them, from our hearts and from our luggage, and we write a story. A good, award-winning story about 'survival' in the face of adversity. We're awarded a cheque and half a publishing contract. Our ordinary is someone else's extraordinary. My greatest literary fear remains, to this day, that an Iraqi person who's lived through the war will read that 'award-winning' story and see all the emptiness inside.

We don't need refugee writing as much as the Nancies need it from us. They need our pain and our survival in equal measure. They need the survival they can claim credit for. They don't want to hear the story if we are not surviving. They'll engineer their memory towards forgetting the ones who have drowned, the ones who have not arrived, or arrived only to achieve nothing of capitalist significance, or nothing that will soothe their guilt and ease the wounds caused by their awareness of their crimes. To thrive after arriving is soothing to white guilt, without much effort required. They grant the visa and they sign the piece of paper, so they get the credit, even though we are the ones who unfuck our brains, bury our trauma deep and pay our parents' bills. We drag ourselves through the depression we gained through unpacking our trauma for some cheap, award-winning memoir. A standing ovation. Applause and a few tears when an excerpt is read from the work that nearly killed us. We wish we hadn't. We've triumphed over our own demise, but we didn't. I never needed this battle in the first place.

Helen Razer, a white writer, tweets about how the literary community praises people of colour exclusively for accounts of lived experience, while it lets 'white blokes' do all the high-end systemic critique. We demand autobiography only from the oppressed. She calls it intellectual apartheid: 'POC are confined to memoir and misery lit by honky arts bureaucrats.'[2] I wish this left me with anything intelligent to say in defence of why I do this. Is she calling out the honky arts bureaucrats, or is she calling out me, the person who actively and wilfully engaged in this cycle and gave the honky everything they wanted?

In the past, I had been so consumed by the misery literature that I started to exaggerate the bad things that had happened. I wrote stuff from the past in the present tense. I became so consumed I didn't know how to write once I was healthy and happy again. I still struggle with this. A writer's block, but it's because I think misery is the only path open for me. What do I have if not this? What do I have if not a story Nancy can cry to? I started to believe that misery was the only form of writing acceptable, and the only way to create a memory I could recognise and live with. I was commissioned for a piece of memoir last year that came at a time when everything was working out perfectly, so I started to dig into the past for misery because my supply was running low. I was starting to run out of sadness, and my first reaction was to beg the universe to fuck me up again so I could have something to write about. Every misfortune amplified. I wrote the piece, it got published and retweeted. It reached my mother-in-law at the time and she hated it. She said that my writing was painting a picture of me that was untrue. She said I was lying in this memoir, and I was.

The legitimate refugee is a perfect victim. They are never afforded character depth. They can do no harm to anyone else – but reality is not like that. We never talk, in the host country, about what the Arabs have done to the Kurds, or how we denied the Assyrians dignity, or how the Shias were killed by their own. My father applies for asylum in Australia and so does the man who tried to kill him via an execution order. They both have very convincing and true stories, but only one story is told: they are victims of something or someone else. Searching for ourselves, and our narrative, within victimhood is toxic. We end up finding nothing, wasting our lives searching.

We try to understand our identity by reading the misery literature of others, trying to find ourselves there. We never find what we're looking for (because we are complex, and misery literature is simplistic: a basic hero's journey). A hero's journey is how you produce resilience. Resilience is so marketable, so profitable and so attractive. It makes all pain palatable.

This is not an argument against writing trauma. This is an argument against resilience. Resilience is a sham. We move from one pain to the next and, sometimes, we find a moment of pause between what we swing to and from, and there is peace for a short period of time. Resilience has a happy ending. Resilience has stability. Resilience has an 'it's over now, you can breathe, you can start your life' simplicity. I cannot forget the day when I got my Australian citizenship and my passport. I wrote on Instagram, 'This is the day all my problems get solved,' because my understanding of my own problems was reductive. I thanked my past self, gave her a round of applause, for the resilience she had shown in the ordeal leading up to my acquisition of papers. I loved her, I admired her.

An academic once told my class about an experiment where someone willingly gets buried alive for twenty hours, a type of intensive emotional cardio. She said most people make it out with half the brain they walked in with. They lose it. They aren't prepared for what is going to happen, what their body and mind are going to go through. Then she looked at me and she said, 'You. You would come out exactly the same as you went in. This wouldn't affect you. You were trained for this.'

What a useless skill. 'Most likely to survive being buried alive for twenty hours.' Can I put that in the yearbook? Writing about refugeeship in the same ecosystem that generated refugeeship is a special type of delusion, isn't it? I'm never writing another essay again.

1 Dhawan, Nikita. 'Hegemonic Listening and Subversive Silences: Ethical-Political Imperatives', *Critical Studies*, vol. 36, no. 1, 2012, pp. 58–59.

2 Razer, Helen: 'Ikr? Like praising POC exclusively for accounts of "lived experience" and letting the white blokes do all the high-end systemic critique. Soooo dangerously progressive to keep the thinking for whites only and demand autobiography only from the oppressed. Intellectual apartheid.' (Twitter, 4 September 2019, https://twitter.com/HelenRazer/status/1169208377198563328) And: 'Yeah. It's a bit like that. A shortcut to defining whiteness by demanding the ecstasy of guilt. And, FFS. Like there's a shortage of scholars and theorists who ain't white. POC are confined to memoir and misery lit by honky arts bureaucrats.' (Twitter, 5 September 2019, https://twitter.com/HelenRazer/status/1169429360383647744)

Private Performances

Kasumi Borczyk

With thanks to Shujuan Borczyk,
Chong Yang Cen and Guang Shu Zhong

Last month, in the town where I now live, I found myself freely associating certain moments in my day with memories from my childhood. These memories found a way of rising to meet the present moment more and more often until life began to feel as though a facsimile were continually being superimposed onto landscapes that I had already seen.[1]

1 Every afternoon, in our village, we would eat and walk. Your 公公 and 婆婆 would give us our dinner and we would walk around town with our chins to our bowls – only stopping if something interesting caught our eye. I remember, one day, I was strolling through the village with no purpose in mind when an old fortune teller who was passing through town walked right past me and pointed towards my right hand. She told me that she could tell from the way I held my chopsticks that, someday, I was going to live far away. I asked her, 'How far?' and she said, 'Beyond the horizon.' It wasn't until I had come to Australia and found myself staring at the menu at McDonald's, wondering how long it would take me to be able to learn to read it, that I remembered what she had once said. I still don't know if I believe that she really knew just from how my fingers held

the chopsticks, but, when your 婆婆 was young, she also went to a fortune teller, who told her that she would have five children and that only one would end up looking after her and her future husband. So, you see, maybe there is some truth to it after all.[a]

a At the time, when the famine started, we were living on the side of a highway. Soldiers used to pass by on their way to Tibet, carrying their backpacks in one hand and a sack of bread in the other. 'Pillow-bread' we used to call it, because the train rides were long and cold and you would rest your head on them to fall asleep, sometimes reaching around and tearing off a piece to eat until your pillow got smaller and smaller and your head was on the floor but your belly was in the sky. One day, the soldiers had no more pillow-bread. We would find flour wherever we could to make biscuits for the soldiers on their way. Slowly, there was less and less flour. We would strip the bark off the trees and ground it into powder to make the biscuits until there was no more bark on the trees to strip. Sometimes, soldiers would return tired and hungry and looking for something to eat. When we told them that we had nothing to offer them, that we had five children ourselves, that even the animals were hungry and that even the trees were naked, the soldiers looked like they could cry. One day, we saw a young soldier boiling some water on the other side of the road. I noticed that he was beginning to take off his belt, so I stuck my head out the window and yelled out to ask what he was doing. He said that he was going to boil it until the leather was soft enough to chew. I put my head back inside because I couldn't bear to watch him try.

All of this most likely began when I started speaking to my online therapist about why nothing is painful but everything still hurt. For one hour per fortnight, I would tell her about the sensation of holding an arabesque in ballet class as a child and contorting myself, millimetre by millimetre, towards perfection as if my body were being bent between an anvil and a hammer by God's will, and a crest of white hair behind the fractal fuzz of a computer screen would nod encouragingly and ask me what I mean by[2]

---

2 God, I felt like such a nuisance! I lived with your 舅父 and his wife in their house in Meadow Heights. I stayed there until I met your father and I couldn't speak a word of English for months. My sister was collecting stamps back home in China, and I remember asking my brother if I could go through his drawers to find some old letters so that I could peel the stamps off and send them to her. A few days later, his wife accused me of stealing money from the drawers. You know, my grandmother always said, 'In the florist's home, she arranges bamboo sticks,' meaning that you will always take for granted what you have in front of you every day. These words came back to me during those first few months in Australia because I couldn't imagine taking anything for granted – not even for a second. Even then, my life was still better than what I had left behind.[b]

---

b We were told to gather whatever metal we could find. Did we question why we were doing it? We were advancing our nation; there was no time to stop and think. They placed big brick furnaces where our crops used to be and, every day, we would melt down whatever metal they brought to us. Sometimes, we would come home from work, dead tired, but there was no time to sleep! We had to keep an eye on the furnaces and check if we needed to add any wood to keep them burning! For half a year, we hardly slept. The metal came out in big lumps. We didn't know what to do with it or what it would be used for, but we continued to keep the furnaces burning. When we thought we had melted everything we could find, our neighbour – a Communist Party member – came around to every house to see what scraps of metal might be left. When the authorities came to our house, they made my mother give away her copper pots. She loved those copper pots so much that she cried. In the end, they even took away the brass prayer bells that hung out the front of everybody's houses. Only a demon would touch the prayer bells, but, every time our neighbour took a prayer bell away to the furnaces, he would say, 'It's not my problem; I'm just doing what I was told,' as if that could save him. One day, he even noticed that our roof was supported by strips of scrap metal. He said, 'You know, if you just take out every second strip, your roof will still be standing,' and that is how we lived in those days – a breeze could blow us over but, somehow, we were standing.

God. After each session, I would enjoy the contact high of touching parts of my symbolic order. Up until then, the truth that lies behind all things felt as though it had only ever made its presence known to me through the creaminess of cataracts. My parents were not religious, but their desires were loosely governed by the benevolent God of the Free Market. Social mobility presented itself as divine salvation, which is why I was sent to the kind of all-girls Anglican school where starchy white shirts and competitive spirit were akin to accoutrements for some new, neoliberal denomination. My mother worked in the Ford car-assembly plant in Broadmeadows[3] until my brother was born, and my father supported us by bulldozing houses and removing asbestos or toxic waste from big and important buildings

---

3 My friend Ling told me that Ford was hiring factory workers at the time and that you didn't need to speak too much English to get a job there. The work wasn't so bad.[c] Every day, we did new things and assembled different parts of the cars. One day, my job was to spray-paint the car doors, and I told my site manager that I couldn't spray them because I was already pregnant and I didn't want to breathe in the fumes. He told me that he didn't pay me to get knocked up.

---

c Let me tell you a story. Your grandmother and I were working in communications at the time. Our days were spent typing out messages in Morse code, like this: *Dut dut dut duuuuuut dut dut dut.* One day, our supervisor gathered us into a room. He told us that we were to say how we really felt about the party. He said, 'We want to know so we can improve.'

He said, 'It's okay, you can share how you really feel because we want to know.'

And then he said, 'Or you can tell us what other people in your team have been saying.'

And then he said, 'Has anybody in your team been having bad thoughts or saying bad things?'

There was a young man in our team, a very friendly guy, who loved to write – just like you! He fell in love with a beautiful young girl in our village who he once studied with. Now, this girl's mother was a poor woman. She would sell tea leaves at the port to sailors who were passing through. There was one sailor in particular who would buy tea leaves around Melbourne. I spent at least a few of my formative years being very confused when the daughters of property developers and architects would bring glossy magazines featuring Metricon-style McMansions for show-and-tell, and I would be forced to grapple with how my own father could possibly destroy things that looked so beautiful. I fantasised constantly about living in the kind of home that had fluffy ornamental pillows, a pantry full of snacks that didn't smell like biosecurity threats and parents that congratulated you for 'trying', and then I spent a few more years reckoning with whether or not the lesson I had chosen to teach myself – that we are not all winners by virtue of existing – had any merit at all.

---

from this woman and took a shining to her beautiful daughter. Noticing an opportunity, the woman began to bemoan the fact that they were so poor and how she couldn't afford to send her daughter to school. The sailor agreed to pay for her daughter's tuition fees in exchange for her hand in marriage when she graduated. The daughter went to school, where she met our young writer. They fell in love and would walk home together every afternoon so that she soon forgot about her promise to the sailor. When she graduated, she returned home to visit her mother and the young writer received a letter from her saying, 'I'm sorry but I'm preparing to marry.' He went crazy. He went mad. He took a train to her home town on her wedding day. He told us all at work that he had to find her. When he finally saw her, he began to cry. He said, 'We used to walk home together every afternoon! We treated each other so well! How could you do this to me?' The girl knew that what she was doing was wrong, but there was nothing she could do so she began to cry, too. In the end, the young writer left her village with a note saying that he wished her well in her marriage but that she would never see him again because he was going to kill himself. You would think that this is where the story ends, but this is China we are talking about!

Our story always stretches backwards and forwards for thousands upon thousands of years. Instead of taking his own life, the young man decided to write a novel about it instead. Without telling anybody, he stayed at home every day after work writing and writing and writing. Eventually, he showed some close friends his work and would read little sections out loud to us. He was even pretty good. He wrote like a poet. He was a very smart man. Eventually, people started to talk because it's a strange thing, after all. Every day, he wrote and wrote and wrote until he had a manuscript so thick, so full of words, he would carry it tucked under his arm. Anyway, that day we were all gathered in the one room, we were all too scared to talk. When they asked if I had anything to say, I kept quiet and said no. The leader told us that we had to find somebody in our group to denounce by the end of the day. He asked me, 'What are you thinking? What's in your head?' and I said nothing. I thought, *They're not going to take me away. There's no way.* We sat in silence for hours. We were sitting still for so long that, eventually, we all needed to go to the toilet but were too scared to leave. The young writer was the first to finally go to the toilet and, as soon as he left, somebody said, 'I denounce him! He has been writing and writing every day for

Like in all marriages that exist in that unbridgeable gulf between two cultures, the silence between my mother and my father was only briefly erotic before it odorised everything between them with a kind of nameless anxiety. Cultural barriers did not allow them to fight by airing out their bereavements from time to time before allowing them to percolate anew. I imagined a healthy kind of power struggle in my Australian friends' parents, for whom verbalised resentment was at least a sign of emotional investment. Our family shared moments of quiet communion. My father called me Mishka – 'little mouse' – and my mother would wake me and my brother by jumping up and down on our beds and singing in nonsensical Cantonese, 'Wake up! Wake up! Wake-ity uppity wack wop!' They never

---

---

months and nobody knows what he is writing about. I bet you he is writing a manifesto!' I kept my head down and said nothing. I needed to go to the toilet. He never returned from the toilet and I never saw him again, but I sometimes think about the small passages of his love story that he read to me. They were very good. He was a very good writer.

fought, but their drawn-out silences had all of the anticipatory drama of waiting for rotting fruit to fall from its tree. They shielded us from the crossfire of adult relationships but, occasionally, I would catch them obscured from each other by furniture – my mother rolling her eyes, my father shaking his head – and I'd understand something in that moment about the incommunicable.[4]

---

4 When I was growing up, whenever a husband returned from the hospital with his wife and their new child, all the neighbours would stick their heads out the window and ask, 'What is it?'

If it was a boy, you would yell: 'Boy!'

And if it was a girl, you would yell: 'Bathwater!'[d]

---

d I remember walking past the hospital one day during the famine. I saw a nurse in uniform holding what looked like two glazed peking ducks hung upside down, one in each hand, and heading towards the bin. I had to look twice before realising that they were stillbirths. In those days, babies were dying before they were born from hunger. It was like they were saying, *No! I don't want this life! I refuse to live like this!*

My partner once noted that I'm unable to talk about my emotions without prefacing them with 'I think I feel …'[5]

---

5 Like I want a small life.[e]

---

e My 母親, your great-grandmother, always said, 'Where money falls, beauty lands.' In those days, life was[†]

† As though this symphony of perceptions will remain fundamentally unshareable, and communication is what we call the failure of trying to share it, anyway. He asked me why feeling was a two-part process that I wasn't able to arrive at through instinct alone. Intellectualising emotion is kind of like mapping a trail of pigeon shit and trying to impose on it some sacred geometry – which is not to say that it cannot be done, just that we may not know enough about pigeons. I have begun to experience the world from the perspective of difference, and, whenever memories of my childhood begin rioting upwards towards the light, I find myself witnessing the memories of a memory, creating new ones based on how I think the act of witnessing them makes me feel. When I was a child, my mother used to tell me jokingly, 'Where money falls, beauty lands'; I recalled this phrase years later as my tram passed the Smith Street and Alexandra Parade intersection, when 'Fortune favours the bold' also passed in and out of my thoughts like a wandering albatross. I can recall this moment on the tram with greater clarity than any actual moment of my mother repeating this phrase to me and, now, thinking about it again, it strikes me as curious how some memories remain simply memories while others become statistics and others still become something akin to emotions, transformed into private performances. I remember thinking, that day on the tram, that implicit within every aphorism is the capacity for the opposite to also be true: that what is beautiful is also what is abject and unadorned, and that I could someday aspire to the unambitious,[6] to cultivating the least significant version of

6 Myself? I feel like I want a small life. Some people want to be on top of mountains, living on top of everything. But, if it were for me, I would be happy just swimming at the bottom of a little stream because[f]

---

f It's better not to talk about such things … I guess we were some of the lucky ones.

Death & The Devil

Ruby-Rose Pivet-Marsh

In my room, there is an altar: bits of fabric, jewellery, shells, dried flowers, candles, tarot decks. It is where I keep my loved ones – photos of those who have passed on and of those who have not but who need the extra care.

At some point, I took the photo of my brother down from the altar. I couldn't protect the both of us anymore – or maybe I just got tired of trying to.

▪

In the tarot, the card called 'The Devil' symbolises the shadow self, attachment and addiction, among other things. It is tied to the sign of Capricorn. When my brother was little, he had a necklace with a pendant made of steel. It was bent into the shape of the symbol for Capricorn. He wore it until, eventually, he lost it. He doesn't believe in astrology or the occult, but, when I bought us matching zodiac necklaces (his, Capricorn; mine, Scorpio) as adults, he treasured his for a while.

The 'Death' card symbolises endings, change, transformation and transition. It is also associated with the sign of Scorpio. After a particularly shitty time, I get a scorpion tattooed on my ankle. I call it my protector.

▪

There are things my brother doesn't remember, or doesn't remember completely, either because he was too small or because he doesn't want to (after all, *I* remember them). Things like the two of us sitting on a bench in a police station wearing pyjamas our gran made, our feet not touching the floor and me reading to him so we could both pretend that we weren't there. I think maybe I prefer that he doesn't remember, and maybe that is selfish rather than selfless. Whichever it is, I have been carrying those memories on my back and in my legs and along my arms for the both of us. I am an older sibling, if nothing else. Right down to the bones. Further, even.

He has been balancing on a tightrope between *recovered* and *recovering* for two years – or, I guess, closer to three. He is good at it by now: agile and nimble. When a work accident tests his balance, he doesn't so much as wobble. But he runs. He runs on the cracked bluestone down to the river and, there, he keeps running. And running and running until he can't run anymore. Sometimes, he drives down to the beach, flings himself into the ocean and lets the saltwater soothe his nerves.

We used to stay at the beach, which is actually many beaches, at Gran's house every school break, as our parents couldn't exactly take two weeks off work just because we weren't in school. Every school holiday, the beach. Even in winter.

Death and The Devil dancing in the ocean under the rain.

▪

A year after the accident, he is still only when he lies in an MRI machine. He is meant to have the ends of his sciatic nerve burnt off but, instead, an epidural delivers steroids to the base of his spine. It helps for a little while. And then it doesn't anymore. The following week, I am inside the same machine and the planes of my body are being inspected. An effort to locate the pain so it can be repaired.

An ex-girlfriend told me that was part of her reason for breaking up with me. The possibility of him relapsing and turning up at the hypothetical home we might one day share, asking for help, was too much of a risk for her.

I don't think that was actually a reason at all, but it was a good way to hurt a person. A brilliant way to make sure that, when things ended, they remained that way. I have seen her only once since: walking down the street while I sat inside the 220 bus, which made me slip into immediate panic. My brother says he saw her on the 223 one night but she didn't seem to recognise him with his hair short, colour back in his face and his clothes fitting his body instead of hanging off him.

∎

Recently, Mum found our reports from primary school. Every single one of my brother's personal statements, from grade prep all the way through, starts with things like:

- *I must be better*
- *I must try harder*
- *I must improve*

One time, he told me that grade two was when he decided that school wasn't for him. His handwriting looks mostly the same these days.

∎

We are at 501 Receptions for a celebration. At some point, my brother and I go for a walk. Dad is too drunk and Mum is annoyed, so we leave to smoke outside the nearby Sims supermarket. I can't get the lighter to work. My brother, no more than sixteen, lights two cigarettes, passes one to me in silence. We settle near the ATM. This is the centre of our known universe.

Death and The Devil leaning against the wall,
not talking. Smoke passing between them
and then disappearing in thin wisps.

A friend who is no longer really a friend sees us from her car and beeps as she passes. We walk back along Barkly Street, chewing gum as we go. He takes Dad home. I go to work at the pizza shop.

▪

My brother is sitting at the kitchen table that is not really in the kitchen, talking to Mum. *My GP said addiction can be hereditary.* I try to bite my tongue. Of course it is. I can't help it.

He asks me why I am so angry.

When I was a kid, I was in therapy because my emotions were too big and I didn't know where to put them or what to do with them. By the time I was in grade two, I was up to my second therapist. She told my parents they couldn't reward me for going to sessions because I was a bad kid having the wrong responses to the world around me.

After that, I carried my emotions around in my chest, wrapped up tight. They took up so much space that I could never get enough air in where it was needed. My heart would strain as if it were a cloth being wrung out and throw itself against the cage that held it in place. Barely. Just. Trying to get out.

▪

I am in Saigon Pho with Mum. Before the market burned down. Before the fancy burger joints. Before the towering giant towers of scaffolding. Before. Before. Before …

I am facing the TV but looking beyond the screen. I am in the place no-one can reach me. Mum takes me to the doctor because, at some point, I start hyperventilating and crying into my soup instead of bringing the spoon to my mouth.

The doctor orders an X-ray. He tells me *lots of young women feel this way* when it doesn't show anything unusual. Except he doesn't explain what *this way* is, and I'm still sitting there, unable to pull air in and unable to get my eyes to focus.

Now, many years later, thanks to a doctor who listens and explains things to me, I take medication to tame my breath. But this means that the pain has found somewhere else to bear down. Everything aches and, sometimes, more than aches. More like my body screaming when I move. Also when I don't. I start smoking in a way I never have before. It feels good. Until it doesn't and I fall in the shower. I hit my head, hard, on the edge of the bathtub. Suddenly the world comes back into view.

I flick through my journal – one I haven't been keeping up with as much this past year as I would like to. Weeks at a time are missing and, for long stretches, the bits I *have* managed to get down all start with things like:

- *woke up in lots of pain (crying)*
- *pretty big pain day*
- *exhausted*

I am trying to track the pain: when, where, how. But it is everywhere, always and in all ways.

▪

House-sitting one weekend for a friend, my partner sits behind me on a beanbag, kneads the knots along my spine. *All gristle.* No bones, no muscle. Not really, not anymore. I make a joke about the body keeping the score but I know that, really, it's true. Later that same night, they kiss my back and say the freckles on it make up the shape of a dancer. We wake up tangled together.

▪

We went to a mediation just before my brother left detox. He kept trying to make eye contact with me, but I couldn't look at him. The room was a fishbowl: small, made up of glass and with barely any oxygen inside it. That was how our childhood pet goldfish died. The table was round, and in the centre was a Tupperware box of biscuits that went mostly untouched. His case worker said I was *visibly traumatised* and that I should go to therapy. Again. He gave me the name of a drug and PTSD psychologist. I went to see her and, during our sessions, I spent most of my time picking the SNS off my nails. Chips of lime green fell from my fingers and onto the couch; I scooped them up as best I could and put them in my bag.

I carry my mess with me. My brother has never been to therapy.

Death must go first so that The Devil may follow.

■

Our parents went to South America as the recent riots started up in Chile. Or, rather, as the violent government response ramped up. Before they left, when my brother had snuck out to smoke after dinner, they showed me where their wills were and asked if I was ready to be responsible for them. I said I always assumed I would be. Our father couldn't go back and not join the marches; our mother couldn't let him do it alone. Everything was too dire, too important. It still is. I had just assumed this went without saying. I did as I was asked; I prepared. I hid the jewellery along with some cash. I memorised the places where papers are kept. I wondered which version of our father would be returning.

Dad used to work on container ships because it was a way out from under the dictatorship that started when he was fourteen. When we were kids, he had long hair that fell past his waist – dark and curly. When my brother lets his hair grow out, it is the same. This was how I learned to plait hair: sitting behind Dad on the couch, turning his hair over in my tiny hands until it made a single long plait down his back. When I was nine, I gave Dad nits and Abuela cried over the phone as Dad told her she had to cut his hair.

I used to have dreams about drowning. In one of them, my father and I would be pirates on a ship. We would spit over the edge of it, watching the ripples our saliva made while the ship was anchored still. And then I would fall in. Or maybe he would push me. Either way, I would sink down, down, down into the dark green of the ocean until the dream went black and I felt as though I was floating just above my mattress.

There is a photo from my first day of school. Dad and I are sitting on my bed and he is brushing my hair. In another photo from the same day, I am in my uniform, ready to go. My brother, just small enough, is sitting inside my backpack, still in his pyjamas, clinging to my shoulders.

Dad used to wear three gold hoops in his right ear. One day, I asked my brother if he, too, thought our dad was secretly a pirate when we were growing up. The holes in Dad's ear have long closed and so, now, I grow my hair long and I wear three gold hoops in my right ear.

He said yes.

▪

Sometimes, Mum has my brother put his face next to mine so that our cheeks touch. She studies our faces, points out the ways we look the same, the ways we look different. The places he and I are our father, the places we are her, the places we are neither – or, perhaps, where we are both at once. Unlike mine, my brother's eyes are light, like pieces of amber glinting under the desert sun. Amber is one of the rarest eye colours. Only about five per cent of the world's population have it and, mostly, they are people of Asian and South American descent.

We both had teeth pulled from the same places in our heads. Removing them makes space in the crowd. He didn't keep his retainer in after braces, like I did, so they shifted back. Then other things changed the way his teeth looked. I decided to change mine, too. I put a gold crescent moon on my smallest tooth, the right lateral incisor that didn't quite grow all the way. The crescent fell off prematurely, just two months later. The gems I added afterwards fell off, too: one accidentally swallowed when it dropped into a sandwich, crunching so hard when I bit down on it that I thought I had chipped my tooth, the other washed down the sink at my partner's house along with the white foam of toothpaste.

▪

Once, at a cafe in Seddon, Mum asked whether I was angry. She said it was okay if I was. So I cried silently and into the plate (poached eggs, sourdough, sides of salmon and avocado) because that is what I do when I am angry. Anger is usually something else. Apparently.

Death makes a small spell for The Devil
(dried rose petals and lavender in a canvas bag)
and hopes that it helps.

▪

My brother texts me twice

For pain management with your gp
For pain management with your gp

A few hours later

norflex neogesic celabris

The names are misspelled, and I am already taking a different skeletal muscle relaxant, but I know he means well.

▪

It is a new moon, or a full moon. The moon is doing something, either way. I am dusting off my altar and rearranging it. I gently put the photos of my loved ones back up. I pause. I drag a chair to my wardrobe and balance on it so I can reach the top two shelves. I dig until I find what I am looking for: a metal tin stuffed with photos. I shuffle through them like a deck of cards. I find the one I am after. The Devil is small and smiling and wearing a teal fleece jumper. He is holding a plastic magician's wand. The room is dark and the light around him is a hue of blue.

I light a candle.

Replica

Hannah Wu

Not being fish, how do we know their happiness?
We can only take an idea and make it into a painting.
To probe the subtleties of the ordinary,
We must describe the indescribable.

— inscription on *The Pleasures of Fish* by Zhou Dongqing
(late thirteenth century)

The art studio is not really an art studio but a compact living room in a commission housing flat. Concrete stairs slope up through grey hallways to the eighth level; graffiti unfurls across the walls towards the front door. Our art teacher is a scraggly man named Chen, whose warm eyes peer out of wire-rimmed glasses. A smudge of ink dots across his cheek, tufts of hair swirl around the peak of his balding head.

Paintbrushes in our palms, he crams us around a dining table covered with white plastic tarpaulin, a ceramic filled with black ink marooned in the centre. A small shrine with incense sifts smoke in the corner of the room, Guan Yin's sharp nails stretched skywards. Pears atrophy in a brown bowl, heaving their organs into rot. Grime climbs up the walls like moss.

In the first week of summer, we draw out our days by copying out straight lines with calligraphy brushes. Chen demonstrates his technique seamlessly by twirling out several identical strokes across a piece of paper. Each line is supposed to be of equal length, the width to be weighted with flourish, controlled with our wrists. *Flick the wrist!* he instructs, and we flick our wrists. The boys eventually get bored and start flicking paint at each other.

He instructs us to copy out the same brushstrokes over and over, repeated until our pages are swollen with wiggly ink, then strung across red string overhead like a banner. Humidity pours in from outside as a lazy ceiling fan fends for itself. A laminated, blown-up photo of Wang Xizhi's calligraphy is Blu-Tacked onto the wall for reference.

We form dots several times over, merging into straight lines, slipping through horizontal strokes, until we clumsily form Chinese characters, wonky with our collective effort. Repetition becomes pedagogy, an exercise that engraves the memory of action into the soft bends of our hands. Chen walks around the classroom with a cigarette hovering between his fingers, smoke bleeding towards the sky, looping into nothingness. He inspects our work with pleasure, places a palm on each of our shoulders, delicately imparting that we will get better with practice.

This is an image that I had lived inside of, held my breath inside of.

■

Prior to the nineteenth century, calligraphers in China were traditionally literati-scholars and learned to write through the meditative practice of directly copying the works of previous calligraphers.[1] The process of copying was a means of methodically learning technique, studying the moral virtues contained within poetic texts to form social bonds with other artists.

In order to learn the art, the calligrapher had to imitate; art practice was not thought of in relation to creation or originality, but as a practice of teaching, passing on and inheriting traditional knowledge through generations.[2] Importance is placed not on invention, but on the expressiveness of gesture, the ability to emulate, and on the social relations that are formed in the process. Past and future generations are connected through the practice of replication.

■

Light collapses in on itself in the early hours, refracted blue through the window into the room. Slip out from the apartment, skip down the stairs and out into the open street. The rustle of leaves while the sky is still sleeping. Take the shortest route possible, walk briskly to keep out the bitterness.

It has become a daily ritual to walk by the river, or as it is commonly referred to, the aqueduct, the fake river. Incisions have been made into the land to form a concrete canal, a hollow basin for rainwater to flow through. The sides are lined with concrete, graffiti on the river's edges, an endlessly unfolding public gallery of text and images.

The water is high from rainfall, flowing leaves and twigs and debris through its veins. This river, a silver thread, stitching over rocks and stones.

■

It is morning when I am speaking with Danny on the phone, our bleary syllables squeezing from slow mouths, sequencing from lips to receiver to static to ear. I am walking by the river vein, brown from the slow mud and silt of yesterday's rainfall. Strands of birdsong weave through the trees, wet leaves sluice drops of moisture into curves.

It starts to rain again, really hard, until I am completely drenched, concrete turning from grey to black. The river is running again, slipping over rocks seamlessly, the surface forming dimples as each drop hits the water. Rain saturates my bag, seeping through my jacket and belongings. I am a long way away from home when I tell Danny that I am leaving to see my family.

■

There is an image that remains clear in my mind. Of many people standing in a large fishpond: short and tall, wide and thin. A small child is carried on a father's shoulders, hands clutching the man's forehead. Black hair, the burden of white skies and drooping trees surrounding the fishpond's border. Jade-green water, creasing at rhythmic intervals.

In *To Raise the Water Level in a Fishpond* (1997), performance artist Zhang Huan arranged for rural labourers to climb into a fishpond, raising the water level by one metre. This is a project of poetics. Tangible change is inflected on the environment through a collective effort, an accumulation of bodies, weight sinking into liquid. They are united in this exercise; they work together to raise the water level. But, when they leave, the water level drops back down to its initial height and the labourers continue with their lives. The moment passes and things return to how they once were.

▪

古人云
As the ancients said

死生亦大矣。
Birth and death are two ultimate events.

豈不痛哉！
How agonising!

每覽昔人興感之由, 若合一契；
Reading past compositions, I can recognise the same melancholy from the ancients;

未嘗不臨文嗟悼, 不能喻之於懷。
I can only lament before their words, without being able to verbalise these feelings.

▪

Moss glimmers through the cracks in the walls. Low sunlight glides through the recesses of fronds, flower buds kneeling on the path from the oily banks of shrub. My father and I walk through the winding fern trail that unfolds behind our family home in silence. Blackberry bushes dot the crescent of land and, as we walk, he plucks the small fruit from thorny brambles, placing them into my rounded palms. Cicadas circle their melodies around this gesture of care. We walk this way for some time.

Walking is the rhythm of motion, of repetition, the articulation of the body at the point where speech might disappear, where it is replaced with the back and forth of tread. The hinges of our limbs stretch and bend with symmetry. There seems to be a mutual understanding in this act.

My father is a man of few words, a gentle, self-sacrificing man, but for as long as I have known, he carries the form of silence that is withholding, where the movement of thought is visible behind his long pauses. His delicate gaze gives this away, the way that he examines others, his eyes flickering out towards the world and then away, into a world of his own. His face is lined with the traces of long hours of labour, cracked with exhaustion, a timid smile that reveals little else otherwise. Perhaps this is why I have always been frightened by the gap that exists between the unsaid and the said – the tension that hovers between what is felt and what we might try to enclose through language.

To my surprise, his voice breaks me out of this reverie.

You know, if you hold things in, too, they will re-emerge in a different place.

I can only stare at him in response.

▪

[I]n all desire to know there is already a drop of cruelty.[3]

▪

Wang Xizhi (303–361) lived during the Jin Dynasty; he was the calligrapher who composed the historically celebrated *Lanting Xu* (*Preface to the Poems Composed at the Orchid Pavilion*). The legend behind this event suggests that Wang and his fellow literati played games, drank wine and composed poems by a winding creek. Thirty-seven poems were written in total.

The calligrapher's craft was understood as developing a form of communication with the divine; he wrote messages from the heavens, lamenting the transience of life and death.[4] Calligraphy commits the signifying practice of the artist's gesture to paper, considered a form of improvised speech recognisable by the eye, not just by the ear. The next morning, Wang tried but could not recreate the preface to the same quality. The enchantment of the moment had passed.[5]

Scholars today widely accept that none of Wang's original works have survived over the centuries. The initial handscroll has been documented as buried with an emperor during the Tang Dynasty, and the objects that were later revered by museums were, at best, copies of copies of copies of copies.[6] The reproductions are exalted in status; mistakes from each different version of the script have been copied, as well as the seals and adaptations that were added by other calligraphers over time. The thousands of replicas have radically changed from the initial iteration of the scroll due to the natural errors of reproduction, but it has been contested whether Wang even wrote the preface itself.[7] Duplication allows a work's form to continuously metamorphose over time through usage. According to this model, a slow process of change is privileged as an artistic value rather than direct subversion.

■

My mother hands me a thin notebook when I am very young. The cover is a monstrous pink glaze, an ode to an adolescence spent in knock-off Sanrio stationery stores. Scratches of a mechanical pencil are made against the first soft pages, twisting out an underlined date. This memory is drained of sound, as if someone has pressed a mute button, moving through a dilating drift of images.

She trains me in how to convert a feeling into hovering silence, how to metabolise a private thought into writing, so that it might be concealed from speech. She teaches me to guard this, to hold this close. Writing as discipline, a form of withholding. An old habit that served as a form of coping at a time when speaking openly was not always a possibility. I wonder how far back this extends.

She pulls out a suitcase of diaries from her time during the Cultural Revolution. There must be a hundred modest red notebooks folded into the suitcase, some neatly dotted with illustrations of baby deer, black lines and simple shapes. Holding up a small notebook, she exhales and flips through, ink ribboning across old, yellowing paper. She articulates that she had always wanted to be a writer but never had enough time, gives me a look that leaks behind her gaze.

Speech slips away. These interior lessons in writing become an exercise in indirect strain – the distance that silence makes as a holding zone. We fall into the gaps, the spaces and differences in our exchanges, until it all collapses above us.

▪

Writing Diary with Water (1995) is artist Song Dong's ongoing meditative practice, wherein he writes daily entries with a calligraphy brush onto a block of stone. He began practising calligraphy on stone during the Cultural Revolution, when his family didn't have the resources to access ink and paper. As the water evaporates off the stone, the words disappear, fade into the air. A secret, invisible diary, constituted by the process of documentation and undocumentation. Events are inscribed, written in water, but no physical residue remains. Only memory.

▪

當其欣於所遇, 暫得於己, 快然自足,
We enjoy momentary happiness when pleasures captivate us,

不知老之將至。
But we hardly realise how fast we will grow old.

及其所之既倦, 情隨事遷, 感慨係之矣。
When we become tired of our desires, and the circumstances change,
grief will arise.

▪

Lying curled in my mother's bed, I wake up at home, stare into the dark. At night, cars pass the window and move beams across the wall through the gap in the curtains with their headlights. The familiar objects in the room are cradled by darkness, a dresser stacked with tendrils of jewellery pushed up against the wall. Assemble limbs into coil, but I cannot sleep. Light pearls into dots, sound wreathes into a hum. Shadows become beautiful again.

My mother writes in a letter to me: *I think about you all the time, since the last conversation that we had. But you never answered me.*

▪

I was once afraid of the friction in her voice, afraid of her unremitting expectations, afraid of the point at which disagreement shifted into conflict, afraid of the sound of tension coursing through a room. Her voice is bathed in echoes as it reverberates in my head, the gleam of her words knifing through the air. It undulates in pitch and volume, as noise accrues.

When we speak, we often talk past each other, smudging our translations of breath. Cadences fall; empty echoes leave residue. Memory is stored as tension. Remember the way that meaning brushes past the folds of language, the caresses of syllables, through tongues, cheeks, speech.

Days after our conversations, she writes letters if she has been thinking about the indirect resonances of our words, if she feels that she hasn't made herself clearly understood. *What is unsayable, and why is it so unsayable?*

▪

I end up writing my mother letters that I never send. Perhaps, time is the meaning that we impress upon movement.

▪

雖世殊事異,
Even though time and circumstances will be different,

所以興懷, 其致一也
The feelings expressed will remain unchanged.

▪

In European museums, masterworks are preserved through the restoration of the original oil painting. Original parts of a restoration are treated as relics, the object itself revered. In calligraphic art history, reproduction functions as a form of preservation, whereby forgery is thought of as an inherent part of calligraphic art history, rather than as replicating the 'originals' that constitute art history. The masterwork is not distinguished as a static object but seen as alive: as a changing, multiplying organism that continuously lives on through its duplication.

Calligraphers were simultaneously collectors and collaborators; when works became objects of a collection, they were likely to become objects of study, adaptation and copy.[8] There were several formalised styles of copying – copying in a freehand manner, copying through tracing, imitating from memory and inventing by imagination. Standard practice saw calligraphers adding seal stamps to their own handscrolls and applying their stamps onto the works of other calligraphers. Calligraphers would extend previous works by adding their own poems onto the handscrolls or would remove sections, resulting in a singular handscroll containing poems from different dynasties and from many different artists.[9] Multiple layers of meaning are disconnected from each other by time, yet they are still connected by the body of the work. The histories and traces of previous calligraphers are physically layered onto the handscroll's unfolding, adaptable form.

The authorship of most calligraphic works has been contested due to the mutability of the handscroll as a medium. The work of art becomes participatory, malleable; it constantly changes through the process of being encountered and passed on by others.

▪

When it rains, the house leaks in four places. It has been raining for eight days. We place buckets and towels on the wooden floor under the holes. Drips slit through the air in some places, seep through the wall in others. We wait for the sky to stop leaking.

I imagine that an endless ocean exists above. That, as it filters through thin clouds, water splits itself in half, into quarters, into eighths, into sixteenths, into thirty-seconds, into sixty-fourths, into 128ths, dividing its form until there are millions of minor tears falling from the sky.

▪

BOMB Magazine: Do you think your work responds to your living conditions?

Li Binyuan: I don't think there's much of a response to my 'living conditions' – or you could say my work is actually a state of living. I often feel like I'm working even when I'm not; I enjoy getting caught up in the 'non-work' – stopping for a break, or just being still.

Most of the time I'm in this state of being lost in a vacuum of thought. It's a sort of inward-looking practice, like a disengagement from individual feeling. But of course the experiences of thinking and living commingle and influence one another. This sort of interplay is like a primal force that urges me to create.[10]

▪

A particular interpretation of Wang's work can be seen in contemporary artist Qiu Zhijie's *Writing the 'Orchid Pavilion Preface' One Thousand Times* (1990–1995). In this blend of video and photography, Qiu thematises the process of repetition by dutifully copying out Wang's masterwork. As time passes, the characters transform from neat, fluid forms into a blurry mass of black ink through their layering. The objective of copying is not just to recreate or learn from the masters, but to obliterate them, too. Aesthetic and linguistic meaning is disintegrated in the process of copying, forming incoherence out of a previously established, coherent system. Qiu invokes the past masterwork, accelerates the process of replication, and the work destroys itself through its own reproduction.

Yet, even though Qiu dissolves the words through his treatment of the materials, the existence of Wang's work has been preserved beyond its materiality. This erasure is only another interpretation.

▪

仰觀宇宙之大
I look up at the immense universe

俯察品類之盛
I look down at this poetry

所以遊目騁懷, 足以極視聽之娛, 信可樂也。
As our eyes wander, so do our minds.

▪

My mother sleep-talks. She mutters loudly and sighs, wails and snores. The walls are porous, allowing me to trace the auditory contours of her breath. I hear this leak through at night, when wishing for a third, fourth, fifth side of the pillow to turn over. Even while resting, she is unrestful. I practise strokes of calligraphy in empty air, motioning these gestures towards the roof.

Dreams are flickering behind my eyelids again but, when I wake, I forget them instantly. Half-asleep, I hope for unwakefulness as their distant shadows loom somewhere behind consciousness.

1 Fong, Wen C., 'The Art of the Scholar-Officials', in *Beyond Representation: Chinese Painting and Calligraphy 8th–14th Century*, Metropolitan Museum of Art, New York, and Yale University Press, New Haven and London, 1992, p. 119.

2 Ledderose, Lothar, 'Introduction', in *Ten Thousand Things: Module and Mass Production in Chinese Art*, Princeton University Press, Princeton, 2000, p. 11.

3 Nietzsche, Friedrich, *Beyond Good and Evil*, trans. R. J. Hollingdale, Penguin, London, 2003, p. 160.

4 Fong, 'The Art of the Scholar-Officials', p. 122.

5 Ledderose, Lothar, 'Chinese Calligraphy: Its Aesthetic Dimension and Social Function', *Orientations*, vol. 17, no. 10, 1986, p. 38.

6 Clunas, Craig, *Art in China*, Oxford University Press, Oxford and New York, 1997, p. 137.

7 Holzman, Donald, 'On the Authenticity of the "Preface" to the Collection of Poetry Written at the Orchid Pavilion', *Journal of the American Oriental Society*, vol. 117, no. 2, 1997, p. 306.

8 Watson, William, 'Review: *Challenging the Past: The Paintings of Chang Dai-Chien* by Shen C. Y. Fu', Journal of the Royal Asiatic Society, vol. 3, no. 1, 1993, p. 171–173.

9 Ibid.

10 Fuca, Yuan, 'River of Time: Li Binyuan Interviewed by Yuan Fuca', *BOMB Magazine*, 22 August 2018, https://bombmagazine.org/articles/the-river-of-time-li-binyuan-interviewed/

Present and Accounted For

Jon Tjhia

Things contain things that contain other things. Every substance, item and creature is a gathering of its ancestors.[1] Seconds are hidden in minutes hidden in hours hidden in days hidden in weeks hidden in months hidden in years, and all of those things are hidden in bodies, which are also then hidden in other ways. This, though, is about things in arrangement, visiting with each other.

There is so much movement in the world, so much weighing in the hand to find out how much. People say, 'Vote with your wallet.' I have ten

---

1 A leather belt archives ash and ocean, soil, sun, corn and grass; the cow and its lifetime and forebears; the labouring bodies of its farmers, butchers, tanners and their meals, seasons, habits and forebears; a family of by-products, bacteria, steel blades, bones, feeders, fences, shit, water, insects, tree barks and chemicals. Passage to the point of sale and the fingers that slide it around your waist and whatever's after you. A never-ending dream within another, a Droste effect, a stained infinity mirror?

dollars in my pocket. The blue polymer note is an inscrutable ballot slip. Today's donkey vote:

one unrefrigerated 1.25-litre bottle of Pepsi Max,[2]
one 134-gram cardboard tube of Pringles (Sour Cream and Onion),[3]
two Paper Mate Exam Standard 2101 HB pencils[4]
and a Micador 3040 miniature eraser[5]

inclusive of:
all materials (dozens of them in complex constellation),
extraction and transportation (from the corners of the planet, no doubt),
manufacturing (labour, infrastructure, energy, waste management),
processing (in precise proportion and process),
warehousing and distribution (from Malaysia, China, interstate),
marketing (recognition, expectation and trust),
accounting (always),
legal and political lubrication (grow up! but also, do not grow up),
and a mark-up at the point of sale (to keep the lights on).

I'll confess: when I realise how casually I wield this power of assembly, there's a brief involuntary trill of sick pleasure. It's like having the ear of the people in charge.[6] (The last time I used a pencil was election day.

---

2 Polyethylene terephthalate, wood pulp, bleach, inks, glue, carbonated water, caramel IV, aspartame, acesulphame potassium, phosphoric acid, citric acid, sodium benzoate, caffeine, flavour; made in Australia.

3 Woodchips, bleach, wastepaper, clay, plastics (crude oil and by-products, cellulose, natural gas and by-products, coal, salt), aluminium foil, steel, inks, dehydrated potato, vegetable oils, wheat starch, rice flour, mono- and diglycerides of fatty acids, maltodextrin, salt, whey powder, MSG, disodium 5'-inosinate, disodium 5'-guanylate, dextrose, onion powder, sugar, flavour, non-fat milk powder, sour cream (powder, citric acid, lactic acid, malic acid), cultured non-fat milk, sodium caseinate, yeast extract; made in Malaysia.

4 Wood composite body (basswood or alder), graphite powder or clay binder core, plasticised coating, inks; made in China.

5 Unknown PVC-free plastic, low-density polyethylene; made in China.

6 A fluttering feeling of conducting an orchestra. But in this metaphor, are we, in fact, the musicians or the paying audience or the indifferent bodies outside the building?

I'm interested in writing as I'm interested in speaking: with the possibility of future retraction.) Cash or card, we're awash with similar arrangements: relationships made mostly on our behalf and mostly, if tacitly or unwittingly,[7] at our behest. I swallow a mouthful of Pepsi Max, and in three seconds I'm done with every one of its sensations. I used to think I loved 'nature' because it was full of minute variations that amounted to a calming noise. Then, I thought I loved it because it meant spaces where you could escape being bombarded by language. Now I wonder if nature is exempt from assembly: it is, in fact, what it is.

▪

Materials are transected, transformed, transferred, transacted, transfused.[8] When I ask her, Coco says she believes that memory's unmanageable excess will render it essentially moot, while materials keep passing dust back and forth, always eroding and accreting. This gives 'things' an endurance over 'feelings'.

Feelings are transected and transformed and transferred and transacted and transfused, too. They sit inside like sediment, leaving fossil-like outlines and depressions, shaping habits like a stone in a creek. Searching for their telling contours, we press about with our fingers, always trying to know what lingers beyond our understanding.

How do you hold up your end of a conversation with the dead? What do you have to offer on the subject of freedom? I walk out of the apartment. Through the closed door opposite mine, I hear a father's voice: 'No. No!' I walk down the steps and pull the building door[9] to latch behind me.

---

7 When Marxists talk about 'alienation', they're referring to the estranged labour of working people. But search for 'consumer alienation' and it's all about market research, tracing dissatisfied consumers' angst towards brands. So how do we index this? Consumer confidence?

8 Nothing new under the sun – just musical chairs, right?

9 Hardwood, glass, steel, brass, zinc, paint.

Phoning from interstate, Natalie tells me that, when she dies, she would rather her body be 'catapulted into oblivion' than buried or cremated. She's never expressed this desire to anybody else. Is it possible, she wonders, and more importantly, can it be done without harming anyone? On the internet, she reads about the Mongols catapulting cadavers over the city walls of Caffa in the Middle Ages, during a siege, potentially delivering bubonic plague to the city's residents. This story is often used as a prototypical example of rudimentary biological warfare. She does not want her body to be hurled at anybody in particular, or with any intent aside from the action itself. I imagine her cheek pressed to the darkened screen of her phone as she speaks, leaving a faint imprint.[10] It seems to me that oblivion is not very far away at all – it's just a little beyond sight. I think again. It's not really oblivion for the body, either – just someone else's problem.

If I understand it correctly,[11] there's some idea that the universe is underpinned by a tendency towards 'thermal equilibrium'. That is, the Big Bang represents a big expression of heat that will ultimately average out across all matter, making it sort of … inert.[12] I've read of similar ideas about the fate of history. Kneeling on dirt, I face a mirror skywards and reflect light from the sun back towards space, careful not to blind any airborne bodies. Energy is passed around, transformed but never lost. Every state is a visitor. My body is often overheating in a way I cannot regulate. It's really hard to imagine feeling too hot when you're cold, or feeling too cold when you're hot. This is hierarchy.

---

10 Natalie is 914 kilometres from me but, beyond a small amount of visible distance, absence becomes flat and unfathomable.

11 I wouldn't trust that I do.

12 In this way, seeing the entire universe is simple. Mark a point on a matchstick (you are here), strike it alight and watch it burn all the way to the end.

■

In the cemetery, the dimensions of old tombstones recall the aspect ratio of my smartphone screen. Like Instagram Stories, they're a little nudge: *remember me?* You can do a TikTok dance on my grave. One person's inscription is another's caption is another's counterpoint. Just admit it: *I was looking to be loved.*

About love, Amita once offered me the axiom, 'What's for you won't go past you.' It's weird to think the surface of a road has some softness. Or 'give'. What is the aspect ratio of my car's windscreen? Driving slowly on a fast road[13] feels illicit. I was inching along the Eastern Freeway with plenty of time to look around. A dead magpie then a dead cockatoo. Near the Bulleen Road exit, a dead kangaroo, legs up, a big pink 'X' spray-painted across its stiff barrel chest.[14] The lines of the bridge and the trees ripple behind petrol vapour from a truck's chimney.

I like when air bends light. I like that geological feeling you get when a freeway takes a hill in its stride. A casual vivisection reveals the ground's layers. *Don't worry!* On flat land, concrete slabs face the road with a repeating pattern, made to disperse the echoes of a thousand small explosions. In this way, crushed and reconstituted rocks impersonate real rocks, but also they are kind of real rocks. If there's a metaphor here, find it yourself.

Move the map a dozen clicks west. Princes Park Drive curves north, separating the living on its west side (an expanse of soccer fields, hundreds of walkers-joggers-kickers-riders-stretchers at dusk) from the dead on its east side (Melbourne General Cemetery). It's cold, just past the winter equinox, and branches reach naked into the thin air. There are more than

---

13 Asphalt, cement, sand, air, water, gravel, chalk; histories of automotive development and of standardised weights and measures; colonial displacement of First Nations peoples, formation and enforcement of settler laws, administrative subdivision; lives lost, accident research, vehicle sensors and video surveillance, zoning, road rules, the courts, insurance companies, population distribution and housing development; habits, time.

14 ♡ X

300,000 bodies[15] in the cemetery, which is a quarter of the size of my old suburb (home to 5000[16]). There are separate areas organised by religious denomination. There's an Elvis Presley Memorial Garden, thankfully – lest one of history's most famous cultural icons be accidentally misplaced. In the Prime Ministers' Memorial Garden, a memorial to Harold Holt (presumed drowned) reminds us 'HE LOVED THE SEA'. Derrimut, a Yalukit-Willam Boon Wurrung leader who figures in many stories of early colonial Melbourne, did not belong to the available religions. He is buried in the Chinese section. But there is speculation that the Chinese goldminers' appetites for salted fish catalysed the seizure and sale of the Boon Wurrung reserve.[17]

Just inside the green iron fence running the western perimeter, in the Roman Catholic section, there's a row of forty tombs belonging to the Sisters of Saint Joseph of the Sacred Heart. They run in two lines of twenty, mirrored at the head where a single row of black granite slabs stands, engraved with gold lettering on either side. The stones mark the names ('Sr. Lucia Capicciano', 'Sr. Agnes Therese Hickey') and death dates ('Died 25th January 2013', 'Died 1st March 2011') of those interred therein; some graves contain as many as five bodies. These acknowledgements feel either humble or perfunctory. Towards the northern end of the row, nine graves remain empty, headstones unmarked but for a golden cross at the top and 'RIP' at the bottom, offering the sentiment of a blank greeting card or an advertisement. That, or it's just knowledge. What's for you won't go past you.

---

15 'The construction of three mausolea from the 1990s has given the cemetery a new life.' Ha! See: Southern Metropolitan Cemeteries Trust, 'Our History at Melbourne General Cemetery', https://smct.org.au/our-locations/about-melbourne-general-cemetery/mgc-history

16 According to 'new research', the 'average' person can recognise 5000 different faces. See Sample, Ian, 'Psychologists' Face Off Reveals Humans Can Recognise 5,000 People', *The Guardian*, 10 October 2018, https://www.theguardian.com/science/2018/oct/10/how-many-faces-average-person-recognises-5000

17 Clark, Ian D., '"You Have All This Place, No Good Have Children ..." Derrimut: Traitor, Saviour, or a Man of His People?', *Journal of the Royal Australian Historical Society*, 1 December 2005, https://www.thefreelibrary.com/'You+have+all+this+place,+no+good+have+children+...'+Derrimut:...-a0140053899

■

Visiting friends nearby, I ride past the former rope factory in Footscray on Kinnear Street and remember the horrific arson attack that killed three people there a few years ago.[18] David, Tanya and her daughter Zoe. David and Tanya would regularly secure the room – a small brick storage area, their squat – from the inside using a chain and padlock. People heard their screams (there are houses and blocks of flats across the road) and tried fruitlessly to extinguish the fire with buckets of water. After police completed their investigation, charred belongings were removed with a bulldozer.[19]

The green sheet-metal wall of the factory occupies a long section of the street. In one short portion, a couple of metres wide, the metal looks distressed: paint grows bubbled, blanches into patches of lime fringed with rust brown, bands into black. I turn away quickly. The westward wall of the building faces onto a weed-filled gravel lot. It is also made from corrugated iron but in dull silver overlapping layers, on which chunky white graffiti letters say 'ROCK THE SYSTEM'. Layered underneath this, the silhouette of a city skyline, and in front of that, flames.

I have started noticing similar sheets of corrugated iron nearer to home. In an alley that runs through Carlton North, from Richardson to Park, behind the houses on Amess and Canning, I count ninety-two roller doors, nineteen garage doors that swing open, two that slide to one

---

18 David 'Bluey' Griffiths, 39, Tanya Burmeister, 32, and her daughter Zoe, 15. 'The sister knew he had been homeless but she believed that at the factory, where he was squatting, he had been "trying to turn his life around".' Webb, Carolyn, 'Homeless Victim of Footscray Fire Was "a Loving, Caring Person", Says Sister', *The Age*, 14 March 2017, https://www.theage.com.au/national/victoria/homeless-victim-of-footscray-fire-was-a-loving-caring-person-says-sister-20170314-guxj5d.html

19 'The room too had been crammed with meagre belongings. Another resident said the squatters had been "trying to make a go of it", with clothes hanging up, succulents in pots out the front and a mat at the door.' Mills, Tammy, Mannix, Liam and Bucci, Nino, 'Footscray Factory Fire: Man Arrested over Blaze That Killed Three People', *The Age*, 2 March 2017, https://www.theage.com.au/national/victoria/three-die-in-fire-at-rear-of-factory-in-ballarat-road-footscray-20170302-guokzq.html

side, thirty-nine pedestrian gates and one regular door. Where the alleyway opens onto Park Street, there's a round painting above the final roller door. It marks a red flame on red brick. Around the corner, on the wall, an antique proclamation in green lettering: WE RECOMMEND BRIQUETTES / FOR WARMTH & COMFORT.

It's not that I think everything is loaded with talismans and clues. I cross the grass and round the corner and walk up the three terracotta steps into my building. Through the closed apartment door opposite my own, I hear the father's voice, more agitated than before: 'No! No.' I walk through my door and turn the latch.

▪

A prolonged lack of vitamin C produces unstable collagen, a protein that strengthens and elasticises skin. Old wounds will bleed spontaneously.[20] Irene says: 'When function fails, something else is revealed.' In collagen's case, blood. Every time I see my parents, Dad squeezes a bag of oranges and hands me an old passata jar of juice to take home. Every time he does this, Mum tells me to dilute it with water so the sugars don't rot my teeth. In June, my parents tell me that Dad's currently uninhabited ancestral home, where the ashes of his forebears are kept, will be emptied due to problems with theft. Metal pipes have been stolen, and urns taken, presumably to sell to tourists as authentic antiques. They tell me the family has organised to burn the photographs of his ancestors. Not in a dramatic way. I don't really understand. Dad has a medical issue I don't want to tell you about. It's like a stone in a creek.

▪

---

20 Joan Didion: 'That passion for the documentation of irrelevant detail is characteristic of the afflicted.' See: 'Jealousy: Is It a Curable Illness?', *Vogue*, June 1961, p. 96.

What do you have to offer on the subject of freedom? What would it be like to live a life led by pleasure? What's there to say about a cemetery? Before sending the *Voyager 1* spacecraft beyond our atmosphere, we should have made a Golden Record of unhitching yourself from time. A Golden Record of ignoring the lemons rotting in your kitchen. I wouldn't be surprised to learn that NASA had quietly attached a body to the wayward spacecraft – a Golden Record of 'show, don't tell'.

People are often sceptical about things that are free and enjoy the sense of security that a formalised relation – transaction – offers.[21] There is a feeling that a transaction confers rights. Rights can be mistaken for freedoms. Late in the evening, Ben talks about the difference between 'freedom from' and 'freedom to'. Every afternoon, a woman walks by the dead-end semicircle of Canning Street and appraises the items left out as perpetual hard rubbish, which sits beneath a 'NO DUMPING OF RUBBISH' sign. Today, a broad black cowboy hat glued with strings of beads and fake pearls. The carrot-coloured metal supports, feet and handles of a wheelbarrow; a tall steel electric urn without a lid; a boxy armchair upholstered with worn taupe velour; a small blue cardboard shoebox; a black shade for a floor lamp; a thin rectangle of unmarked fibreboard. Assess and turn the perpetual social compost of durables and things people are not quite sure what to do with. The pile isn't peer pressure but peer permission. Or maybe people, trusting in the unknowable resourcefulness of unknown strangers, think of this as an informal service.[22]

Sitting on the grass beside me, Connor tells me he's been wasting time on Carol Bowman's Reincarnation Forum.[23] He doesn't entirely believe or disbelieve in past lives, says that's somewhat beside the point. I make a decision not to remember anything anymore, or at least not to carry it

---

21 Raoul Vaneigem: 'The fight for pleasure in oneself and in the world doesn't pass through money, but, on the contrary, its absolute exclusion.' See Sterling, Bruce, 'Elderly Situationist Enjoys Baffling Interviewer', *WIRED*, 3 January 2012, https://www.wired.com/2012/01/elderly-situationist-enjoys-baffling-interviewer/

22 See footnote #7 regarding alienation.

23 The Reincarnation Forum, https://www.carolbowman.com/reincarnation-forum

around – set it down as language instead. I'm not built for a life ruled by pleasure. Catapult yourself over the wall that forbids you. Who wants to be stacked five-high forever?[24] To hold up your end of a conversation with the dead, pick up a mirror.

▪

I was about to tell you how surprised I was to notice the yellow-tailed black cockatoos (first, the falling leaves, tree-branch chunks and seed casings, then the joyful scratch of their voices) and how, the last time I'd seen them floating over my neighbourhood, I felt so happy I cried.

I ask Jess about last times. She says that what troubles her is the idea of being unaware of the fact. 'This haunts me. We live out our last times all the time without even knowing that's what they are. Would we do things any differently if we did?' I turn the pencil between my fingers.

My friends advocate for some kinds of silence. Irene speaks of silence as both an unfortunate inheritance and a potential-filled space. Michael, whose mother has recently developed Alzheimer's, describes silence elementally:

> When she says things, they don't make sense. She tries to say things that please, but they are out of the flow. Her silence is a kind of relief for me sometimes. I don't know if it feels that way to her. When either one of us says something, the meaning vanishes – it can't be trusted. But sitting side by side in silence – that makes me feel close to her. I can feel her presence in my childhood and young adulthood rising up, regaining its form and coherence. I imagine it like a solid rock, large enough for the both of us, by a river.

---

24 Lauren Oyler in a now-deleted tweet: 'everyone keeps saying the same things over and over!!! say something else'. But what?

These days, his mother barely speaks. It's 2.25 am and the military are once more running drills over my neighbourhood. Helicopters cut the air. I sip a glass of Pepsi Max and read an email from Masako. She explains 暗黙の了解 (anmoku no ryōkai): 'You just have to say it, even silently, and you're held in this cacophony of soundlessness. It means "silent understanding".'

I think that's how you hold up your end of a conversation with the dead. Or with materials. Or desire. Silent understanding.

'To those I don't want held in this cultural embrace,' Masako continues, 'it just means "shut up".'

Thank You for Calling

Brandon K. Liew

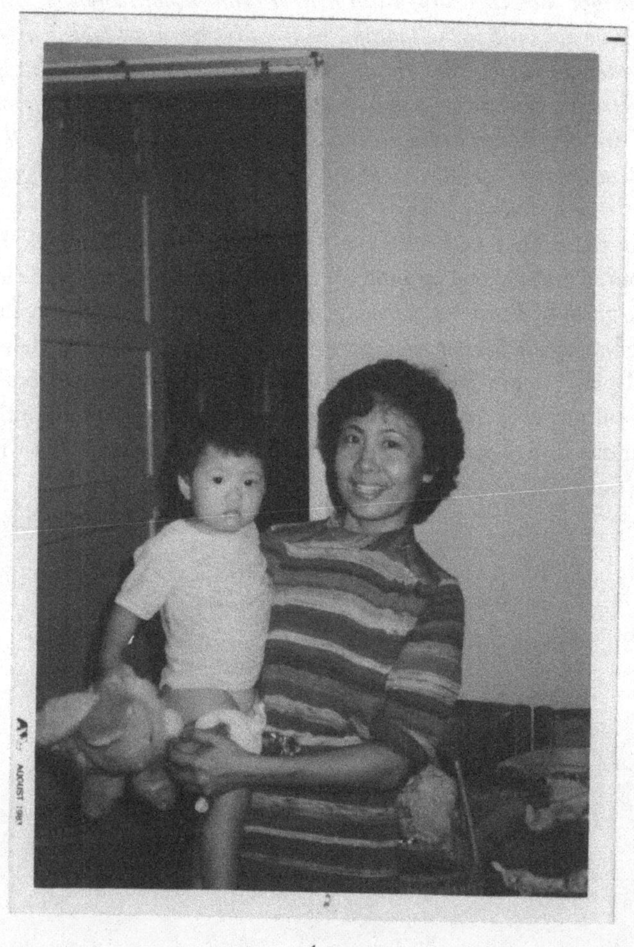

2016

I am in my mid-twenties and David Bowie has just died. The phone is ringing constantly. I find myself repeating the same drivel every time I pick it up. Thought detaches from body.

Hello, thank you for calling Shakahari – this is Brandon speaking. A table for two? Tonight? Give me a moment and I'll see if I can fit you in; it's a little busy tonight. Bowie – well, I can neither confirm nor deny that. All I can say is, if he did visit our restaurant, he would have sat at table fourteen and ordered the croquettes. Well, let me see. It just so happens that I have space on twelve from seven thirty to nine, would you like that? You're welcome. As I said, I can neither confirm nor deny such a thing. Yes, of course – I'll see you at … seven thirty. No worries, thank you for calling Shakahari Vegetarian.

I recite these lines back into the ears of each desperate diner. Half of Melbourne has snapped up a long-forgotten rumour and everyone longs to see the ghost of Bowie on a Friday night. The seat where he sat, the floor that he wanked on.[2] A perverse, performative pilgrimage of the Melburnian kind. I play the broker, the medium for this seance. I come from a long line of cultural brokers. Ziggy Stardust screams at me in contempt through the antique hi-fi. I am in my mid-twenties and the phone is just ringing all the time.

---

1 Grandmother beaming in the old house.

2 He wanks on the floor in 'Time', from the 1973 album *Aladdin Sane*. I think about how rude this is every time I mop table fourteen.

2008

I am fifteen and we have been running this restaurant for almost three decades. I begin by washing dishes and then by waiting tables in the upper section close to the bar. Later on, I am pouring wine and counting the daily take. Eventually, like my mother and grandmother before me, I am managing the floor and closing up on Wednesdays, Thursdays, Fridays, sometimes the weekends. The regulars know me and they always tell me how happy they are that the business is still in the family. The celebrities don't talk to me until they are dead. In one of my English classes at school, I point out that Helen Garner wrote us into in her bestselling novel *Monkey Grip.*[3] My classmates are impressed even though none of them have read nor care about the book. *Monkey Grip* takes place among the hippies and bohemians of Carlton in the 1970s, many of whom loitered at our restaurant, a sort of quasi-experimental countercultural meeting place. That is to say, we had a lot of weirdos.[4] We are the oldest vegetarian restaurant in the inner city; 'Shakahari' in Sanskrit means 'vegetarian'; vegetarian in the seventies meant 'alternative'.

Yes, our menu is fully vegetarian. I would recommend the Avocado Magic to start with, and perhaps the satay for the mains. The satay has been on there for decades. We took it off once and there was a huge uproar; everyone complained incessantly, spoilt children, so Kim Un has been making it ever since. That's right. No worries at all, thank you for calling Shakahari.

---

3 There is a rumour that she used to write in here, too. She hasn't been in lately, so I haven't had the chance to ask about it.

4 Still do.

5

At fifteen, I do not understand what Shakahari means nor do I really care. Grand-uncle Kim Un worked here as a dishwasher after coming here as a poor Hokkien student and took over the place from the devotees of an Indian guru who opened it. The guru was an incredibly spiritual man, I hear.[6] After arriving here with all the other migrants in the seventies, Grand-uncle became something of a hippie and persuaded Grandmother and Grandfather to fly in and help out. And because of that, now I help out. Grandmother still works Tuesdays and Thursdays. She is seventy-six. Grandfather is now buried in a church garden near Ripponlea.[7]

1985

Grandfather and Grandmother are in their forties when they get the call from Grand-uncle Kim Un to help out. For many years, they ran a pub together in Penang named The Barrel, where Grandfather accrued gambling debts and his friends never ever paid their tabs. It was an easy decision to move. The White Australia policy is put to rest and Grandmother eventually manages to secure a visa to Australia as a skilled worker, specifically as one of the only chefs specialising in Nyonya cuisine.[8]

No, we are not an Indian restaurant. Um … it's more pan-Asian-inspired now, I guess, whatever flavour profile that our chefs are inspired by at the moment. Yes. We've been open for many years here in Carlton. Seven days a week, but we close for Sunday lunch. That's okay, thank you for calling. We'll be right here.

---

5 Grand-uncle Kim Un looking sharp in his black suit before departing Penang for Melbourne in the 1970s.

6 Guru Muktananda and his followers in 1972.

7 I cremated him and scattered his ashes at the Anglican parish of Balaclava and Elwood. He used to love that garden.

8 I like to think that Harold Holt and Gough Whitlam were fans of traditional Nyonya food.

9

Grandmother is ten years old when she starts cooking noodles in George Town at the Chinese Recreation Club,[10] where she lives on the first floor with five of her siblings. Her three brothers and two sisters support the family by working as waitresses and singers in the club, and Granduncle Kim Un borrows enough money to study chemistry at the University of Melbourne. Only the boys are given places in school so Grandmother teaches herself to read. She meets my suave Grandfather serving him coffee. They get married shortly after a whirlwind romance and I serve their piping-hot vegetarian laksa throughout my twenties.[11]

---

9 Grandmother and Grandfather taking it easy at the most notorious pub on the island, The Barrel.

10 The Chinese Recreation Club (CRC) was formed in the late 19th century in response to white-only sports clubs in British-occupied Penang. The attached restaurant in particular became well known.

11 I dive into a bowl of Grandmother's noodles in the kitchen and I catch myself wondering if her first bowl tasted the same. Her fingers are slender but her noodles are fat and firm. Was it always that way?

12

1988

Mother is managing front of house and Father is washing dishes in the kitchen. A big red phone rings on the counter and she routinely answers it, as if a call from God themself. Table for two, Thy will be done. The God of Lygon Street is vegetarian and Uncle Robert makes their salads by the window.[13]

Hello, thank you for calling Shakahari. We are open this Easter weekend, care for a table? Celebrating something? Of course, sir. We have an extensive Australian wine list, or you can bring something of your own— You want to bring water? *Uh, we have— I mean, that's fine, I suppose.*

---

12 Mother talking to God.

13 Shakahari used to be next to Jimmy Watson's on Lygon Street before moving next to La Mama Theatre during my years.

14

Father and Mother are both university students and they are supposed to be working and studying, but they are rarely ever studying. They spend time in the kitchen at odd hours together and, because of that, I now spend time in the same kitchen at odd hours alone, doing both their jobs. I think that is unfair. They get married after conceiving me in the kitchen and I arrive in this place as a first-born offering to the God of Lygon Street (Blessed be Thy Satay).[15]

Recently, Mother threw a dinner party for her old Shakahari workmates. They got together, drank all the wine and stayed up all night reminiscing about little things like hauling plates up the tiny orange stairway and minding the insufferable customers.[16] Some of us had gone on to become famous artists and philosophers; some were happy, some were not. Some had never really left the place. Some struggled to remember if they were really there at all, as if they had floated through a shared unconscious dream.

---

14 Uncle Robert on the left and Father on the right, preparing the satay.

15 I try to be more than a circumstance of yesteryear.

16 They are all still as insufferable, except the ones who are nice to me and tell me to write books that I will never write.

17

I am twenty-five when I am woken up by a voice on the receiver telling me that the restaurant is on fire. I arrive on the scene at three in the morning to find the restaurant intact, but the theatre next door is charred and smoking.[18] I ask the police officer cordoning off the scene if we can open for business. He gives me a look and shakes his head disapprovingly.

Hi, thank you for calling Shakahari. We will be closed temporarily due to unforeseen circumstances but you can leave a message for us after the tone, and we will endeavour to take your bookings as soon as we can. We hope to see you again shortly. Thank you for calling.

As I clean up the rubble around the storeroom at the back, I wonder what would happen if the fire had spread. Grand-uncle Kim Un's farmhouse had burnt down completely many years ago on account of either a country bushfire or arson, depending on who you ask. Kim Un and John were devastated; they lost almost everything. Among the ashes, a priceless curation of antiques, books and recipes, perhaps heirlooms, who knows.[19] But the restaurant stood then, and remains still, next to the blackened theatre. The buildings themselves never amounted to much, anyway, so rickety and ancient. Service feels like the re-enactment of a period drama and customers look to me for sage advice while I plate their vegan lasagne, as if I channel the avatar of the guru who had stood in my place.[20] I finish cleaning up while the firemen are still on the roof assessing the damage. What matters is that we are unsinged. We open the next day.

---

17 The old kitchen was a beautiful mess.

18 An electrical fault. Liz has been working hard at La Mama's restoration. They have since reopened and the building looks magnificent.

19 I have never seen the old farmhouse, but I have seen their faces when they think about the fire and that tells me more than enough.

20 We do have a large antique painting of the avatar overlooking the dining room.

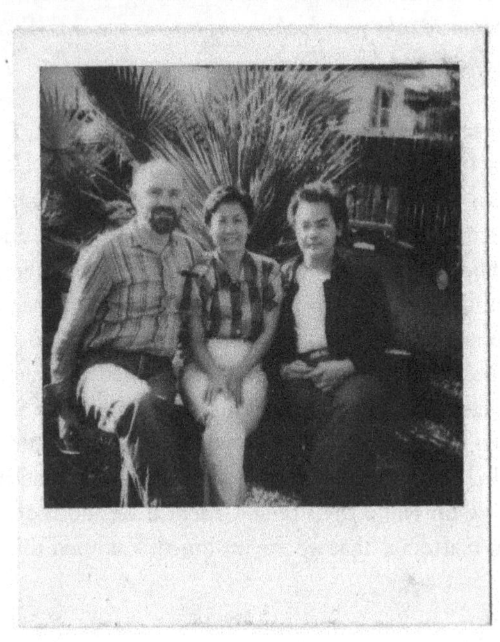

21

Grand-aunty is in the Alfred Hospital and I am translating between her and the ER doctor about her leg that no longer works. She had finished her shift at the restaurant and walked as far as Flinders Street before collapsing in broad daylight. A kind of muscle failure, or 'chef's foot'. They don't know what is wrong exactly, but they tell us that it is to be expected that something will go wrong when you work five days a week standing in a kitchen for most of your life. No-one in the ER is surprised – least of all Grand-aunty, who, to my exasperation, treats it as a retirement trophy. She spends the week in hospital and then the next six months on a fold-out sofa in my living room, before recovering the use of the leg and eventually returning triumphantly to her station astride a sizzling wok. But this, too, is brief. In the meantime, the kitchen is short-staffed and the roster is thrown off by a failed appendage. The workload falls onto the still-functioning appendages that remain in the family. A broken machine is either restored or replaced.

Thanks for calling Shakahari. We will be open as usual for Valentine's Day this year, with a special menu for lunch and dinner to celebrate this special occasion. We will be open every day this week including Sunday lunch, and we look forward to having you with us. If you would like to leave a message or make a booking, please leave your name and number after the tone and we'll get back to you shortly. Thank you for calling.[22]

---

21 Grand-uncle John, Grandmother and Grand-uncle Kim Un, who has transformed into James Dean.

22 Valentine's Day has always been the busiest seating during the year for us. Who can resist heart-shaped croquettes?

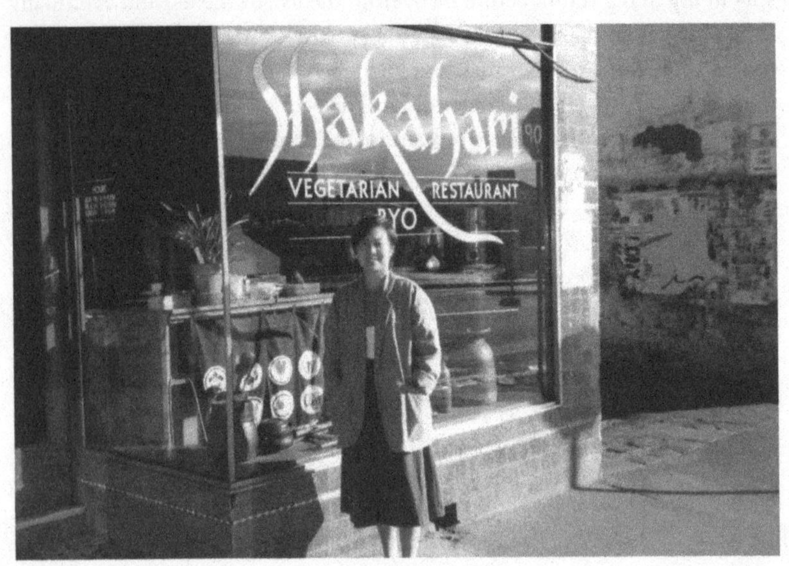

23

2020, winter

I am locked down in my house, almost thirty, when all restaurants in Victoria close on account of a viral pandemic. *No-one is immune*, they say, *stay home*. That's an order. On the first day of the lockdown, I venture from across the city to Lygon Street to rescue our vegetables from rotting in an empty kitchen.[24] I shutter the door and load my car with buckets of raw beansprouts. The water in the buckets swishes and spills in objection. 'You won't last in there three days on your own; you have cheated your fate. Consider yourselves lucky,' I tell them.

Thank you for calling Shakahari Vegetarian. In compliance with Victorian public safety regulations, we will be closed for the time being. There will be no takeaway or dine-in services for the moment.[25] *While we aren't sure how things are going to pan out, we will try to keep you updated, so please call back at a later time.*

The beansprouts are put to purpose in my soup, but there is little to be done about everything else. We fall apart in the quiet.

---

23 Grandmother taking in Lygon Street as she stands tall in front of the shop window.

24 Victoria entered Stage 3 restrictions on 30 March 2020. The statewide lockdown would continue until 12 May and resumed again on 8 July until late October. We made three or four illegal trips to salvage ill-fated produce.

25 We've never really been a 'takeaway' kind of place.

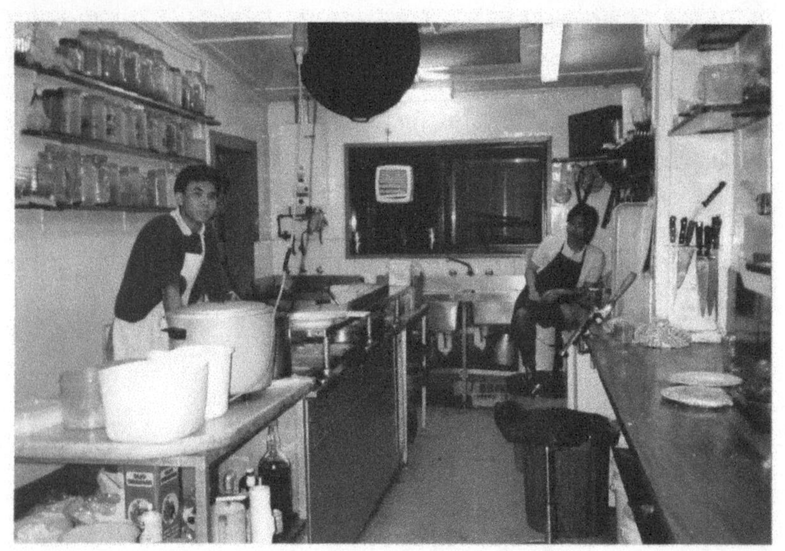

26

I am sitting in the living room listening to a eulogy given by Cousin Pang, who is a full-time preacher. Uncle Robert lies in a casket behind him, solemn, collected. I am not, and neither are Mother and Grandmother as their eyes tear up at the screen.[27] The final days of Uncle Robert are peaceful. For us 10,000 miles away, they are anything but. I find it difficult to think coherently but manage to write down a few sentences and send them to Cousin Pang, who ventriloquises them in a much more preacherly way at the funeral.

Since Grandfather's passing a few years now, Uncle Robert had been the last real father figure, the last real role model for this branch of the Khaw family, for the eldest sons Jason and myself. I don't think we could ever ask for a better father and uncle. I think the strength of his character will live on through the decisions that we make in our lives. Both he and my grandpa have left very big shoes for us to fill. I can only try to do my best to do right by my family as well. Thank you for being here. Thank you all for coming.

The cremation takes place and this moment passes. Among the ashes, a lingering curation of memory and feeling. With the restaurant closed, there is little for us to do but develop idle hands and sullen thoughts. There is no-one left to cook for and no-one left here is hungry.[28] The cat develops an anxiety disorder. The phone is ringing all the time.

---

26 A younger Uncle Robert on the left, looking tired at the end of his shift.

27 The three of us mourn an uncle, a brother and a son respectively over Zoom. We tried looking at emergency flights but it just wasn't an option. I couldn't put anyone at risk.

28 Uncle Robert ran a number of successful bakeries, restaurants and cafés. They have all since closed.

I am twenty-one when Father leaves Australia and I never see him again. In the same year, I graduate with an English degree and not much else in mind.[29] I moonlight as a copywriter in the break room in between shifts. The thought of leaving crosses my mind maybe once or twice. There is no sense to sentimentality. One day, we will run out of customers or run out of satay. One day, we all run out of time. I tell myself, *You better figure out what it is that you want before any of this happens.*[30]

---

29 I wasn't excited about anything.

30 I stick around for another three years before deciding to continue my studies overseas. In 2019, I return to Melbourne on a research scholarship.

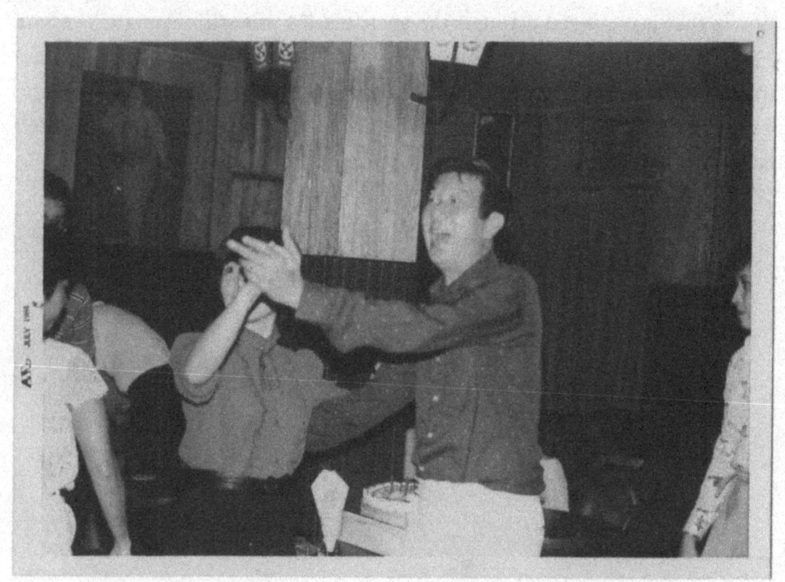

31

It is close to midnight and I send everyone home so I can close up the restaurant in peace. The tables are clean, the sinks empty, back door locked, ovens off, coolroom shut, tills sorted, wine pumped. We had a busy day and I am dreading the train ride home. I turn the music up and finish counting the sums for the take so I can balance the debts for tomorrow. I put on my coat and clutch the keys in my pocket. As I turn towards the door, I realise that I forgot to turn off the gas fireplace that is flickering in front of table fourteen.

The shadows dance on the orange-brown wall, jolting to the ghost of Bowie that is conjured through the speakers. In this stillness, late at night, I sometimes sit and watch this for a while and think about all the other spirits in the room who are dancing without a care in the world. They hold hands and twirl in circles around the room and the expressions on their faces are always that of birds, overjoyed.

---

31 Grandmother and Grandfather dancing in their restaurant.

Archives

Teresa

Veronica Gorrie

Archives are the keepers of our traumatic past. For us Aboriginal people, the first people of this land, the archives are vital in piecing together our past, in order to proceed and forge our way through the future. They hold many secrets the colonisers wished we never unravelled, but unravelling is all we do. Family secrets and cruel memories documented within the archives have played important parts in history; if not for the archives of the past, the lives of our ancestors would have been diminished, lost forever, without a trace of evidence that dispossession ever occurred.

The dispossession and displacement of my people have been occurring since colonisation. The forcible removals of Aboriginal children from their families were the result of the government implementing legislation that empowered the colonisers. Legislation such as the colloquially known 'Half-Caste Act' of 1886 and child-removal policies were enacted not to assimilate my ancestors but were instead acts of genocide. The only good to come of all this were the ward files the government kept, the movement sheets. Names and locations of institutions that housed these children. Names and locations of white families that used these children as child slave labourers. An inventory of items of clothing and blankets that were issued to them. It must be emphasised that specific details pertaining to the identities of the colonisers had been blackened out in order to protect them – to provide them with anonymity.

In 2020, the then-Minister for Aboriginal Affairs announced the Victorian Stolen Generations Redress Scheme and, shortly after, a callout for expressions of interest was advertised. I applied and was advised I was successful. I now sit on the steering committee for the Victorian Department of Premier and Cabinet's office for the scheme. Although Victoria was the first state in this country to implement the barbaric colonial policy of child removals, it is the last to rectify the wrongs.

Being on the steering committee not only provides me with insights into the reparation process, but also allows me to have a voice, a voice for those who can no longer speak, a voice for all those marginalised. Not as one who has been stolen, displaced and dispossessed, but as their descendant – as a descendant of the Stolen Generation.

Teresa was the older sister of my grandmother. Teresa was twelve years old when she was stolen; my grandmother was eight years old, their sister Myra, ten, and their little brother Ronnie, only six. They were stolen from Lake Tyers Aboriginal Mission (now known as Lake Tyers Aboriginal Trust) on 11 November 1941. They were taken to the Royal Park Depot for unwanted children and, soon after, Teresa was given to an old white woman and forced to live with her in Ararat, Victoria. Two years later, Teresa was dead. Sometimes, I wonder: if Teresa had a voice, what would she say? I imagine it would sound like this:

My name is Teresa. I died aged fourteen. I shouldn't have. But I did. I am buried in Ararat; I have been here since 1943. Seventy-nine years. I should be used to it by now but I am not, as this is not my home, this is not my land, and this is not my Country – and, in all honesty, I probably won't be able to rest until I am taken home. My home is Lake Tyers Aboriginal Trust. It used to be called Lake Tyers Aboriginal Mission or, in my language, Bung Yarnda. I want to go home. I have been here so long now. My skin has liquefied and the dirt has caved in on me. My once-infected body is now a corpse, bony shards. I saw many die the same way but I never thought it would happen to me. I was careful.

I had long black hair and big brown eyes. I had long legs and I ran fast. I could have been an athlete. I could have been anything. When I went to school on the mission, I ran so fast I beat the boys. I could have married my first crush, my first love. I could have had children and grandchildren. I would have been a great grandmother. But I am none of these.

She didn't care about me. I was just a slave to her. Her slave. She made money from me. She pretended to care but, once the doors were closed, she was just like every other white person: mean and controlling. She always threatened me – be good, do this, do that or I will write a letter and you will go back. I wanted to go back, back with my sisters and brother. She forced me to write letters and articles to the local newspaper, The Argus. *She wrote most of them but used my name at the end. She wanted the white townsfolk and the citizens of Ararat to like me. I didn't care if they liked me or not; I planned on running away as soon as I could, but she was always watching me, except for when I was at the laundry, where she made me work. She made a lot of promises that she broke. She was a liar.*

She told me that she was going to get Myra, Linda and Ronnie to stay with us, too. This never happened. A broken promise – I never saw them again. I'm a liar.

Teresa is buried at the Ararat Cemetery under a gravestone that reads 'Therssa Gorrie'. Not only is she buried hundreds of kilometres away from her ancestral and traditional Country, Gunai/Kurnai Country, but she has been buried under the most indignant of circumstances, as this is not her name. Her name is Teresa Helen Gorrie. When I applied to access her ward files from the state government, the very same institution that stole her eighty-one years ago, I didn't receive folders containing pages and pages of old English and racist commentary about her movements within the system. I received just one page, and it is this one page that drove me to apply to be on the scheme's steering committee. I felt compelled to bring to life this one page.

Her short life had been reduced to a single page, unlike the reams of paper and the plethora of information I received upon gaining possession of my grandmother's and father's ward files from the Department of Health and Human Services (formerly known as the Department of Welfare) years earlier, which haunt me to this day. The barbarous vernacular used in these files has left an imprint on my brain that I can never unread or unsee. But to fully comprehend my ancestors' lives and to make sense of not only the trauma that they endured but the intergenerational trauma that has been handed down to me were necessary – and, more than that, imperative. I needed to know that the injustices they were subjected to were to no avail and that their existence and survival were significant. That their lives mattered. Flipping through pages, weaving through the timelines of their existence, is almost unbearable, but it is indispensable.

The ward files from the archives are traumatic to read, but the hurt and despair I feel do not compare to all that my ancestors must have endured at the hands of the colonisers. As survivors of cruel injustices, we must challenge their oppressors, our oppressors, and fight for the right to egalitarianism. Only then will our trauma, like a festering gaping wound, scab over and begin to heal.

As part of the steering committee, I have traversed many parts of the state of Victoria – many towns and many communities – to speak to survivors and other descendants of the Stolen Generation. I am privy to their answers to the simple question, *What will it take for you to heal?* Although it is encouraged that they do not recount their stories and experiences for fear that they be re-traumatised, in some cases that's all survivors want to do. They want somebody to hear them; they want to talk. And, by god, it's gut-wrenching to witness and to hear, consoling them as they cry. I cry.

I cry not just because of their harrowing accounts but because of the strength of my people. This has been said by many others before me, Aboriginal people, my people through all our adversities, and there have been many – invasion, massacres, genocide, epidemics of disease, dispossession, displacement, and the rape and torture of Aboriginal women and children. We are still here.

Soon, the steering committee will hand over to the Victorian Premier and Cabinet office the final report containing all of its recommendations, and I am hoping that they are all implemented. Only when survivors, members and victims of the state's Stolen Generation are duly compensated for their loss – loss of culture, loss of language and loss of kinship – only then will I be thankful to the colonisers. But not for bequeathing many Aboriginal families, including my own, with lifelong traumas. I will be thankful for the evidentiary records that have been archived because, without these, our oral testimonies of the past may have never been proven.

I will begin my family's healing by having Teresa exhumed and repatriated to Bung Yarnda, to a final resting place alongside my grandmother and their siblings. Having her finally reunited with them will allow us, too, to feel more whole. I don't want to wait another seventy-nine years.

Whole Bodies

Ryan Gustafsson

It's winter and I'm seeking sun, in a little library in North Melbourne. I'm at VANISH – Victorian Adoption Network for Information and Self Help – going through their collection of reports, newsletters and newspaper clippings. It occupies just a small section of the organisation's meeting room, on the second floor overlooking the street. I'm grateful others have been moved to act in the name of posterity and preservation, staked themselves on futures unforeseen. I think to myself that this is how we begin to stay, together. That this creates a space for dwelling, for sifting, for depth: to see traces of lives stacked, bound, held together by staples rusted over time. That it demands my whole body, such that old photographs of reunions, lodged and forgotten between folds of paper, have a lap to fall onto.

There is little on South Korea in the collection, which is not unexpected. Despite the fact that, in 2023, Korean overseas adoption will be a practice spanning seventy years, this history remains frustratingly inaccessible. An open secret traversing multiple organisations, clinics, agencies and countries. Lifetimes. Characterised by knowing but furtive looks, averted eyes, speculative fiction. Apologies for speaking, apologies for speaking English, for understanding English only. Pleas to strangers. A story filled with stories. Roughly 200,000 of them, if all you are counting are adoptees. Mine, both like and unlike the others.

How many languages would we need to understand the difference between being missing and being lost? How many attempts at translation, how many undead ends?

I have struggled to know where and how to start. How to tell a story with no clear beginning. How to begin to assemble an archive when its materials are always elsewhere, where traces are to be excavated from between the lines. When nothing is in order, but nothing is never nothing. To start not just with silence but with the unverifiable. To inhabit multiple universes while only being able to be in one. To not know who or what is missing. To be the missing, and to wonder how your absence assumes a shape, occupies a corner, a room. Whether it fills a day, perhaps a month. If you and your absence have a name.

I've returned to Korea several times in recent years, and I am coming to understand that truth is not to be found – it is a process of unravelling and being unravelled, it is movement without end. That my history is also the history of others, and that our stories sometimes tell us more about processes, optimisation, the efficiency of systems and their mythologies, than it does about who we were or might have been.

And so when I ask about their histories, adoptees begin with *as far as I know* – and I think about how knowledge is measured in distance and time, terrain and memory. And I wonder if knowledge can also be measured in terms of intensity or desperation. Desire and hope. How it is also tempered by caveats. How we persevere in speaking from a ground that is never not shifting.

When I was younger, I used to oscillate between wanting to keep every single thing and wishing to completely destroy evidence of the way I was seen. Tossed between desiring continuity or erasure. Suspended between being the leaving and the left. Believing that to destroy an object was to refute it, its authority and its revelation. Because it shows too much. Because it is too domineering in how it holds all the ways in which I am undone. As if they retain what they reflect. As if reminders bear responsibility for the things we wish to forget. As if anything can serve as a container for shame.

Isn't the desire to keep such a fundamental and conflictual urge, a struggle for intimacy, for closeness, for externalisation, but also for destruction? To be in company. To be held, even if in abeyance. An attempt to render sensible and intelligible what we cannot remember. To assemble, for the sake of future order, a thread to come. What futures do we stake in what we keep of ourselves, in how we keep them? What footholds do we feverishly carve out, in the hope that they may take us towards a desired self? The one we most wish to believe in. Along the way, I discovered that disappearing and continuing to materialise can occur at the same time. That we often have very little control over either.

What weighs more heavily on us: what we keep or what we give away?

As my fingers carefully work their way through the materials sprawled in piles across the table, I am struck by the library's stature despite its size, by the decisions that have preceded it, the tenacity that undergirds it. How the collection could be expanded to fill not just this room but the entire floor of this grey building, seep through the walls, encircle the trunks of the trees that line the street. But *this is the meeting room*, I'm reminded. The materials must be filed away. A support group is scheduled to meet here later in the week.

I am learning how to let affect form part of the story, how to let it tell what it tells. To let it be the telling. To accept that stories not only point to what has been excluded but carry traces of the energy expended in exacting that exclusion. I am trying to learn how to stop short of memorialisation. To relinquish control. To desire something softer than a monument. Because an archive must build not just knowledge of a past but a route to writing oneself into the present. Because it must be capable of holding ambiguity.

Yet there is a seizing of power in the act of collecting, in the attempt to speak to the world with something the world itself has created. There is humble defiance in the taking ownership of all that we do not know we have lost. Even when institutional history is also personal dislocation. When it documents what it means to be cleaved. Production alongside destruction. Even when it is unclear who or what needs collecting.

What is here because other things are not?

I have tried to retrace steps, not strictly my own, to return to where I have been. To place tentative hope alongside a refusal to accept disappearance. To commit to disorientation. To proceed as if tracing loss does not, sometimes, lead to its amplification. To always remember, when stumbling across new information, the difference between luck and worthiness. To expect nothing while hoping for a world.

I wanted to recall the sensation of heat and sweat from all those hands that carried me, from those chests against which I rested my head. From Masan to Jinju in South Gyeongsang province, to a babies' home all the way up in Seoul, and then to a foster home. From those shoulders over which I could have seen what was leaving – and, if I felt that pressure, then I too was felt by them, my scent and their senses. Our weather. Did we hold on or did we all know not to, already, then?

Last year, I interviewed an adoptee in Seoul who, despite hearing it multiple times, could never seem to remember the Korean word for 'adoptee'. As if lips, tongue, teeth and roof of the mouth all conspired to twist out of turn. As if to remind us that, through a barely perceptible shift in perspective, what had appeared as floundering is transfigured into something closer to dissent. And I marvelled at this recalcitrance, this little *no* that had so much to say.

How impoverished our narratives, with neither start nor end, pieced together slower than the lives that outrun them. How multiple our voices, differentiated yet painfully singular. How generational our time, how collapsed our arc. How late we are when we return. *If* we return. How old and how young. How uncannily we age. And how easily we forget, when we discover this place that has changed so dramatically, that we too are barely recognisable. Here, but gone. That loneliness knocks you out of time while you endure living within it. With all of our others.

But I was once part of three generations, seated in a row. Mixing mushrooms and sizzling rice in stone pots. Sharing the same meal, we compared our hands. A glimpse into a world and a lexicon cleaved from me. I am held by stories untold, and we are sometimes what is lost in the telling. I am named by circumstance, in a grammar I still do not understand. I don't remember the touch but I remember the resemblance, itself a kind of touch, itself a type of (un)tying. Our bodies, ever momentary, penning a tenuous line. Gone, but here.

In the collection at VANISH, there's a stack of newsletters from the Concerned United Birthparents (CUB) in the United States. Founded in 1976 by Lee Campbell, CUB was the first advocacy and support organisation of its kind. Flipping through some issues, I notice a whole section devoted to a list of names and contact details. The header reads: 'soft shoulders'. And I wonder how this would translate in Korea, for those living with their silences and our absences, weighed and buoyed by them – what forms of softness does survival command?

I think about a Korean mother I met during my last trip; she was searching for her son. A group of us gathered in a quiet café in Mapo-gu. She passed around plastic cups of sliced fruit, which she had carefully assembled and brought from home. Staring intently at me, she faintly shook her head as she relayed to a friend – who was translating – that she had been waiting for so long. Decades. I held her gaze for as long as I could bear because we knew I was not him, and that meant everything. But so does this: we are here, which is not nothing.

How many searchers does it take to transform the lost into the missing?

When you go looking, it helps to have a name.

I want an archive as a window that we assemble, carefully and collectively – to provide a way of seeing, a landscape across which eyes may meet. As a seat, a surface on which to unfurl. A moment for rest, an unpaved strip of land. A reprieve, on the side of the road. For all of our names, and for all of the others, those we have been, those we are becoming, and those we are leaning on. To render visible what is disappearing, to reveal beginnings as the endings that they were. To take the sting out of searching and its unendingness, each of us in our too-often siloed ways. To take us *as far as we know*.

I want to hear the unheard *no*, the *no* that did not make it into the world. That got stuck, somewhere between past and present. The *no* that issues not from the throat but blisters forth from the skin. Ours and mine. It demands our whole bodies. I don't know, but I imagine it sounds a bit like my mother's voice.

An archive, but only if we remember what it cannot hold, that it always remains empty. That emptiness too, as much as what surrounds it, teaches us that life is always lived elsewhere.

I am telling you I need you. I will wait as you sift and collect and you gather, and you take this thing that envelops size itself, and you transform it into something we can curl our tongues around. Without apology. I need to see your arms full. To hear you ask of loneliness that it take us somewhere. I want to see the weight of discovery and the not-knowing that accompanies it. I want to hear you put your name to it. Any name. As long as it's yours.

Five Stelæ in Commemoration of Forgetting

André Dao

<u>**A sea of sirens.**</u> In 2016, an estimated 5079 people died crossing the Mediterranean Sea from North Africa to Europe. The sea in which those black and brown bodies drowned is patterned with laws: a patchwork of anti-smuggling regulations, the Refugee Convention and the maritime rules drawing lines on maps marking out territorial waters and continental shelves, and the International Convention for the Safety of Life at Sea, which says that '[t]he master of a ship at sea, on receiving a signal from any source that a ship [...] is in distress, is bound to proceed with all speed to the assistance of the persons in distress'. Without rest, operations of one kind or another crisscross this patterned surface: rescue operations, border-control operations, anti-smuggling operations, commercial shipping. The black and brown bodies are carrying out their own operation, too, even if it is normally described in other terms: *fleeing*, *seeking asylum*, a *crisis*, a *plague*. For this operation – call it 'Operation Breach Fortress Europe', or 'Operation A Better Life For My Unborn Child', or 'Operation Colonialism Coming Home To Roost' – the black and brown bodies' essential tool is the Thuraya satellite phone used to call the Maritime Rescue Coordination Centre (MRCC) in Rome. The call sets off a sequence of signals: the MRCC sends out a broadcast warning to all ships in the region using the World Wide Navigational Warning Service.

These ships – which include vessels from Italy's Operation Mare Nostrum, the EU's Operation Triton (border control) and Operation Sophia (anti-smuggling), NGOs like Migrant Offshore Aid Station and Médicins Sans Frontières (MSF), and merchant ships – are all equipped to transmit Automatic Identification System data, broadcasting the vessel's position, speed, course over the ground, destination, flag and identifiers every two minutes. Listening to this sea of sirens is the Global Pulse – a 'flagship innovation initiative' set up by the UN Secretary-General to harness 'big data and artificial intelligence' for the 'public good'.[1] The Pulse, working with the UN Refugee Agency, has trained a machine-learning algorithm on these signals – which really means that a team of human beings manually tagged 77,000 data points to identify which ones related to rescue and non-rescue patterns. The Pulse calls the resulting rescue patterns *rescue signatures*. The resulting archive is called *the gallery of rescue signatures*, a grid of squiggles. Sometimes, the squiggle is relatively straightforward: on 28 July 2016, the rescue ship *Aquarius*, run by MSF, travelled in a more or less straight, north-easterly line across the sea. Other times, the squiggle is furious, as if its author were trying to scratch out an unwanted sentence: from 6 to 10 August 2016, the *Aquarius* zigzagged and looped back on itself, retracing its own path through the water. From this archive of rescue signatures, the algorithm derives the signature of all rescues: the typical latitude, longitude, speed and course over the ground of a rescue at sea. It is said that this information will help save lives in the future. What is not said is that other lines have been erased from this archive: the lines of jurisdiction and the patterns of rights and responsibilities that makes some bodies illegal; that facilitate the crossing of goods and gold over the same waters; that, in December 2018, forced the *Aquarius* (by then the last rescue ship operating in the Med) to cease its operations, and which eventually led to the prosecution of dozens of rescuers on charges of collaborating with people smugglers – charges carrying prison sentences of up to twenty years. What else is not recorded in the signature of all rescues? What does this archive of lines remember about the journeys of migrant bodies, and what does it forget? Jacques Derrida tells the story of the archons, chief magistrates of Ancient Greece. Official documents were filed in their homes, so that the archons were 'first of all the documents' guardians. They do not only ensure the physical security of what is deposited and of the substrate. They are also accorded the hermeneutic right and competence. They have the power to interpret the archives.' Derrida continues: 'Entrusted to such archons, these documents in effect state the law: they recall the law and call on or impose the law.'[2] Who is the archon of the archive of rescue signatures? Surely it is only the algorithm that has jurisdiction here – only the algorithm can make sense of these lines. The algorithm can *only* make sense of these lines. It understands nothing else. As Derrida says: 'The archivization produces as much as it records the event.'[3] The algorithm is the archon – a common translation for *archon* is 'ruler' – and the law it keeps is algorithmic. Orit Halpern picks up on Derrida's story in her history of computational thinking, *Beautiful Data*. She says that computerised data changes the way we think, ushering in a new kind of objectivity based not on deeper truth but on correlating observable behaviours – the recognition of patterns in a sea of sirens. Computerised data changes the way we record the world; it makes possible, or at least it makes it possible to imagine, a world in which everything is recorded. Of course, not *everything* is recorded. Not *every* part of everything is recorded; *part* of everything is recorded – the observable parts, the quantifiable parts, the digitisable parts. For a rescue to become a signature, it must first become an outline of itself – a line, a squiggle. The technical structure of an archive is not only technical: it determines what is archivable. Which is to say that the dream of recording everything is just that – a dream. To record every rescue, the event is reduced beyond recognition and beyond comprehension. 'Twas ever thus: there has never been a perfect memory machine. But now, as Halpern says, 'we have mechanized that loss, made it no longer a pain to be felt but a site for further technical projects; at its extreme horizon, devoid of anything but its own technical imperative, this drive becomes "radical evil". This "radical evil" is, of course, the failure to imagine a future through the loss of all points of reference; an automation of recording that facilitates death.'[4]

The museum of statelessness. Seven years ago, along with four friends (we were a group of lawyers, journalists and advocates), I started speaking to people who had been imprisoned inside Australia's immigration detention system. We trained ourselves as amateur oral historians by reading: first, the testimonies collected by Voice of Witness, a US-based charity co-founded by writer Dave Eggers to 'amplify unheard voices';[5] then author Studs Terkel's monumental *Working*; and, finally, Nobel laureate Svetlana Alexievich's *Voices from Chernobyl*. Eventually, after many interviews, after Reza Barati was beaten to death on Manus Island, after Sayed Ibrahim Hussein drowned in the ocean off Nauru, after Hamid Kehazaei died of septicaemia from a cut on his foot sustained on Manus, after four-year-old An Hoang Le (detained in Melbourne since he was two) died of leukaemia, after Mohamad Nassim Najafi died of a suspected heart attack in the Yongah Hill detention centre, after Ali Jaffari immolated himself in Yongah Hill, after Fazel Chegani was found dead on Christmas Island, after Omid Masoumali immolated himself on Nauru, after Rahib Khan overdosed on pharmaceutical drugs on Nauru, after Kamil Hussain drowned while on a daytrip from the detention centre on Manus, after Faysal Ishak Ahmed died of head injuries from a seizure at the detention centre on Manus, after a myriad of other violences that did not quite meet the threshold of being recorded in the Australian Border Deaths Database – we published a book called *They Cannot Take the Sky*, a collection of stories moulded from the oral testimonies of thirty-five people who had more or less survived those violences. At the time, we wrote that the book was a 'record of Australia's mandatory immigration detention system from the point of view of the people it incarcerates'. We also said that it was more than a record, that it was about more than detention – that it was about love, family, death, resistance and hope. We relayed the words of Abdul Aziz Muhamat, who told us about a detainee on Manus who only responded to his government-issued ID number: 'Look, man, no-one is pretending here,' said Muhamat. 'Why should we pretend? We forgot our names.' We wrote that the book exists for Muhamat to speak his own name. It was well reviewed, and well received by refugee advocates, migrant-literature enthusiasts, scholars. It didn't sell particularly well, but it does crop up from time to time in academic articles about refugee self-representation. It won awards. The book became a part of what Viet Thanh Nguyen calls 'the industrialization of memory';[6] it was a modest contribution to the war to control the territory of remembering and forgetting. On the basis of this contribution, we received money to do more (that's a memory-industrial complex for you). We got seed funding to make a digital archive of testimonies by stateless people. We spoke to more seasoned memory-workers – radical archivists, oral-history experts, stateless activists and artists – to develop a methodology that would be participatory, that would be 'best practice', that would produce an archive that was meaningful to both stateless persons and to institutional mechanisms of justice (royal commissions, international tribunals, criminal courts, etc.). We did our homework: on the comprehensive, monumental archive (see: the Yale Fortunoff Video Archive for Holocaust Testimonies, and the Australian Generations Oral History Project at the National Library of Australia);

on the small, contained, one-off project archive (see: the Cambodian Women's Oral History Project, and Detention Remembered); on the investigative archive (see: Forensic Architecture and their investigations into human rights abuses in Israel, Syria and beyond); on the idea of producing a map of statelessness in Australia (see, in a negative sense: the fact that the Australian Government cannot provide accurate numbers of stateless persons in their own detention centres; and see, more positively: the woven maps of Rabouni, the administrative centre for the network of Sahrawi refugee camps in north-western Africa, which refigure the camp as a space for independent self-government, and which were hung as tapestries in New York's Museum of Modern Art). In the end, doing our homework was not enough. We spent two years speaking to current and formerly stateless people – individuals from Iran, Iraq, Afghanistan, Palestine, Myanmar, Nepal, some in detention and others with visas or even citizenship in Australia or New Zealand, all of them denied a home in the place that was their home, all of them belonging to a place in which they did not, as a matter of law, belong. As a matter of memory, of family, of the smell of the rain or the feel of the soil or the taste of food – that was different, of course. The stories we collected were rich in that gap between law and memory, or between citizenship and belonging. Yet, as a group, nothing held these stories together except for those laws that caused such pain. And the more we realised that, the more we realised that the archive we wanted to make was too artificial; we had wanted to make an archive that was alive, but it seemed as if we were working on something stillborn. So we fell back on the individual stories and published them as a suite in a literary magazine, with images from an artist to tie them together aesthetically, if not organically. This left us with the perennial questions. Who were these stories for? How long, and for whom, could they live for like this – as individual stories – without the warmth and protection of a home, without a powerful archon watching over them? Is the story itself, as a form, the problem? To be stateless, said Hannah Arendt, is to have been stripped of the 'right to have rights'.[7] How does individual testimony counter such systematic destruction – how can 'I remember' ever overcome what Milan Kundera called the 'desert of organized forgetting'?[8]

Can the ghost in the machine speak? Somewhere near the city of Gulu in Northern Uganda, a woman calls in to a talkback-radio program to complain about the poor sanitation in local refugee settlements. 11,000 kilometres away, in downtown Manhattan, a team of data scientists, analysts and engineers are listening to this conversation. None of them speak Acholi, the language the woman speaks. The team in New York are in the Global Pulse's headquarters, and they are not so much listening to the Ugandan woman as extracting a signal from the noise. They are testing a prototype, the Radio Content Analysis Tool, which uses machine-learning algorithms to 'analyse public radio content in Uganda and explore its value for informing development of UN projects and programmes on the ground'.[9] There are over 2000 hours of broadcast a day on all of Uganda's radio stations. The Tool takes all that noise and filters it down through a combination of machine-learning techniques, like speech recognition and keyword filtering, and human expertise in the form of rapid evaluation by human analysts alongside transcription and translation. Essentially, the Tool makes available to a UN bureaucrat a highly simplified report of topics discussed on Ugandan talkback radio – useful, presumably to pick up on broad trends. But that is a far cry from what we would normally think of as listening to a person. Yet, in promoting the Tool, the Global Pulse suggests otherwise: it says that the Tool 'brings in people's voices' and 'leaves no voice behind'. Its language is echoed by the Pulse's chief data scientist, who has said, 'Before 2030, technology should allow us to know everything from everyone to ensure no one is left behind.' The immediate example he gives is of 'nanosatellites imaging every corner of the earth allowing us to generate almost immediate insights into humanitarian crises'.[10] Here, again, is the fantasy of a totalising record. It is a seductive fantasy – powerful enough to co-opt that which might be thought to resist it. In 2014, then–UN Secretary-General Ban Ki Moon appointed an Independent Expert Advisory Group to advise on a key plank of the UN's post-2015 development plan: the so-called data revolution for sustainable development. The advisory group's final report, *A World That Counts*, makes rights central to the data revolution. But the first right listed is one that doesn't really exist: the right to be counted. You won't find it in the major international human rights treaties, nor is it ever fully explained what the right to be counted means. But it seems, from the rest of the report, that the right to be counted is thought of as a necessary condition for other rights. There is a play on the meaning of 'count' here. You have to be counted to count – that is, to matter, to have rights. If you're not counted, you're invisible. Arendt be damned – it's not citizenship we need but total surveillance. This is a strange reversal, perfectly illustrated by the glossy photos the Global Pulse uses to promote the Tool: individual women, always outside (in an open field or on the shores of a lake), with radios clutched next to their heads as if the radios were huge mobile phones. The absurdity of the photo – that the women, ostensibly empowered, finally, to speak, to participate in how they are to be governed, are actually clutching devices for *listening*, not speaking – reveals more than just the banality of humanitarian marketing. It reveals the truth: that the Radio Content Analysis Tool speaks *to* the women, telling them they are being heard, and that it speaks *for* them, representing them as data points in a data set. If the women were to speak for themselves – though there is no indication in the photos that they do, for their mouths are invariably closed – then the radios that they hold so closely will not hear them. As Gayatri Chakravorty Spivak might have said, the data subject cannot speak.[11]

The ancient library. The Athenians recorded their archons on stelæ, free-standing marble columns inscribed with the archons' names and the years of their reign. This was a public list, possibly erected in the south-western corner of the Agora, mirroring the official record held in the nearby archives. What purpose did this public record serve? Classicists can only guess. Even the names and dates are only educated guesswork, pieced together from fragments of marble dug up in the 1930s. It occurs to me now that a far better technology for remembering is – was? – oral storytelling, stories spoken from one generation to the next since time immemorial. The speaking is the key to it, for in the speaking the stories change – so imperceptibly that no-one is fully responsible for or even conscious of the changes, adapting to transformations in the country, absorbing strangers who need to be absorbed, forgetting conflicts that need to be forgotten – all the while, this changing and forgetting is held together in a skein of unbroken remembering. All of that is lost when things are written down. Writing has its own compensations: certainty, trade, commerce, development – in a word, so-called civilisation. Still, though you can reject the premise that these compensations are 'progress', you can't deny that we live in a world of writing. This is Alexis Wright's wager in her novels and non-fiction: there is no going back to the way things were. This is why she wants to build a 'self-governing literature' from what she has 'learnt from our ancient library contained in the land'.[12] I take her to mean that the ancient library, and its spoken telling, is no longer enough – not enough to secure Country against the predations of a written, and therefore rational and commercial, culture – so she takes the risk of writing down things that had once only been for the speaking. It reminds me of another who made the same wager – less successfully, as it turns out. The Old Man was at the centre of a native title dispute over land just north of Broome. I was a stranger in that Country, working for the whitefella judge presiding over the dispute. One of the key witnesses was a professor of creative writing, an early pioneer of metafictional writing techniques. In his youth, the Writer had, like other white Australians of his generation, gone into the outback in search of a way to be at home on stolen lands. He found what he was looking for in the Old Man, a charismatic storyteller who held court under a mango tree. The Old Man told a story about how he had come to look after the land north of Broome. It was not the Country he was born into; at first, he was also a stranger in that place. But the old people of that Country were dying out – that is, their children had been stolen. And here was this healthy young man who had eloped with his wrong-way wife, in need of Country. So the old people showed him the ancient library, taught him its stories, and he began to look after it. By the time the Writer showed up in Broome in the 1970s, the Old Man was an established figure in local politics. Along with other senior lawmen, the Old Man was involved with the push for land rights – otherwise known as the long struggle to get settler law to recognise Indigenous laws, a struggle that essentially involves making the ancient library legible to, perhaps even commensurable with, another archive that is less ancient but backed by greater force: the English common law. This is where the Writer came into it: the Old Man decided it was time for the stories to be written down. So this was his wager: in moving from the oral to the written, he gave up the technology of remembering-forgetting that might, over generations, have seen him and his family fully absorbed into that Country. Instead, he took up a different technology, one he hoped would be more amenable to the whitefella archons. He was right – and then he was wrong. First, the book that the Writer wrote with the Old Man made the Old Man famous. Many young people from the cities, most of them white, came out to Broome to work with the Old Man and his family to protect the land. That was more or less the way things were until the Old Man died. His family continued his work. Then a gas company showed up. They wanted to build a huge hub just off the coastline and had money to spend. Some of the stolen children of those old people started to make themselves heard (a number had been speaking for years, but no-one was listening). *We've always been here*, they said. *Even when we were stolen, we came back to Country.* So there was a dispute. In court, the Writer was called in to give evidence about the Old Man, because the Old Man could no longer speak for himself and the Writer's book had come to stand in for him. A Queen's Counsel cross-examined the Writer. Is metafiction real or imagined? How much of what is written down in the book true? Why would the Old Man say there were no children left on Country when he knew that there were? Wasn't the Old Man just a charlatan? A thief? Why should we think of this book as anything more than a land grab? In the end, the written word betrayed the Old Man. The records showed that he had arrived in the area in the 1930s. He might have known the stories of the Country and he might have spent the rest of his life looking after that ancient library – the court didn't rule either way on those things. But whatever the stories and the looking-after meant, they were not, for the purposes of whitefella native title, a traditional connection. They did not go back long enough. The Old Man and his family did not belong to that Country north of Broome, where the court held its hearings in the pindan scrub, in the shade of a sacred boab tree. The court did not say where they did belong.

The shape of their absence. Critical race theory is in the news again. Which is funny, because one of the field's groundbreaking works, *The Alchemy of Race and Rights*, begins with author Patricia J. Williams watching the news in her terry towelling robe, depressed and despairing: 'I don't know how to find something to write about in the pain of this deadly world. There is more in the news than even my depression can consume.'[13] So, you see, it's quite funny, in a bleak kind of way, that Williams' brilliant, generous, paradigm-shifting scholarship is now part of an even darker, immensely stupider, news cycle. It's funny because, when Williams finally does find something to write about, it's her great-great-grandparents: 'I look for her shape and his hand.'[14] 'Her' is Williams' great-great-grandmother. 'His' is the thirty-year-old lawyer who bought her, aged thirteen. The man who raped her, who made her bear his children, his property. Look, I know – that doesn't sound very funny. But you have to wait for the punchline. (This isn't it.) When Williams says she is looking for 'his hand', she means his words – in his legal writing and in his judgements, his signature on bills of sale for his slaves. When she says she is looking for 'her shape', she means the absence of her great-great-grandmother from the records. There is no grave, no body, no record of death at all. The hand is writing, is law, is the record, is force, is violence, is coercion. And the shape is the void where a person might be, erased by the violence of the hand. But the shape is also the tender place in Williams' own life, the missing heart of all our lives, deformed by our collective amnesia. In this way, the hand reaches out from the grave: 'The force he was in her life, in the shape of my life today.'[15] Williams, the would-be alchemist, wants to reverse this flow; she wants to use her hand, her writing, to fill in *her* shape: 'I have tried to piece together what it must have been like to be my great-great-grandmother.'[16] (Don't worry, the punchline is still coming.) The third or fourth time I read that chapter, I realised belatedly that I have been trying to fill in the shape of my own ancestors, my paternal grandparents – my Ông Bà Noi. Only my grandfather is dead; my grandmother is still alive, calling me on WhatsApp from her apartment on the outskirts of Paris. But the shape of my life today has been determined, in part, by the forces that made them absent from me – an absence of geography and language and history. Forces we sometimes call *war* and *coloniality* and *capitalism*. For ten years, I have been trying to write about them – to transform their absence from the records, from the literature that I grew up reading, from my daily life, into a presence. This is what I have tried to do across essays and short stories; an unpublished memoir and an abysmal, orientalist novel (thankfully, also unpublished); and, finally, a book assembled, monstrously, from broken-off parts of all those failures. Williams might call this alchemy. There are other names for it, too: *speaking with ghosts* (Avery Gordon, via Derrida),[17] *critical fabulation* (Saidiya Hartman).[18] Whatever you call it, it's a fraught enterprise. The ghost doesn't speak back. So you appropriate the Other by assimilation (Spivak, via Derrida). So you give in to the temptation to 'fill in the gaps and provide closure where there is none' (Hartman).[19] Once, someone – not a family member, but someone connected to the memory-work I perform on detention and migration – said that I hadn't listened, that I'd heard what I'd wanted, and that that not-listening had been like stealing their life all over again. When I tried to explain myself, they said, 'I hope you stop making excuses, and take this as an opportunity to learn.' So here I am, learning. Though I don't think I'm learning what I was supposed to learn. I'm learning that all this interviewing and writing, all this remembering and imagining, it's to ward off a world that is already here – the world of the total record, of the perfect memory. (Get ready, here it comes.) Which means remembering against memory. Which means listening and not-listening, getting it wrong and making it up. Which means failing over and over again. (There – get it?)

1 Global Partnership for Sustainable Development Data, 'United Nations Global Pulse', https://www.data4sdgs.org/partner/united-nations-global-pulse
2 Derrida, Jacques, *Archive Fever: A Freudian Impression*, trans. Eric Prenowitz, University of Chicago Press, Chicago and London, 1995, p. 2.
3 Ibid., p. 17.
4 Halpern, Orit, *Beautiful Data: A History of Vision and Reason since 1945*, Duke University Press, Durham and London, 2014, p. 76.
5 Voice of Witness, 'About', https://voiceofwitness.org/about/
6 Nguyen, Viet Thanh, *Nothing Ever Dies: Vietnam and the Memory of War*, Harvard University Press, Cambridge, 2016.
7 Arendt, Hannah, *The Origins of Totalitarianism*, Meridian, Cleveland and New York, 1951, pp. 296–298.
8 Kundera, Milan, *The Book of Laughter and Forgetting*, Penguin, New York, 1986, p. 159
9 UN Global Pulse, 'Using Machine Learning to Analyse Radio Content in Uganda', 2017, https://www.unglobalpulse.org/document/using-machine-learning-to-analyse-radio-content-in-uganda/
10 Oroz, Miguel Luengo, 'From Big Data to Humanitarian in the Loop Algorithms', UN Global Pulse, 22 January 2018, https://www.unglobalpulse.org/2018/01/from-big-data-to-humanitarian-in-the-loop-algorithms/
11 Spivak, Gayatri Chakravorty, 'Can the Subaltern Speak?', in Cary Nelson and Lawrence Grossberg (eds), *Marxism and the Interpretation of Culture*, Macmillan, London, 1988, pp. 271–313.
12 Wright, Alexis, 'A Self-Governing Literature', *Meanjin*, vol. 79, no. 2, Winter 2020, p. 96
13 Williams, Patricia J., *The Alchemy of Race and Rights*, Harvard University Press, Cambridge and London, 1991, p. 5.
14 Ibid., p. 19.
15 Ibid.
16 Ibid., p. 17.
17 Gordon, Avery, *Ghostly Matters: Haunting and the Sociological Imagination*, University of Minnesota Press, Minneapolis, 2008.
18 Hartman, Saidiya, 'Venus in Two Acts', *Small Axe*, vol. 12 no. 2, 2008, p. 8.
19 Ibid.

This Is Probably Sedition

Elizabeth Flux

There's a battered box on the shelf where I keep my rage. This is not a metaphor.

The box is made of hefty cardboard, its history of use and reuse mapped across it in mismatched tape. On one side there's a large sticker – upside down – that reads 'FRAGILE'. When the package arrived, I left it sitting on my desk for days, unopened, before finally taking a knife to it. Nestled in the packing peanuts were five boxes of slides and a garish orange holder to view them through. I pick a slide at random from the box labelled 'Night View' and, though the image is from the late 1970s, the familiarity of the scene is immediate: neon signs and high-rise buildings, people waiting for a bus. I slot in another. And another. Soon, I skip the viewer altogether, holding the slides directly up to the light, squinting at them so I can get through them more quickly. Less than halfway through the first stack, there it is – the hill housing the hospital where I was born. I carefully pack it all back up again, put the box onto the shelf where it will stay for the foreseeable future.

It's a cheap toy – tat for tourists.

It's glimpses of a place I know from a time before I knew it.

It's Hong Kong in 100 frozen moments, and I'm going to keep it forever.

■

I thought democracies died quickly or loudly, but it turns out to be more like drowning. Death in the water isn't how we picture it; it isn't loud splashing or a frantic struggle for air. Instead, more commonly, someone simply slips below the surface – and, by the time anyone notices, it's too late.

■

My claim to my place of birth has always felt shaky, even though I speak the language, even though half of me technically belongs there. I moved away at the age of two and, as I've grown older, my hair has lightened and my features have moved more towards my Western half – I look like a gwai mui ('ghost girl'), the colloquial name given to young white women. But these worries always fade almost instantly the moment I land.

Being in Hong Kong feels right.

It's a strange thing when somewhere is both your home and yet not: you don't do the normal tourist things; you occupy a strange limbo between everyday routine and the novelty of travel. My feet know the path from the double-decker bus to my ah poh's apartment, then back down to the 7-Eleven; my memory flicks to a lazy summer day as a child when I sat on a bunk bed watching the traffic move, far away, on the street below. I know the best places to buy groceries. I can navigate the markets nestled into residential apartment blocks, where tourists rarely set foot. I know Hong Kong well and not at all; all my time spent there feels less like travel and more like a look into an alternate life I might otherwise have been living. In my mind there has always been a next visit – maybe in six months, maybe in two years, but always somewhere in the not-too-distant future.

It's an idea that is hard to let go of.

Hong Kong is slipping away and it feels like the world doesn't care. Every so often, something big enough will happen to break through the ceiling of international-worthy news – a two-million-strong protest, the arrest of pro-democracy politicians – and then it will again fade into the backdrop, the slow drip of horrors there only to see if you look for it or are emotionally invested.

How long Hong Kong has been fighting for its independence is perhaps impossible to say. At its simplest: it was part of China, then it was handed over to the UK in 1841, then back to China in 1997 with the promise of fifty years of autonomous rule – a Hong Kong governed by Hong Kong people. That promise slowly started to dissolve as China sought to have more of a say in the running of things. In 2014, Hongkongers fought against a move by Beijing to limit which people could be elected Hong Kong's chief executive to a pool preselected by China. In 2019, Hongkongers took to the streets in their millions to fight against a controversial extradition bill. The bill was shelved and, for a brief moment, it felt like a win – but then COVID hit and, while the world was distracted, Beijing brought in a national security law that effectively gives China carte blanche to crack down on anything it doesn't like, anything that can be thought of as 'dissent'.

The wording of the law, which was passed in June 2020, is vague – deliberately so. 'Secession', 'subversion', 'terrorism' and 'collusion' are all crimes under the law, but what exactly falls under each of these things? Is writing an article for a foreign paper collusion? Is any form of criticism subversion? What degree of criticism counts as punishable: words spoken to a loved one, words committed to a diary, the words I've written so far? How can you avoid committing a crime if you don't know exactly what is forbidden?

▪

One of my favourite things to do in Hong Kong is to look up. Buildings are taller or shabbier or homelier or brighter depending on what part of the city you are in. My phone is full of pictures from my last visit – colourful walls, uniform windows, sunlight peeking between identical skyscrapers. There are the eight-storey buildings with no lifts and a ground floor of restaurants hosting a lazy trickle of customers twenty-four hours a day. There are the apartments that stretch to pinpoints up in the sky. At night, some streets light up with neon signs that layer on top of one another so much that it looks like day. In residential buildings, you see laundry hanging out of windows, over balconies, giving a story, a personality to each otherwise-identical home.

It's a display like this that got a man arrested in June 2021. Hanging out of his window was not laundry, however, but a black banner with white text in both English and Chinese. It read: 'Liberate Hong Kong, revolution of our times.' Prior to the national security law coming into effect, this was a popular protest slogan; now, it's illegal.

■

Is it illegal for me to write that slogan here? One of the early criticisms of the national security law was that its wording didn't limit its reach to just Hong Kong. The answer is foggy but worrying.

In July 2020, Amnesty International posted an article unpicking some of the law's key ramifications, flagging that it

> asserts jurisdiction over people who are not residents of Hong Kong and have never even set foot there. This means anyone on Earth, regardless of nationality or location, can technically be deemed to have violated this law and face arrest and prosecution if they are in a Chinese jurisdiction, even for transit. Accused foreign nationals who don't permanently reside in Hong Kong can be deported even before any trial or verdict.

Every sentence of this essay is gruelling to get out; it feels like I'm carving it directly into my skin. Remembering past trips hurts now as it serves as a reminder that there are unlikely to be future ones, and putting criticism into words feels like inviting danger. But that's the point of the law, isn't it – to make it difficult to say something.

Within days of the legislation being passed, I wrote an article for literary journal *Kill Your Darlings* because I didn't know what else to do; I needed people to know what was happening. A lot of people listened. And then the world moved on. The news cycle moved on. As I always knew it would.

That didn't make it any easier.

I thought the national security law's ratification would be the nightmare, but the true grief has come from watching, impotently, as events unfold, as freedom is eroded, and nothing is done. Every so often, a country offers scolding words, a bit of solidarity, but then another day passes, another news story rises. Then something else happens in

Hong Kong to remind anyone outside still watching that all of this isn't stopping any time soon.

Since the national security law was brought in, democracy and press freedom have been rapidly eroding in Hong Kong. Under the new authoritarian aura, a colonial-era sedition law has resurfaced and been wielded to crack down on free speech. There's no room to criticise those in charge, to ask for freedom is to invite punishment, and being arrested for words, for wanting what was there only years before, has quickly, disquietingly, become almost normal.

∎

Seeing the vice tighten around Hong Kong day by day used to make me cry, but I feel like that part of me has dried up. So I turned to objects. They're solid, tangible – unchanging. The first thing I bought was the slides.

My favourites are the ones in the box marked 'Hong Kong'. In it, there are places I've lived, places I've visited, places I've since seen filled with protesters trying to hang on to what's theirs. I like these images because they'll never change; no matter what happens next, there is a record of what came before. But I worry about looking at them too much because I fear they will move in front of my own memories, superimpose themselves onto scenes where they don't belong. Already, the videos that play in my mind, of the visits scattered across my childhood, have become fragmented with time – movement settling into still images, veracity questionable.

∎

My relationship with *things* has always been complicated; I struggle to separate the feelings from the object they are associated with. This makes it difficult to throw anything with even a hint of sentimental value away – and I assign sentimental value far too generously. I also get tangled in symbolism, even though I know the world isn't that tidy.

I am fully aware that my logic doesn't track, but still:

A friend gives me a T-shirt that she thinks I'll like. It doesn't look right when I try it on, and I know I'll never wear it. But I keep it, folded in the cupboard, because throwing it out means throwing out her friendship.

Irrational.

I never give anyone a watch or a clock as a gift because it feels like putting a timer on our relationship. If it stops, that's it.

Irrational.

I'm given a jar of sweets to take home after a birthday party. I now have to keep the jar otherwise my friend won't have another birthday and it will be my fault that they died.

Extremely irrational.

When I was three, my ah poh came to visit and brought with her a little ornamental house containing flowers and beads that, whenever I shook it, looked like they were floating on air. I've carried it with me from home to home for decades.

In 2020, it started to leak – but I couldn't see where the crack was, couldn't see how to fix it, and so it has been sitting on a cloth in the laundry sink ever since. This is irrational. It should go. Throwing it away does not mean I don't love my ah poh; similarly, the fact that it only began to leak the same year that Hong Kong started descending firmly into destruction is *not* a metaphor. It is a *coincidence*. And yet.

The metaphor-that-isn't-a-metaphor would feel far too heavy-handed were it not for the fact that it is real. The broken house stays with me, slowly leaking, while I can do nothing about it.

It's only in retrospect that I realise it was a coping mechanism. First, I cried. Then I raged. I frantically scrubbed my seditious middle name from my online presence wherever possible; I can't show up to Hong Kong or China with an ID card that says '天安, 1989'. Then I start listening to the daggy Hong Kong pop songs my mum used to play in the car, over and over again. I learn how to cook the breakfast macaroni that is available on almost every street corner. I message family members asking for recipes. And I start hunting down *things*.

A friend sends me art related to the 2019 protests and I hang it on the wall, put a smaller print on my desk. I come across a HK$5 coin as I'm digging around the bottom of my bag looking for a pen and it sits on my desk. I find myself absently flicking it across my fingers as I make phone calls, or grip it tight as I read. When I pick it up, I don't put it back down until it has grown warm in my hand, body reaching equilibrium with metal, giving a bit of my own warmth to – what? A token.

I don't know what I can do from the sidelines. Well, actually I do know: nothing. I have no power, so instead I collect things. Maybe if I have enough things, if I gather all the pieces together, I can hold on to something that is slipping away more each day.

▪

The same week I finished writing this essay, in June 2021, Hong Kong newspaper *Apple Daily* finally shut down, after months of targeted government harassment and the arrest of its founder, Jimmy Lai, for reportedly organising an unauthorised pro-democracy demonstration in late 2019. He was sentenced to fourteen months in prison for 'unauthorised assembly'. Hong Kong jails are rapidly filling up with activists.

Apple Daily printed over one million copies of its last issue and Hongkongers, no longer able to take to the streets in protest, no longer able to mark the anniversary of the Tiananmen Square massacre, no longer able to express discontent in any real, visible way without fear of repercussions, bought out every copy. When no more copies were left, they started buying back issues.

It was bittersweet. Fewer words reporting on atrocities in Hong Kong would go out into the world. This wasn't just about one newspaper being taken down; it served as a warning to everyone else. To think twice. To know there are consequences. To toe the line.

Five days later, on 29 June, journalist Andrea Lo tweeted:

> I am at the Hong Kong Central Library doing research for a project on the newspaper archive floor & have been told Apple Daily archive searches have now been suspended. This started a few days ago

This was followed half an hour later by:

> they said it is because 'it's under NSL review'. sorry for burying the lede, i am pissed off & upset

The national security law wasn't supposed to be retroactive; incumbent Chief Executive Carrie Lam publicly vowed that the law would only apply from the moment it came into effect: 30 June 2020. *Apple Daily* was founded in 1995.

Erasing history is nothing new. It happens during most revolutions, during most regime changes. There are many reasons for wanting a blank slate, but most of the time it comes back to one thing: trying to control the story. Words written over the top of other words, squeezed in between older lines and ideas, make the picture muddy and complex. Give people too much information and they'll be able to question things, to decide for themselves. It's easier to make people accept ugly realities if they don't know there's an alternative – if the only words they're allowed to know are yours. With no opposing views allowed, and with enough time elapsed, it has the potential to work. Citizens might forget what came before, not know what freedoms they had lost. It might even begin to seem normal – right, even – that someone can be taken into custody for simply displaying a plea for liberation on their balcony.

But, at the same time, millions of copies of the doomed paper are now scattered throughout the apartments of Hong Kong and have been mailed across the world. Many copies, eventually, will be thrown away. Some will degrade over time. But enough will survive. The words – their record of events – are out there, and they can't be fully controlled, redacted or erased.

■

On the final day of my last trip to Hong Kong, I caught a bus to the seaside village of Stanley. The day was perfect – in hindsight, suspiciously so. By the water stood a grand, colonial building that dates back to the 1800s. I search for it in the slides. It's not there. There are temples, and street markets, and microseconds captured of the lives of people who just happened to cross the photographers' paths, but this landmark is missing. It's only later I realise it's because, in the late 1970s, Murray House wasn't in Stanley; in the early twenty-first century, it was moved, brick by brick, from Central to its new location.

We value and fear history – whether it is held in bricks and mortar or on flimsy transparent plastic – for a reason. It holds power. It can steer the story. The national security law has made it more dangerous to put new words out into the world. I would worry that writing this essay is enough to stop me from ever returning, but, even before I typed a single letter, I was already too scared. I am afraid every time I retweet a news story about an arrest, or a protest being banned, or a critique of what's going on over there – and those aren't even my words. It feels foolish to be worried, but that is, I suppose, part of why the law exists, why it's so deliberately vague. My hope, though, is that if enough people care, if enough people make noise, we'll notice those at risk of slipping beneath the surface. As things currently are, I know I can't go back.

It's ironic. Before 2019, Hong Kong was somewhere I'd never felt in danger. Night felt as safe as day. But the more that even innocuous words are punished, the more important it feels to keep saying them: to share the voices of those speaking up. To not stay quiet. To not stand idly by. To remember.

Otherwise, all we're left with is This:

Hong Kong
is

part of China

Knowing Even as We Are Known

Barry Corr

Of all settler buildings, the archive is the most tomblike: a catacomb of dead letters, words, commas, full stops, dust-shrouded sheets piled on pile. As an Aboriginal person, I see the settler archive as – to use Sigmund Freud's terms – unheimlich, uncanny, a fearful place. Traditionally, when our people died, we destroyed their belongings to ease their passing, to not hold them back. Perhaps, when settlers invented writing, they did not realise the entrapment caused by words; maybe that was when the settlers lost magic, becoming what they are today. Archival writing, for me, is a magical trail of words tracing in and out of a labyrinthine house of magic, a house of memory, a house of sleep and dangerous dreams. In its darkness, it can conceal the true nature of the dead; it can hide their secrets; it can catch, entangle and hold back those who it wants to keep; and, occasionally, it turns to cast the dead into the flickering light of accountability.

A statue of former New South Wales (NSW) governor Lachlan Macquarie faces St Matthew's Anglican Church in Windsor, a town in the Hawkesbury Local Government Area in north-west Sydney. Windsor has a particular affinity for Macquarie. Windsor is a 'Macquarie town'. His statue stands in his Great Square, looking at his church. Thompson Square, his other public place, is lauded by some locals as the birthplace of Australian egalitarianism.[1] Such is Macquarie's standing in the Hawkesbury that his statue was erected during Windsor's 1994 bicentennial celebrations despite Macquarie being in India when Hawkesbury settlement began in 1794. The statue depicts him wearing the uniform of an infantry officer, and his sabre, more suited for a cavalryman than an infantryman, reveals much of the real-life person's theatricality. Macquarie slouches over a blank map, a wish-fulfilling tabula rasa for a terra nullius. He is only a slanting glance away from the final resting place of magistrate William Cox.

The mausoleum housing the remains of Cox and his first wife, Rebecca, is easily missed among the tightly packed graves around St Matthew's. Its post-and-lintel style and classical proportions reflect the classical origins of the magistracy and the archive. The Athenian republic's chief magistrates were the archons, and the archive (derived from the word *archon*) has, today, come to refer to both the building and the historical records kept there. Despite having a different etymology from the Ark of the Covenant, the archive in settler societies similarly carries binary expectations of right and wrong, of truth and secrecy, of concealment and revealment. The archive is foundational; it legitimates government and authority. Etymologically, the Greek *arkhē*, also carries the meaning of 'beginnings'. It is only a small step for settler societies to conceptualise the archive as the taproot of the ever-branching, ever-aspiring tree that they imagine as civilisation. But this is a shallow view of the archive. When one pushes through the dark, dry, dusty crumbling papers, one comes to the Deep. It is that upon which the settler archive lies uneasily – that which has always been here, long before what settler societies imagine as the 'beginning'.

Born in 1764, Cox was a half-pay officer who, on transfer to the NSW Corps, was fortunate to be appointed regimental paymaster.[2] Joseph Holt, a transported Irish rebel, wrote in his memoirs that Cox paid the soldiers in kind: tea, sugar and rum rather than coin. While Cox was the colony's second-largest landowner after John Macarthur, his debts dragged him down and he was recalled to Britain.[3] Holt records that, during this collapse, Cox entrusted a chest to him: 'I don't know what was in it but I may truly guess [...] This chest was very heavy.'[4] The contents of the chest may have re-established the Coxes on Clarendon, a 400-acre grant made conveniently to Cox's children in 1804. Cox never faced trial, resigning his commission to return in 1810. In the same year, Macquarie appointed Cox as magistrate in the Hawkesbury. Macquarie probably had little problem with Cox's financial irregularities. As regimental paymaster during the 1790s, Macquarie regularly drew the regimental pay up to three months in advance, investing the funds with Indian moneylenders and keeping the interest for himself.[5] As a reward for building a road over the Blue Mountains in 1814 to 1815, he received the first grant of 2000 acres on the western slopes. Cox was not an exclusivist; he valued talent and benefited from the convict system. Clarendon, writes historian Edna Hickson, 'had all the appearance of a self-contained village. Over fifty convict servants acted as smiths, tanners, harness makers, wool sorters, weavers, butchers, tailors and herdsmen.'[6] The Cox dynasty expanded up the Nepean following more grants to his sons at Mulgoa between 1810 and 1816. Cox became the largest landholder on the Hawkesbury, the senior magistrate in the Hawkesbury, and the commander of the Hawkesbury garrison. The perquisites of office were sweet for Cox.

Cox and Macquarie played significant roles in the 1816 Frontier War on the Nepean and Hawkesbury rivers. The archival records of their activities – or the lack of those about Cox's, in particular – have, for two centuries, seeded the settler mythos of Hawkesbury settlement. The early guardians of the settler archive had no idea that another Western binary, that of the binary code of zero and one, would pierce their historical secrets. The etymology of the name of Australia's archival search engine, Trove, points not just to treasure, but to one that has been hidden, lost and then re-found. Whether settler Australia can confront Trove's revelations is another matter. The true seed of the colonial archive is not a stately tree, such as Cox's long-gone oaks at Clarendon, but rather a carefully manicured and bejewelled 200-year-old bonsai, sheltering within the walls of an ever-shifting hedge maze.

Asymmetric Warfare

An insatiable thirst for land defines all settler invasions. Aboriginal society, notes military historian John Keegan, was not warlike and was poorly placed to resist the settler invasion when it came in 1788.[7] Smallpox quickly put an end to the resistance that began to mount around Sydney in 1789. Fighting shifted to the slopes of Prospect Hill in the 1790s, spreading with settlement to the Hawkesbury in 1794 and then moving with settlement up the Nepean Valley. Tuberculosis, influenza and gonorrhoea were the invisible handmaidens of settlement. Consequently, Aboriginal resistance was necessarily measured, with focus placed on breakers of traditional law. In contrast, settler responses were indiscriminate, escalating waves of violence with predictably horrific results.

Between 1810 and 1816, Macquarie began filling the gap between South Creek and the Nepean with grants of large pastoral estates for the well-to-do. Increasing stock numbers, soil exhaustion, crop pests and diseases intersected with a drought that began in 1812, sparking conflict.[8] Sporadic fighting broke out in the autumn of 1814, stretching from Appin to Cox's Mulgoa farms. While Macquarie encouraged restraint among the settlers in 1814, his position had, by 1816, become as existential as that of his predecessor, former governor Arthur Phillip, in 1789.[9] The release of smallpox into the Aboriginal population in 1789 was hardly coincidental in the context of dwindling food stocks and increasing Aboriginal hostility. Macquarie's dispatch to Earl Bathurst on 18 March 1816 provided graphic details of the impact of the drought and gave notice of a military expedition to punish Aboriginal warriors responsible for killing five settlers in the Cowpastures.[10] As in all asymmetric warfare, consideration must be given to the way that Aboriginal warriors took advantage of the drought to attack settlers.

On 30 March, *The Sydney Gazette* reported that hostilities had moved downstream, with an attack on the Lewis farm on the junction of the Nepean and Grose rivers. The graphic details of this attack likely horrified the *Gazette*'s readers. Significantly, the corn harvest was not blamed as being a reason for the attack.[11] Then, on 9 April, Macquarie ordered detachments of the 46th Regiment into the field. One of its captains, W. B. G. Schaw, scoured both banks of the Hawkesbury, ineffectually pursuing fifteen warriors; another captain, James Wallis, found an Aboriginal camp of men, women and children on the Cataract River and killed fourteen of them. The camp was probably not hostile.[12] On the advice of one of Macarthur's wife's men, a lieutenant, Charles Dawe, surprised an Aboriginal camp, killed at least one person and captured a fourteen-year-old boy.[13]

Macquarie's proclamation on 4 May 1816 was made as the detachments of the 46th returned from the field. This ruling, which effectively enacted martial law, broadened operations so as to include settlers and minimised the potential of murder charges being laid for the killing of Aboriginal people. Aboriginal access to farms was also restricted. Magistrates and troops at Sydney, Parramatta and Windsor were ordered to support settlers in driving off hostile warriors. Finally, Macquarie set 28 December as the date for the annual feast at Parramatta and for the settlement of hostilities.[14]

In late May, drought-breaking rains caused the Nepean and Hawkesbury rivers to flood and forced in Serjeant Robert Broadfoot of the 46th, who had been scouring the Bringelly and Cooke districts, without reporting any contact.[15] In mid-June, the fighting shifted to the Hawkesbury. Two assigned servants were killed on a Grose River farm on 19 June.[16] The end of June saw more rain and flooding. In reporting the killing of Joseph Hobson on 8 July, *The Sydney Gazette* revealed that Hobson was the last settler left on a line of farms on the Kurrajong Slopes, the others having been driven off by Aboriginal warriors.[17]

Absence and Abrogation

The colonial archives of NSW differ significantly from the Athenian archives in that they are a record of invasion. There is a self-reflective relationship between the *process* of settlement and the *language* of settlement. The historical records of the nascent colony were largely written by men, most of whom were free, and nearly all of whom were self-made and enjoying opportunities denied them in Britain by class, birth and wealth. Self-interest dictated that the horrors of extermination be concealed as settlers reconciled invading Aboriginal country with Britain's orders 'to conciliate [Aboriginal peoples'] affections, enjoining all Our Subjects to live in amity and kindness with them'.[18] Fortunately, there were – and there are – those whose actions or observations, whether in moral outrage or in simply passing comment, throw light, however fleeting, onto this darkness.

Cox's memorandums to Macquarie in the second half of 1816 appear to have been removed from Macquarie's archive by an unknown person. Sometime after 1890, however, they came into the possession of Sir William Dixson, a wealthy collector of Australiana. Perhaps they were directed to Dixson by another unknown hand; perhaps they found their own way there. Regardless, they became part of a set labelled *Documents Relating to Aboriginal Australians, 1816–1853* bequeathed by Dixson to the State Library of NSW in 1959. Within the Dixson Library they remained largely unnoticed – but, two centuries after being written, Trove has revealed their contents.

Cox's 11 July 1816 report detailed operations on the Kurrajong Slopes beginning with the arrival of Broadfoot's detachment from Mulgoa. On 8 July, Cox formed a party of settlers, constables and Aboriginal guides to make a sweep of the slopes. This was the day that Hobson was killed. No contact was reported, and guards were left at farms.[19] On 15 July, Cox wrote at least two reports to Macquarie. The first recommended stationing three military parties 'for some time' at the Grose River, Windsor and Portland Head; Macquarie responded on 19 July, sending pouches, belts and ammunition for three armed constables. The other report contained the names of four Aboriginal men – Cockey, Butta Butta, Jack Straw and Port Head Jamie – who had been killed. Officially, these were the only Aboriginal casualties on the Hawkesbury in 1816. How they died was not explained, the implication being that they were killed in combat.[20]

Macquarie's proclamation on 20 July extended its predecessor's ambit, leading to the outlawing of ten Aboriginal men. Of these, only three had been on the list given to Schaw on 9 April; the seven additions, five of whom were probably Hawkesbury men, came from Magistrates Cox, Cartwright and Mileham. As well, this proclamation had a particular focus on the Hawkesbury because military detachments were sent to the Nepean, Hawkesbury and Grose Rivers to protect settlers. Macquarie's proclamation gave magistrates, soldiers and settlers three months to sort the matter out.[21]

The killing, in late August, of one of Cox's Mulgoa shepherds and 250 of his sheep can be viewed as a targeted killing, typical of asymmetric warfare.[22] However, while parties were sent out, there were no reports of contact or casualties. It is perhaps not a coincidence that, in the first week of September 1816, Macquarie suffered an 'alarming complaint' in his bowels that required his confinement.[23]

On 9 September, two Aboriginal children from a Cattai farm owned by Dr Thomas Arndell were admitted to the Native Institution in Parramatta.[24] It is likely that they were orphaned in military operations. On 14 September, Cox reported the organisation of five parties of soldiers, settlers and native guides to sweep the Hawkesbury–Nepean Valley for a fortnight;[25] it is logical to assume that the killing of his shepherds and sheep was the cause of this activity. The parties were still in the field in October. Significantly, while Cox commanded the field parties, he only had intermittent contact with them. Broadfoot was the highest-ranking soldier among them – he had been rewarded £100 for capturing bushrangers in Tasmania in 1815,[26] and he was to be the Bank of New South Wales' first customer. The Australian Government's 2020 *Afghan Inquiry Report* highlighted the risk of small detachments under the command of non-commissioned officers taking matters into their own hands,[27] and there is no reason to suspect that 1816 was any different. As well, the serjeants and corporals leading these small parties would be under settler pressure to kill Aboriginal people without reporting having done so. Indeed, these parties made no reports of contact or casualties.

On 1 November, hostilities officially ended. Macquarie offered the survivors of those outlawed the opportunity to surrender and be pardoned. Macquarie's 4 April 1817 report to Bathurst, detailing his success in quelling Aboriginal resistance, was masterful bureaucratese. He blamed the violence on 'the hostile Spirit of Violence and Rapine, which the black Natives or Aborigines of this Country had for a Considerable time past Manifested against the White Inhabitants'. He wrote of his success in 'disarming' and 'outlawing some of the Most Violent and Atrocious Natives' and offering an 'indemnity to such as delivered themselves within a prescribed Period'. He concluded with the hope that his Native Institution would 'ultimately pave the way for the Civilization of a large Portion of the Aborigines of the Country'.[28] No Aboriginal casualties were reported.

Illuminating the Cracks

Piecing together the story of a war that never officially happened is possible only by looking around the edges of the archive, looking for incidental scraps of information, looking beyond the reflections of that which has been left for us to see.

Over the years, the gaps surrounding the killing of Mrs Lewis and her servant as well as the subsequent killings of Cockey, Butta Butta, Jack Straw and Port Head Jamie began to fill, nodule-like. Lieutenant Archibald Bell told Commissioner John Thomas Bigge in 1819 that Mrs Lewis had been killed because the promised remuneration for some work done by Aboriginal people had been refused with 'very rough usage'.[29] This challenges *The Sydney Gazette*'s reporting of the matter at the time and throws new light on relations between settlers and local Aboriginal people.

It was the bowerbird habits of David Scott Mitchell, a bibliophile who obsessively collected regional newspapers, that enriched the archive beyond the imaginings of its colonial founders and exposed the horrors of 1816. The Hawkesbury's newspapers of the early twentieth century held old-men's recollections of stories seared into their memories by the flickering light of kitchen fires that had burnt out long ago. These included, between 1903 and 1910, Samuel Boughton and Alfred Smith, who recounted the stories of the killings as told to them by eyewitnesses.[30] From their accounts, we can draw that Cockey, Butta Butta, Jack Straw and Port Head Jamie were betrayed by either an Aboriginal man called Stevey or, more likely, a settler named Carr; the four men were then turned in to Cox and Bell. One may have been killed while fighting, but at least three were hung – one at Lewis' farm, one at Hobson's and one at the start of Comleroy Road. Cockey was pushed off a dray and shot repeatedly while choking on a stringybark rope.[31] Cox avoided any embarrassing questions by simply writing in his 19 July memorandum that the men were 'killed'.

Accounts left to us by George Bowman (who, born in 1795, may well have participated in 1816's punitive expeditions) and Peter Cunningham (a Hunter Valley settler) add depth to Boughton's and Smith's accounts. In 1825, Aboriginal men killed a settler and his convict servant on the Hunter and then visited the Hawkesbury. Returning via the Putty Road, they chased some mounted settlers and stopped at a hut at Putty, where there were three men known to them. One of the men, Carr, who had been involved in the 1816 incident, was killed; another was beaten badly, and the third escaped to Richmond. An armed party was sent out after them and attacked the camp of a 'friendly tribe' at Burrowell Creek.[32] These are liminal glimpses coming from the edges of the frontier, both in time and space, that ripple the calm of the settler self-image.

Again, it is outside the silence of the official archives that we glimpse a sense of what happened in the second half of 1816. William Romaine Govett, who came to NSW as a surveyor in 1828, described parties of soldiers, settlers and Aboriginal guides crushing resistance in 1816.[33] Boughton's opinion that many Aboriginal people were 'hung without trial'[34] is supported by the missionary Lancelot Threlkeld's recollection of an Aboriginal man being hung and shot in 1816 by 'a party of whites'.[35] The Reverend John Dunmore Lang recalled being 'shown places on the Hawkesbury, where the "commando" system had been carried on, and the natives literally [were] hunted down and shot',[36] a process not dissimilar from Bowman's opinion that the 'military did not attempt to take the Blacks and make prisoners of them but shot all they fell in with and received great praise from the Governor for so doing'.[37] In 1890, Prosper Tuckerman recalled that his father had told him of soldiers killing more than 400 Aboriginal people in one expedition.[38] By the 1840s, there were few Aboriginal people around Windsor.[39] The last recorded killing was of a twelve-year-old girl, murdered in 1846 by 'two gentlemen' at Upper Castlereagh.[40]

Official archival documents such as governor's dispatches, trial transcripts, *The Sydney Gazette*, various memorials and memorandums, and David Collins' *An Account of the English Colony in New South Wales* indicate that approximately forty settlers were killed by Aboriginal people on the Hawkesbury between 1794 and 1825, while fifty Aboriginal people were killed during the same period. While the estimate of settler deaths is reliable, the official records of Aboriginal deaths cannot be trusted. It is only through the records collected and donated to the State Library of NSW by Mitchell and Dixson that we have any idea of the true scale of the operations in 1816. The eccentricity of both men's extraordinary collectiveness and generosity makes them truly liminal: not outliers but islets catching flotsam and jetsam drifting into oblivion.

It is in various rewards and payments – the records of which obviously did not make their way back to Britain – that Macquarie let his guard down and revealed that the operations of 1816 were, in fact, a war. Cox received a payment of 'the Sum of £76.10.7 – Str., being the amount of Provisions, sundry necessaries and Boat-hire, incurred during the recent *Warfare* with the Hostile Natives, for the Military Parties & Guides under the direction of Mr. Cox'.[41] Similarly, the most significant indicator of the scope of Aboriginal casualties suffered in the Frontier War of 1816 can be found in the admission of sixteen Aboriginal children to the Native Institution in 1816 – amounting to slightly under half of all admissions between 1814 and 1820. These figures indicate that the sixteen children were the survivors of indiscriminate night attacks on camps, such as the Appin Massacre.

Delayed Awakening

Collectively, settler societies are both unwilling and unable to recognise, let alone address, the catastrophic and genocidal nature of the frontier. The colonial archive shrouds itself self-effacingly in a faded light before the settler gaze. Settler societies have no means of knowing themselves as others know them. Settler societies also fail to realise that, while the frontier is in constant pursuit of the horizon, it is only one of many waves recycling, repudiating and repurposing old frontiers, leaving settlers with little to dwell on beyond an endlessly receding mirage.

The significance of Cox's epitaph, which is in keeping with the Calvinistic doctrine of predestination, is – like the Cox mausoleum – easily missed. It is probably not coincidental that it is drawn from the books of *Titus* and *Acts*, both written during the apostolic colonising of the gentile world of the Roman Empire: 'Not by works of righteousness which we have done but according to his own mercy he saved us' (*Titus* 3:5) and 'Believe in the Lord Jesus Christ and thou shalt be saved' (*Acts* 16:31). This is not the stuff of Paul's faith, hope and charity. The curious repetitiveness of the two verses is best explained by looking at the chapters from which they come: in both cases, *Titus* and *Acts* reference magistrates, but in contradictory ways. The epistle to Titus, Bishop of Crete, enjoins the flock to 'obey magistrates', whereas *Acts* concerns the admonishment of the Macedonian magistrates following God's miraculous release of Paul and Simon from prison. Cox's epitaph suggests that he was one of the elect carrying out God's will, unencumbered by the constraints of his magisterial role. At the bottom of Cox's epitaph is a line broken by the symbol of a diamond. The etymological origin of 'diamond' is the Greek *adamas*, referring to both hardness and protective invincibility. Dark is the adamant gaze reflected from Cox's epitaph.

Homer and Virgil tell us in the *Odyssey* and the *Aeneid*, respectively, that dreams come from the House of Sleep through gates of polished ivory and transparent horn. To paraphrase Homer, dreams from the gates of ivory deceive and bring no fulfillment, while dreams that come through the gates of horn bring true issues to pass. In navigating the archive, we should look to Gilles Deleuze and Félix Guattari, who tell us in *A Thousand Plateaus: Capitalism and Schizophrenia* that we should expect to find, not a single taproot, but a multiplicity of rhizomes connected to and disconnected from one another. Using their model, it is possible to visualise the archive not as a single entity, but as a multiplicity of entities connected and disconnected from one another by time and space, more a labyrinth than a pathway. The truth of the Frontier War on the Sydney plain is not gathered in one place in the archive; rather, it comes to us aslant, like flickering light from many campfires. Trove, to borrow from Virgil, is not so much a golden bough or a trail of thread, but a trail of words, allowing us to navigate the labyrinthine House of Sleep that is the colonial archive. Too easy is it to be beckoned through the opaque gates of polished ivory in a delusional dream of settler superiority, self-righteousness and indifference. Much harder is it to follow the trail of words through the gates of transparent horn and bring true issues to pass.

1 See, for example, *Community Action for Windsor Bridge Submission*, http://www.cawb.com.au/uploads/1/0/4/5/10456711/cawb_eis_submission_v2_pdf_copy.pdf, p. 31.

2 Cox, Richard, *William Cox: Blue Mountains Road Builder and Pastoralist*, Rosenberg Publishing, Sydney, 2012, p. 32.

3 Ibid., p. 51.

4 Holt, Joseph, *A Rum Story: The Adventures of Joseph Holt, Thirteen Years in New South Wales, 1800–1812*, ed. Peter O'Shaughnessy, Kangaroo Press, Sydney, 1988, p. 82.

5 Ritchie, John, *Lachlan Macquarie: A Biography*, Melbourne University Press, Melbourne, 1986, p. 34.

6 Hickson, Edna, 'Cox, William (1764–1837)', *Australian Dictionary of Biography*, 2006, https://adb.anu.edu.au/biography/cox-william-1934

7 Keegan, John, *A History of Warfare*, Vintage, New York, 1994, p. 391.

8 *The Sydney Gazette*, 11 January 1812, p. 3; *The Sydney Gazette*, 15 February 1817, p. 2; Macarthur Onslow, Sibella (ed.), *Some Early Records of the Macarthurs of Camden*, Angus & Robertson, Sydney, 1914, p. 300.

9 *The Sydney Gazette*, 18 June 1814, p. 1.

10 *Historical Records of Australia*, series 1, vol. IX, The Library Committee of the Commonwealth Parliament, 1917, pp. 52–54.

11 *The Sydney Gazette*, 30 March 1816, p. 2.

12 Wallis, James, AONSW, Reel 6045; 4/1735, pp. 50–62.

13 Dawe, Charles, AONSW, Reel 6045; 4/1735, pp. 29–32.

14 Bannister, Saxe, *Statements and Documents Relating to Proceedings in New South Wales*, in 1824, 1825 and 1826, W. Bridekirk, Cape Town, 1827, pp. 96–98.

15 Barton, Leonard L., *The Military History of Windsor*, NSW, L. Barton, Sydney, 1994, p. 41. Broadfoot was the first depositor in the Bank of New South Wales.

16 *The Sydney Gazette*, 29 June 1816, p. 2.

17 *The Sydney Gazette*, 13 July 1816, p. 2.

18 The full text of the instructions given to Phillip can be accessed at http://www.foundingdocs.gov.au/resources/transcripts/nsw2_doc_1787.rtf

19 Dixson, William, *Documents Relating to Aboriginal Australians, 1816–1853*, ML, reel CY2743; DL Add 81, State Library of NSW, pp. 177–181.

20 Ibid., pp. 182–192.

21 *The Sydney Gazette*, 20 July 1816, p. 1.

22 *The Sydney Gazette*, 31 August 1816, p. 2.

23 Macquarie, Lachlan, *Diary 10 April 1816 – 1 July 1818*, original held in the Mitchell Library, Sydney, ML Ref: A773, pp. 44–49.

24 Brook, Jack and J. L. Cohen, *The Parramatta Native Institute and the Black Town*, New South Wales University Press, Sydney, 1991, p. 69.

25 Dixson, *Documents Relating to Aboriginal Australians*, p. 188.

26 Barton, *The Military History of Windsor*, p. 41.

27 *Afghanistan Inquiry Report*, Inspector-General of the Australian Defence Force, Commonwealth of Australia, 2020.

28 *Historical Records of Australia*, p. 342.

29 Ritchie, John (ed.), *The Evidence to the Bigge Reports: New South Wales under Governor Macquarie – Volume 1: The Oral Evidence*, Heinemann, Melbourne, 1971, pp. 173–174.

30 Boughton, Samuel ('Cooramill'), *Reminiscences of Richmond: From the Forties Down*, Cathy McHardy, Kurrajong, 2010, pp. 109–110, 150–151; Smith, Alfred, *Some Ups and Downs of an Old Richmondite*, Nepean Family History Society, Emu Plains, 1991.

31 Ibid., pp. 150–151.

32 Cunningham, Peter, *Two Years in New South Wales*, first published in 1827, reprinted by Angus & Robertson, Sydney, 1966, pp. 197–198; 'Memorandum for Mr Scott', Original Documents on Aborigines and Law, 1797–1840, Macquarie University, http://www.law.mq.edu.au/research/colonial_case_law/nsw/other_features/correspondence/documents/document_102a/
33 Govett, William Romaine, *Sketches of New South Wales*, first published in the *Saturday Magazine* in 1836–1837, republished by Gaston Renard, Melbourne, 1977, pp. 195–197.
34 Boughton, *Reminiscences of Richmond*, pp. 109–110.
35 *The Colonist*, 27 October 1838, p. 3.
36 Ibid.
37 'Memorandum for Mr Scott'.
38 *Windsor and Richmond Gazette*, 25 October 1890, p. 3.
39 *Windsor and Richmond Gazette*, 30 August 1929, p. 5.
40 Gilmore, Mary, *More Recollections*, Angus & Robertson, Sydney, 1935, pp. 246–247.
41 Macquarie, *Diary 10 April 1816 – 1 July 1818*, pp. 50–59, emphasis added.

Your Face Is a Historical Atlas: Chinese Face Reading for the Past and Future of a Surveillance Society

Lucia Tường Vy Nguyễn

My imaginary court of justice is a place not only for judgement, but for rituals, witchcraft, and magic.

— Morehshin Allahyari[1]

A face appears, with a peach on its nose, ancient coins laid over its eyes and orchids blooming from underneath. On the centre of its forehead nests a dragon, and studded above the upper lip is an ingot of gold that gleams purple and blue. These talismans spin and rotate over the face's contours, swelling and shrinking and glistening in a blue light, hovered over by perhaps the most powerful talisman of all: a cursor.

To use the *Cybermancy 2* face-reading program, you must first enable your webcam by clicking the on-screen bagua, an octagonal feng shui energy map representing the 'eight areas' governing every individual's life.[2] Your face must be centred and well-lit in order to be read by neural networks and prediction tools sourced from a machine-learning library. Vector lines will trace the curves of your face to materialise a series of facial landmarks, each signifying a different realm: wealth, marriage, fortune, child-bearing, health.

Your nose indicates you have some physical or mental health concerns, pronounces the peach on my face.

> *Peach, I'm better at being alone this year than I was last year. Fewer hallucinations. Although … I am conversing with a piece of fruit. A peach that's chromed blue on screen, shaved bare of its fuzz and balanced on the tip of my nose.*

> *I hear you're meant to represent immortality in Chinese lore, peach. Makes sense. We grab you with our hands, our mouths, like immortality were a pound of flesh. Does it even matter, though? Does anything on the Internet[3] ever die?*

Cybermancy 2 was created by Asian Australian artist and software engineer Jane Fan, who modelled its occult-like aesthetics on the ancient practice of Chinese face reading, a pseudoscience that interprets the 'regions' of the face to foretell an individual's fortunes. As outlined in the Ming dynasty's *Compendium of Materia Medica*, a guidebook for traditional herbal remedies, mian xiang ('face reading', known in the West as 'physiognomy') pairs personality traits with prominent facial features such as the eyes, the nose or the mouth.[4] Large lips suggest a proclivity to gossip. A wide forehead portends intelligence and success. Clear skin signifies good life. An overbite reveals a lack of ambition. A square jawline in a woman warns that she will bring unhappiness to her future husband. Whereas the Chinese zodiac assigns animal-related personalities based on birth year, mian xiang pinpoints a human being's position on a grander schematic map of the universe, in tandem with plants, animals and the elements. Within this cosmogony, the face was not only a harbinger of fortune but also a systematic index of the relationship between the human body, the natural world and social life.[5] Face reading thus opens the map of one person's future and an archive of their country's past.

'Although I use game technologies, I wouldn't say my artworks are games, because there is no obvious action and reward. I would call them *experiences* or *interactions*,' Fan tells me.[6] 'As powerful as interactive art can be, the struggle is that the audience perceives it as a "game" to be solved or beaten. This might lead to some frustration if the interaction does not have a definitive conclusion [or] give the user a sense of control, or if it [offers] more questions than answers.'

Fig. 1. Interface of Jane Fan's *Cybermancy 2* program

While *Cybermancy 2* was designed for the 2021 digital art program hosted by Sydney's 4A Centre for Contemporary Asian Art, the 'game' of reading faces is modelled on an older colonial regime through which particular communities – Othered by socially constructed notions of race – were intended to be 'beaten'. A face now demarcated with vector lines and dominate points by biometric technology was once cast in lantern light – perhaps once forced into lantern light. In 1731, the US Government enforced the *Law for Regulating Negro and Indian Slaves in the Night Time*, which required Black and Native American slaves to carry lanterns when travelling at night so that white authorities could identify (and, if necessary, subdue) them. This form of slave patrol lit up the path for contemporary policing and surveillance practices like stop-and-frisk and biometric data collection.[7] Across carceral history, coloured skin has become a canvas upon which sentences of imprisonment and death are written.

'Skin is a sensory matter, a physical extension of the body's ability to perceive harm, desire, safety, risk,' writes American academic Mitali Thakor. 'Skin is a contact point, a boundary zone at which relationality is negotiated.'[8] The digitally rotoscoped skin seen on hyperreal avatars, for example, is 'mimetic of real skin, indicative of the creation of palpable, sensuous connection between the original and the copy [...] The desire to uncover this artificiality, to measure the degree of realness, relies on logics similar to the desire to inspect racial authenticity.'[9] Pseudosciences like physiognomy and phrenology, which attribute mental abilities to formations of cartilage, skin, muscle and bone, have encoded racial biases into the screening processes of our modern surveillance society.

In turn, these colonial power dynamics are coercively reproduced in online architectures and technology – a process that Iranian media artist Morehshin Allahyari has termed 'digital colonialism'.[10] Particular faces are deemed less human than others. On the other side of the lantern and the screen lies something far more insidious.

In his 1946 one-paragraph short story 'On Exactitude in Science', Jorge Luis Borges envisions an ancient civilisation in which a guild of cartographers had 'attained such Perfection' that they were able to draw a map perfectly to scale – one 'whose size was that of the Empire'. But, like the rule of that Empire, the map crumbled over time, torn to shreds by the weather and cast out in the desert to be inhabited by beggars and feral animals. In his essay 'The Analytical Language of John Wilkins', Borges then strays into the taxonomies of a fictitious Chinese encyclopedia, whose absurdity offered a jumping-off point for philosopher Michel Foucault's interrogations into knowledge, discourse and truth. Foucault is perhaps best known for his theory of the panopticon effect, whereby citizens of disciplinary surveillance societies become complicit in the policing of their own bodies. Much like the Empire's map that coincided, point for point, with the real world, the Ming empire sought to perfect an incontrovertible cartography of its own. Face reading rose to prominence in a society already steeped in divination practices, including palm reading and feng shui. Physiognomy was mainly intended to justify a woman's marriageability (or lack of) to potential suitors. From this, Chinese society developed a cult of 'face', wherein one strives to maintain public respect, honour and dignity – to 'lose face' is to be deprived of all of these virtues.

'In feng shui, you can choose or avoid certain furnishings to improve your luck in different parts of your life,' says Fan. 'Orchids or other flowers are usually connected to romance and fertility. Fruit like mandarins and oranges are linked with prosperity because they are round and golden like coins.' *Cybermancy 2* succeeds her palm-reading program *Cybermancy*, which presents the user with advertisements targeting the demographic their palms were 'read' to reflect – that is, it plots points across the hand to advise purchases for the near or distant future. *Cybermancy* drew from Fan's interest in playing with neural networks, whose inner workings are not understood by the general public, much like magic. The difference between magic and science, however, is the latter's interest in explaining – in apprehending – bewildering phenomena.

In the same way that astrology, despite its controversial foundations, endures in the public imagination, rituals and superstitions persevere as means to soothe fears in the face of the unpredictable and unknowable. Government-sanctioned quarantines and panic over sovereign borders have rendered particular maps obsolete. And so we have opened our search engines and traversed a virtual Empire instead.

> *You are young and accumulating assets, feeling the pressure of a competitive economy. Taking care of finances will help you attract a good partner,* **advise the ancient Chinese coins tipping back and forth over my eyes.**
>
> *You have a poorer chance of bringing wealth into your life,* **smirks the ingot on my cupid's bow.**
>
> > *Zoom stocks increased by 425 per cent in 2020; coincidentally, at the same time, I wondered whether I should invest in the market because, well, wealth in the arts can be just as elusive and corrupt and criminal. Most of us in the arts will only observe such affluence from afar, encased and barricaded like a military fortress, like an installation we must not touch. If I cannot touch this wealth, perhaps I should resign myself to its incorporeality – and acquire some NFTs instead.*
> >
> > > *Money draws blood, oil and weapons. The filthy secret codes of this world are programmed on number$ and glyph$$$. And I would gladly press filthy gold to my eyes just to be dead to it all.*

The world's shift from the physical to the virtual during the COVID-19 pandemic has augured a future that is even more intensely surveilled, commodified and – with non-fungible tokens (NFTs) and cryptocurrencies – gamified. Much like in Borges' tale, the force of the weather remains inexorable. We look to the cloud, each face latched on to the screen like a key in a lock. The cloud swells and opens before us into eternally expansive storage structures for archiving the past; these include records of Chinese face reading, whose taxonomy of favourable features has dictated ideals of physical beauty in East Asia. A life of fortune mirrors a genetic blessing. The game of life seems to be programmed with a somewhat simple reward system. But I befriend players along the way.

British Chinese digital artist Lina Deng's body of work, which includes glitching GIF designs and video works like an Elon Musk 'fancam', seeks to interrogate the politics of image circulation and private digital ownership. In early 2021, she designed an Instagram face filter, titled 're cognition', that combines facial-recognition technology, Chinese numerology and reference charts for face reading. The filter sculpts a translucent numbered chart over the user's face, which is diagrammed with crosshairs, dotted vector lines and a crop square framing the centre of the face – the area mian xiang assigns to 'middle age' (ages thirty to fifty). As I redraft this essay, Deng has been living for a few months off-grid – the Instagram grid, that is. Her account is deactivated, her filter persisting as a screenshot on my phone, as a fraying line of inquiry in this essay. A glitch, perhaps, in the cosmology of the digital. Deng tells me that, since face reading is Taoist, it is intrinsically cosmological and spiritual, and thus difficult to reconcile with Western science's emphasis on the empirical and the measurable. This is the very same science that, in eighteenth-century Europe, enabled physiognomy to eventually filter into eugenics, which in turn justified colonial wars and the slave trade across the globe.

'I think that modern science as we know it is just as socially constructed and culturally specific as the "spiritual" practices of astrology and mian xiang,' says Deng.[11] She cites social-justice theorist Denise Ferreira da Silva, who argues that universalising philosophies such as Immanuel Kant's 'categorical imperative' can act as colonial frameworks for racial subjugation by first decreeing that there is an 'ideal conception of humanity'. By nature, the racialised subaltern exists outside this ideal.

'Practices such as mian xiang that do not partake in colonial frameworks are extremely important not only in the preservation of cultural practices but in helping us to conceive of ways of knowing outside Eurocentric architectures,' Deng adds. One of the last stories I remember from Deng's Instagram is the meme of *SpongeBob SquarePants*' Patrick Star chained to a barrel in the middle of a stadium, captioned, 'when u defend astrology in front of a class of STEM students'. Toying with empirical methods of meaning-making offers an antidote to a world rendered meaningless by rampant exploitation and policing under the same hand. Read the palm. Bite it.

One of Western science's particularly egregious impacts is the embedding of panoptic measures into everyday life, in the name of

Fig. 2. re cognition Instagram filter by Lina Deng (formerly @linatheebean)

security. In July 2021, the Australian Parliament passed the *Online Safety Act 2021*, which endows the eSafety Commissioner – at the time of writing, Julie Inman Grant – with sweeping powers to censor abusive or abhorrent online content in order to protect citizens of all ages from the Internet's harms. Yet think tank Digital Rights Watch cautions that this blanket approach to censoring has the potential to implicate the social media accounts of sex workers as well as platforms that have hosted the damning footage of police brutality that mobilised Black Lives Matter and abolitionist movements of recent years.[12] The commissioner can also fine social media platforms for not removing content that breaches Australia's established (and outdated) media classification codes – a punitive threat that would naturally drive platforms to more heavily police their own users. Evidently, applying a universalising, Kantian approach incapacitates individual agency – particularly in the case of sex workers of colour, given some of the most popular genres of pornography are constructed on vectors of racialised fetishisation, of racially identifiable open-access faces spliced into private fantasies.[13] For whom are we providing this online safety? Or, rather, who do we choose to punish not merely in beaten flesh but also in online fictions?

I initially suggested an interview to Deng via a direct message (DM) on Instagram. This was also where we became acquainted with random details of each other's lives, and where many of my friendships and collaborations have grown during the pandemic. This is where I begin to learn how to organise a community.

Internet studies scholar Safiya Umoja Noble contends that what is often absent from the discourse on online abuses is 'a questioning of the historical and cultural development of science and technology and representations prioritized through digital technologies, as well as the uneven and exploitative global distribution of resources and labour in information and communications systems'.[14] In the case of Australia's *Online Safety Act*, the Senate has also failed to account for sex education and harm reduction – calling to mind Thakor's observation that governments, rather than allocating funding to community-based initiatives to address the exploitation of vulnerable communities, tend to opt for prosecutorial and enforcement-heavy solutions.[15] Digital colonialism fuses the punitive with the pleasurable, much like how the Global North's imperialist ventures across the Global South have been connected by a genealogy of greed. Never forget how we mapped the world. Never forget how we drew the Web.

Better to show the courage to fix or end a relationship rather than stay in comfortable unhappiness, whispers the eternal knot fastened on my brow.

> *The Internet began as a military-academic construct intended to connect military units, universities and governing bodies in a network to defend sovereign borders.*[16] *The military love their passwords; the military love their coercion. But do they love their witchcraft?*
>
> > *In ancient Mesopotamia, the Akkadian word for 'password' was the same word for 'omen'.*
> >
> > *The Internet listens to me; the Internet knows what I like.*
> >
> > *It knows my passwords and it sees my omens. Is this a relationship of comfortable unhappiness? All I can say is,*
> >
> > *it's complicated.*

The pandemic has made sharing space difficult and fatiguing – though video conferencing and online forums like Discord have allowed us to try. Amid all this, the captured face has remained our primary conduit for connection: framed on video calls, in avatarised profiles, with Instagram filter effects, and through face detection to unlock our smartphones. The face has become a means of breaking down barriers despite also signifying the obstacles we encounter as racialised persons.

The face, whether composed of cells or pixels, is a site for touch and connection. Deng made her filter to mediate tensions between the face as an ephemeral object (skin grows and dies) and the face's permanence as an archive (of histories personal, familial and cultural). I have my father's nose, my mother's jawline. Such features commune on a face that has been shot, captured and framed by my family since birth. For Fan, there is a reason that particular superstitions and rituals have persisted despite how absurd or meaningless they may seem: 'We keep them alive and believe in them because they're intrinsic to our cultures.' In much the same way, the art we make and the stories we tell are not isolated but connected in a historical continuum. Borges did not draft 'On Exactitude in Science' from thin air, but was inspired by an idea he encountered while reading

Lewis Carroll. Foucault's interrogations of 'truth' were partly inspired by having read Borges. My citations trace a particular genealogy, too.

The face is traced in cyberspace and pieced together into an archive of what we have read, done and said – an atlas of the virtual roads we have travelled – just as our ancestors discovered and colonised physical spaces and sought to make maps that attempted to contain them. But monitors overheat and screens freeze as the (to appropriate Borges) 'Inclemencies of Suns and Winters' wreak havoc on the computerised machine. Moreover, asks sociologist Ruha Benjamin, 'What social groups are classified, corralled, coerced, and capitalised upon so others are free to tinker, experiment, design, and engineer the future?'[17] The question remains. Ancestral knowledge can be passed down across generations through trial and error, though it is unclear whether this trial and error enables authorities to better control the populace or allows the populace to wield better control over themselves.

***In this day and age, finding a job that suits you can be difficult,* warns the dragon crouched in my forehead.**

Shut up, dragon; have you even been reading the news? The economy's not simply competitive – it's crushing those in precarious situations. What does 'a job that suits you' mean? To what end do I imagine?

***Start thinking about whether you want to have children,* advise the orchids digging their stems into my pixelated cheeks.**

Orchids, half of my friends are determined to become parents soon, while the other half tell me they wouldn't dare bring a child into a world like this. I think I agree with the latter. The second my child's face is touched by light, it will be coded with misfortune and surveilled by cameras without consent. Digital technologies are not of flesh and blood, but they have still followed the course of our evolution. They are part of our ecosystem.

But we do not know where we're going. We do not know where the machines will go.

I google 'orchids in Chinese culture'. Alongside the chrysanthemum, the plum blossom and bamboo, the orchid is considered one of the 四君子 *('Four Gentlemen') of Chinese art lore. These Gentlemen signify the cycle of the four seasons, of time ongoing.*

The Gentlemen remind me of four similar men – on horseback – in Christian mythology. But with them comes the end of Empire, the end of time.

I place my fingers on the touchpad and begin to summon.

> *My imaginary court of justice subpoenas cartographers, dragons, flowers. The stenotype will imprint their omens and testaments on a canvas of rotoscoped skin.*
>
> *My imaginary court of justice is in session, deliberating on the future.*

Fan delivers a grim perspective: 'Ultimately, it doesn't matter if you receive judgements from a fortune teller or from Instagram. Either way, you become anxious and self-conscious.' This ~~game~~ interaction leaves me with more questions than answers.

Could not start webcam. NotAllowedError: Permission denied

> *I don't have a password. I can't troubleshoot.*
>
> ***NotAllowedError: Permission denied***
>
> *I don't have an omen on this black screen. I can't see where to go.*
>
> *What does it matter – I've been arguing with numbers. Lina said mian xiang predates empirical theory, so maybe I should just write off this entire reading as some perverse calculus. They got some things right about my past.*

I don't know how perfectly they calculated my future. But the Empire claimed to have mastered cartography.

Perhaps I should ask the Empire what they meant by such Perfection.

They must be listening already.

1 Allahyari, Morehshin, 'Physical Tactics for Digital Colonialism', Medium, 8 June 2019, https://medium.com/@morehshin_87856/physical-tactics-for-digital-colonialism-45e8d3fcb2da
2 Fan, Jane, *Cybermancy 2*, 2021, https://4a-digital.github.io/cybermancy/
3 The writer has capitalised all instances of the words 'internet' and 'web' to signal both as spaces to traverse: virtual locational phenomena that resemble a city or a cadastral parcel to be owned (much like a URL domain is owned).
4 Samizadeh, Souphiyeh, 'Chinese Facial Physiognomy and Modern Day Aesthetic Practice', *Journal of Cosmetic Dermatology*, vol. 19, no. 1, 2020, pp. 161–166; Wang, Xing, 'Categorising the Body and Interpreting Fortune', in *Physiognomy in Ming China: Fortune and the Body*, BRILL, Boston, 2020, p. 217.
5 Wang, 'Categorising the Body', p. 233.
6 All comments by Jane Fan sourced from an interview with the author.
7 Browne, Simone, *Dark Matters: On the Surveillance of Blackness*, Duke University Press, Durham and London, 2015, p. 78.
8 Thakor, Mitali, 'Deception by Design: Digital Skin, Racial Matter, and the New Policing of Child Sexual Exploitation', in *Captivating Technology: Race, Carceral Technoscience, and Liberatory Imagination in Everyday Life*, ed. Ruha Benjamin, Duke University Press, Durham and London, 2019, p. 190. Thakor's research into 'Sweetie', the AI designed to lure in child predators on 'webcam sex tourism' websites, is of particular interest. Thakor notes that Sweetie's facial features are modelled on the faces of young victims of sex trafficking in the Philippines, a network heavily shaped by Western imperialist violence in East and South-East Asia.
9 Ibid., p. 200.
10 Allahyari, 'Physical Tactics for Digital Colonialism'.
11 All comments by Lina Deng sourced from an interview with the author.
12 Digital Rights Watch, 'Explainer: The Online Safety Bill', 11 February 2021, https://digitalrightswatch.org.au/2021/02/11/explainer-the-online-safety-bill/
13 Australian Government, 'Seeking Help for Tech Abuse More Difficult for Culturally Diverse Women', eSafety Commissioner website, 18 February 2019, https://www.esafety.gov.au/about-us/newsroom/seeking-help-for-tech-abuse-more-difficult-for-culturally-diverse-women
14 Noble, Safiya Umoja, 'The Future of Information Culture', in *Algorithms of Oppression: How Search Engines Reinforce Racism*, New York University Press, New York, 2018, p. 160.
15 Thakor, 'Deception by Design', p. 203.
16 Noble, 'The Future of Information Culture', p. 154.
17 Benjamin, Ruha, 'Introduction', in *Captivating Technology*, p. 4.

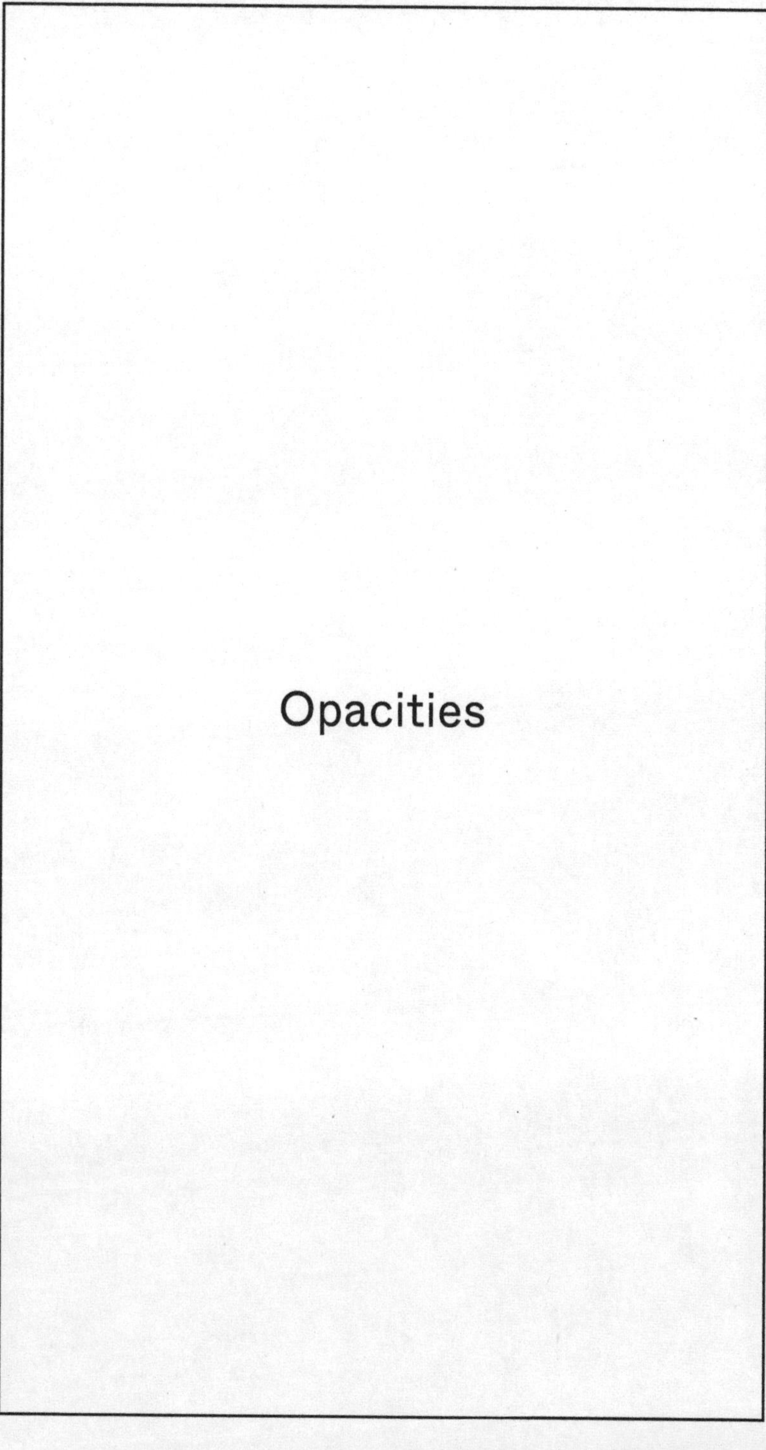

Opacities

Third Cowboy from the Sun

Hassan Abul

Luisa is in her late twenties and sprawled across the passenger seat. She takes expansive drags from a joint while summertime Mexico races past in the window. It's the second day of her road trip with Tenoch, the cousin of her cheating husband, and Julio, his best friend who borrowed his family's car for this trip. They are going to a beach. Tenoch and Julio have just finished high school, and the stretch of time between the present moment and the start of the university semester jitters with potential. The boys are both long and lean, with a bravado that far outstrips their clumsy limbs and limited experience. Luisa is smiling. It's a smile that takes up an incredible portion of her face. 'I saw you last night.' She's teasing them about peeking through the window of her hotel room. 'Did you want to see me naked? See me naked and have a wank?' This is the first moment in *Y tu mamá también* where we see the film's central relationship shift.

I think about this scene a lot. Before this, it had felt like she was being swept up in their wake – they were teenagers, yes, but this was their car, their country, their trip to an isolated beach that only they knew the location of. They invited her, quite forcefully, because they had wanted to tangle with her, because they had liked the look of her. But when she says this, she names the way they have been looking – as though she were a sexy diversion for the holidays – and reminds them that she's equally capable of looking back, of constructing them in her own perspective. After the initial shock, you get the sense that the footing between them has been somewhat levelled: she asks them for their thoughts and experiences on sex, and they meet her there, as truthfully as they can from within the characters they'd constructed in front of her the day before, charolastras with a manifesto.

The summer stretches out behind them.

▪

H. says he's going to spend the summer in Adelaide. The eyes in Melbourne have started to feel sticky, restrictive. He tells me this over the phone, his tongue barely keeping up with the cascade of revelations tripping off it: all the changes he had been bargaining with himself over had been possible all along. I say this clarity is new, I say it seems he found it because he had gotten out of the city for a few days. He says it is, he says he did. He had spent the day at a beach.

It makes an intuitive kind of sense, to me, that changing is harder when you're in view of people who know you.

▪

'Your voice has gotten a lot deeper.' R. and I were walking along Darebin Creek. It hadn't rained in over a week, but the creek was full and the earth still waterlogged, holding on to the memory of heavy downpours earlier in the month. Each step was sticky, with clods of grass and dark mud suctioning onto my boots; I could see my own easy tracks when I looked back. 'I hope that's okay to say – I haven't seen you in a while.' I chewed my lip for a moment, sensitive to the potential probing in R.'s follow-up. I have always been prone to disappearing; people don't usually call attention to it. Because of the way the creek twisted around a bend, a still pool of water formed in the corner, collecting detritus that had flowed in off the street; a cracked milk crate and a couple of plastic shopping bags bobbed gently.

'It's okay to say. I'm glad to hear it.'

■

The first time I watched this movie was midway through Melbourne's second lockdown. An 8 pm curfew was in effect, but it had been getting dark hours earlier for weeks. Like others, I succumbed to the cooking impulse. Doughs that required three separate rises had been previously impossible, since I wasn't available all day to lean over and poke a finger into the surface. Toum, a Levantine emulsion of garlic, oil and lemon juice – the internet said it could be done in a food processor but would taste better whipped by hand. It would just take time. I had the two hours to spend alternating hands when each one tired of whisking. On screen, Julio and Tenoch lay on separate diving boards, legs dangling over the edges towards a swimming pool. They're at the country club Tenoch's father serves as a trustee of; on Mondays, the club is closed and they have the place to themselves. I watched them over a mountain of garlic cloves, crushed and pressed; a jug of lemon juice, the squeezing of which alerted me to a network of tiny fissures crackling across my hands; and a big can of olive oil with a leaky spout. Toum is supposed to become white and somewhat fluffy. You beat it and beat it, and there should be a moment when it all comes together; you watch it closely, making sure you don't whip too far and cause the emulsion to break. The boys are naked, jerking off on their separate boards, calling out to each other the names of girls and women they both know. I look down at the bowl in my lap and the arm furiously beating the whisk and grow self-conscious, aware that I have begun matching their rhythm. They cum at the same time, spurred by the thought of Luisa. Their mutual spunk drops into the pool, globs of white in an otherwise impossible azure. We see it from below, the camera underwater, receiving it.

I never managed to get the toum to the fluffy, white stage. It remained thick, unctuous, a deep yellow.

■

There's a line of thinking in metaphysics called 'process philosophy'. The basic idea is that, rather than thinking of things as in a state of *being*, it's more fruitful to think of them as in a state of *becoming*; change is not just something that happens on the way between fixed, cataloguable states, but an essential aspect of things.

Let's take a swimming pool: you could say it's an artificial pit of water, usually with a tiled interior, made for humans to swim in. This tells us some things about swimming pools; it's the way many of us in the West have been trained to think – 'scientifically', 'rigorously', through the lens of 'utility'. But if we refocus our eyes a little, a dynamism, an existing-in-context, a sense that we are coexisting with it, emerges: the shimmer of the water is an interaction between the sun and the blue sky and the moving water; this interaction is totally dependent on the moment. The structure of the pool is made up of the labour that brought all of the pieces there, and the histories of colonisation and capitalism that led to the fences surrounding it (whether literal or social – who are the people the pool is intended for?). It's the rotation of the Earth on its axis that tilts to create summer, and the pleasure humans locate in cool submergence. There's a precarity here: no part of this is extricable from its wider context, which has the capacity to change at any time. The pool doesn't just exist; it's in the *process* of existing. Viewing things in snapshots is, for process philosophers like Alfred North Whitehead and Maurice Merleau-Ponty, a useful scientific fiction, but *duration* is inescapable.

Aurora Mattia tweets, 'kind of weird to abstract transsexuality into a gender identity when it's literally a durational & shapeshifting form of embodiment'. This is to say: this essay exists in relation to transition. Susan Sontag wrote in her diary: 'I vulgarize my feelings by speaking of them too readily to others.' This is to say: I'm afraid to pin down exactly how.

▪

When I tell D. about *Y tu mamá también*, I can't stop talking about how actively the camera seems to *look* at things. D. and I are 'body doubling' over video call – working together on separate projects while occupying the same space. Being able to glance up and see their face set in concentration anchors me. Sometimes, a housemate opens the door to ask for a cigarette and waves when they see me; it delights me that, in Berlin, there are witnesses to our friendship. Early in the movie, Julio and Tenoch are stuck in traffic; frustrated, they speculate about the cause. We see the backs of their heads – the camera is in the back seat, like a third, less loved member of their troupe. When they pass the actual cause (a pedestrian, struck crossing the busy road and killed), the camera swivels as though set atop a human neck and gazes back through the rear window at the body beneath a sheet; we never see the boys' reactions or even confirm whether they noticed. It's not the point of the scene; their silent friend in the back noticed.

The camera has a tendency to wander away in this movie. When Julio is on the phone at his family home, we're slowly pacing around the apartment, lingering in front of photos on the walls, only half-listening to his conversation. At a roadside restaurant, when the conversation turns too raucous, we get up and walk through the kitchen, thinking about the lives of the staff we see. The camera is suffused with its own perspective, almost personified; it brings the act of looking to the fore.

▪

The gym I start going to when the big lockdown ends does not have any mirrors. Instead, we rely on each other to adjust our stances – your left knee is swinging out, take your grip a little wider, that looked really good. When I'm early to class I ask the owner about some object or another – a tumbled gemstone, a little dish. The whole gym is filled with traces of people who have moved through it. Even the gold glinting in both of our ears was formed by the same local hands.

I know the exact date I started taking testosterone because I had to email it to an endocrinologist to schedule bloodwork. Sometimes, I think about deleting that email. It doesn't feel like something I should know.

I know it was after the first cases started appearing in Melbourne. I know I waited until just after my last in-person work meeting for the year. I know that I felt guilty, guilty, for the gift of growing myself out of sight of others. By the time I sit at my coffee table whipping toum, my pubescent 'stache has sprouted, and I'm grateful that no-one but the mirror sees it. It's not that I am embarrassed, exactly – but I fear that seeing someone's face change when they notice it, or hearing exaggerated excitement in their remarks about it, will rob me of something precious: of seeing it for myself, through my eyes alone.

▪

Part of what makes change difficult in view of those who know you is the degree to which we co-construct ourselves with others. Merleau-Ponty brought forward the concept of 'intercorporeality': the idea that cognition is done with the body and, crucially, done in collaboration with other bodies. Humans have always externalised our psychological functions – see the memory aides in strings of beads in the archaeological record – but, increasingly, we find that we serve as scaffolding for each other, too. There's a social dimension to consciousness; my father asks if I'm interested in communism when I mention this.

The Soviet developmental psychologist Lev Vygotsky said that it is through others that we become ourselves.

▪

Legibility has started to feel like a major project of mainstream transsexuality. I think that this is related to the focus on representation over other forms of action. The way we carve up time has something to do with it, too – the internet is full of videos of people documenting themselves at the one-week, one-month, one-year mark. I watched them, once, before I ever thought of them as relevant to me. YouTube still suggests them to me.

I do not keep records of my own changing form. Édouard Glissant would frame this opacity, this refusal to be measured against an external scale, as a kind of resistance; I'm not sure I am that principled. Mostly, I do not see the point: this whole thing has been too slippery, too experiential and dynamic, to fall easily into an archive. Any attempt would feel false.

Stuart Hall once described the body as a text, and so we are all literary critics. Now that we are within view of each other again, people tell me what is inscribed in my body constantly. C. tells me my leg hair has become impressive. A. says my face has changed shape. H. says, 'Wow, your voice!' My mother says I sound unwell.

▪

Last week, at a renovated ballroom on Sydney Road, I watched the novelist Cate Kennedy tell a story. The regent honeyeater, a bird endemic to the south-eastern corner of Australia, is going extinct. Its habitat has been cleared for human expansion, with conservationists sounding the alarm for decades; now, fewer than 300 remain in the wild. (I looked them up on the tram home: these are of a delicate build, black with yellow speckles, long, narrow beaks and mournfully tilted eyes.) The regent honeyeater relies on song to attract a mate but, currently, there aren't enough adult males to teach the adolescent males the required songs; the tunes the young birds piece together instead are unsettling for the females, making for fumbling, unsuccessful courtship, and so the population dwindles further.

■

The age gaps in *Y tu mamá también* are unavoidable, but I don't exactly know what to do with them, either. Roger Ebert's review describes one of Luisa's roles in the film as 'turning them into beings fit to associate with an adult woman'; there is a deeply maternal energy surrounding each of her sex scenes with Julio and Tenoch, both of which are painfully unerotic. Tenoch is first: when he comes into Luisa's room to ask her for shampoo because he has forgotten to pack his own, she tells him to drop his towel. She instructs him through the whole thing – kiss me; lick me; no, you have to take my underwear off first – and, when he cums after a minute at most, mumbling apologies into her chest, she consoles him, laughing to herself. Her turn with Julio is similar, but ends instead with a determined look of resoluteness from Luisa as she clutches his head full of apologies to her breast. Perhaps she expected it this time.

Tenoch never looks more like a boy than in this scene. There's a panic in his wide eyes as he realises what Luisa has clambered into the back seat of their moving car for, and he yanks the wheel towards a dusty side road where he can stop the car and bolt away on foot. But, once he does, it's towards an elevated position from which he tries to jump and see what is going on in the car. He slips and scrapes his elbow; giving up, he sits on the ground, smoking fretfully and clutching his knees to his chest. The anguished twist of his mouth makes him look like a child denied something and told he would understand when he was older. When Luisa finally emerges, she consoles him maternally – crouching down next to him in her cuffed jeans, loose and lightweight, crooning, 'Hey, Tenoch, don't be that way,' while he pouts behind the shag of hair hanging over his eyes, looking at her only when she isn't looking at him.

▪

My boyfriend gives me his old shirts. At first, I feel like I'm swimming in them, with the sleeves hanging away from my body and catching on doorhandles. I'm a teen boy in a ratty surf T-shirt, holes forming at the neck. My boyfriend gives me two bottles of his favourite lube. Worried they'd stop making it, he'd stocked up; bottles rolled around his drawers when he needed socks. But they would expire faster than he could get through them. This lube is special because it doesn't dry sticky. It's special to me because it's thick and white. When I finish, sometimes I watch it run down the gap between my thumb and index finger. I'm a teen boy, five, six times a day.

▪

Every time I've made a deliberate break from my stifling surroundings in the last year-and-a-half, it's been to look for birds. H. has a book on them, narrow enough to stuff into a men's back pocket but reassuringly thick, with pencilled illustrations and cramped text categorising the curvature of their beaks, the iridescence of their plumage and the pattern to their vocalisations. (For our honeyeater, it gives: 'Calls with clear bell-like notes, some quite sharp, others deep, mellow, musical: "quip-quorrip, quip-kip, quorrop-quip".')

Kennedy says that researchers are trying to teach the songs to regent honeyeaters in captivity. In aviaries set up specially to facilitate mating, they are piping in recordings taken from the wild. I try to find footage of this on YouTube, to see how it's working; soon, clips of avian vocal training fleck the feed of suggested videos, interspersed between tutorials on altering the resonance of human voices.

When I get the mail a few days later, I realise that the cloth face mask I ordered weeks ago is patterned with black-and-yellow honeyeaters.

■

Sometimes, true things are also very stupid. I choke on spit when the endocrinologist tells me there's a hard-to-get cream that makes new dicks grow big. Later, I take a beat to recover when I read that 'jizz' is a legit birdwatching term (it means something like the impression of a bird from its rough shape or movement or behaviour, the undefined *vibe* that makes it recognisable at a glance). No-one else on the train seems to have noticed the ground dropping out beneath me as I reckon with having to live in the same world as phrases like 'the swallow's distinctive jizz'.

I didn't wear glasses for a long time. They were prescribed to me, almost yearly, with the prescription ratcheting upwards in a way I think I was supposed to understand as failure. People were surprised at how I got around despite this and, looking back, I am too – route numbers wouldn't come into focus until the bus had almost driven past, and chalkboard menus could have been offering anything. But, mostly, it was fine. I learned that the 610X bus was always a newer model, more squared-off than the 600, and that Syrah was a safe bet for 2014 wine lists. People, too, had a basic form that could be picked out from a distance: M.'s neck craning sharply down at her phone, shoulders hunched high above most commuters' heads; R.'s immediate and bobbing step to the right after pressing a pedestrian crossing button. J. always radiated openness, gazing out instead of down when waiting. These details didn't register consciously, but some part of me could recognise them in whole.

In 'Encountering Birds: A Phenomenology of Jizz', Stephen Wood writes, 'We have two ways of looking at birds that are at odds with one another: firstly, how they appear to us in the field, often in an instant, and secondly, how they are presented to us, in a museum cabinet, in a bird book, or in wildlife films.' The close-up and static views of the second way, with toe ridges and wings fanned out to show the varying lengths of individual feathers, are specific – and can feel truer for it, for the conventional sense of 'truth'. But they are abstractions from the experience of spotting a bird. 'They give us the expectation that we should experience birds in the field in this way, which is rarely the case.' In the actual encounter, '[b]irds are most often glimpsed in an instant, as a characteristic integration of flight, note, length and colour of bill, plumage and legs' – a kingfisher is a flash of blue between the trees, a cockatoo is angling your neck and shielding your eyes after an arcing shriek, and common mynas are a chain of harassment encircling another, bigger bird.

H. and I almost miss our train home. In the marshy waters near Altona, there's a boardwalk built through a wetland reserve, a good spot for birdwatching. Perched on a stump, one bird eludes our identification. We flip through H.'s guidebook, from index to waterbirds to swifts and back to the index; the beak is sharp and yellow, and the general proportions suggest it is a passerine but we can't find it there. Desperate, we comb through every section, looking for some unlikely genetic outlier. Later, H. messages me: it was a common starling. During the breeding season, its speckled brown plumage turns dark and iridescent; the guidebook rendered this as a small rainbow-coloured bird.

In the light in which we saw it, the feathers were deep and glossy black.

▪

H. reaches over and touches my pubey little goatee. I feel his fingers not on my skin but in the movement of the hair as they brush past. It feels fresh, like the first time I shaved my head and stepped outside and felt the wind sweep her fingers over my scalp. It feels medicinal, like his enthusiasm for these scraggly dark hairs is full of biochemical targeters that bind to my self-conscious thoughts and neutralise them.

There is a trade-off to being seen.

A Brief History of Water

Lou Garcia-Dolnik

I bore witness. No one asked this of me, but I wanted to keep watch of the dying everywhere, so I could figure out how to care for a bleeding sentence.

— Billy-Ray Belcourt, *A History of My Brief Body*[1]

June. Suspiring winter. An apartment with double-hung windows for a street-facing wall and the city moving beneath, quickly, as a river that insists on a kind of intransigent *moving to*: nothing that passes through it holds or, perhaps, here, everything has always already conjured a horizon of movement's potential.[2]

I live the city's entreaty for a futurity as elsewhere.[3] *I walk into the field expecting to be devoured & then I am.*[4] I write nothing. I count the hours diluting, one into the next, as drops decanting into a larger body of liquid, innumerable in the breadth of their sameness. I don't see any one person twice, on the street or in the fast-food joints that puncture the walls of dull, remote corporate offices, except for a neighbour who inhabits another apartment high-rise across from mine and who is also often alone.

Old English: from all + ana, *'unaccompanied, all by one self', literally 'wholly oneself', from* all *'all, wholly', preser ving the old pronunciation of* one.

I return home from days wasted answering emails and ordering coffees to avoid working on a manuscript I know is slipping through my fingers. My neighbour is there. They move as if suspended in liquid, the air that sutures the space between our windows a benthic wilderness within which relationality enacts its directive to behold.[5]

I spend hours in this looking. I don't know if or when they face me, the light that illuminates their space – a table, sofa bed and shelves that house objects of various shapes and sizes I can't make out from this distance – casting a dark grey shadow over the features that would allow me to discern if they face me or not. The night is figured in their image, delivery drivers and industrial lights illuminating back-alleyways approaching as they hold their isolation, distorted by night's refractions.

In the promise of their silent aliveness, *I am held, and held.*[6]

▪

Beholden: to hold by some tie of duty or obligation, to retain ... in duty bound; to owe debt;   to be indebted.

▪

There is a history that sits within me. It is my history: I house it.
Like a memory to which one does not pay visitation, the house lives
leveraged against the ravages of colonial time.[7] Like any house,
it wears a history of usage that transcends the purpose
of its actual use

which is to say my history means to drown me.

If I am living, it's because I've learned to live submerged,

an ersatz, deviant form of freedom.

■

In a falling plane, the body behaves as if sunken.

Take-off, the pilot ascends, air is pressurised by engines and ambient oxygen is ladled through an appliance that sheds heat from cabin-bound air. In that closed system of circuitry and flows, the body can sustain itself for hours. If substantial failure occurs to any one of the aircraft systems, however, the plane might enter a dive.

Limbs float as if belayed by invisible strings, no longer bound to their seats. Objects swim in suspension – detritus from luggage, magazines and seat trays floating in open free-for-all – though the problem is not so much a dearth of gravity but its categorical imperative:

So, what comes down?

If the cabin is decompressed, pressurised air rapidly flows from the plane and voids the lungs of oxygen. Barotrauma: severe damage to the internal organs caused by violent (de)surfacing. *Perhaps this pressurized orientation to memory – one by which we understand the past as a trace that pulsates in a body in the present – is always the case with life-writing.*[8]

Perhaps memory is an atmospheric kind of pressure: it surfaces around the body. Unhouses weight.

■

It is my history: *I house it.*

■

Somewhere on the train line that runs behind my neighbour's apartment, a fire flares. Tall, the flailing limbs of it like a bright beacon. For two seconds it burns, then is snuffed out almost as soon as it's allowed to inhabit its native wildness. Because open fire doesn't belong within the confines of the retardant city, it calls attention. Who lights that fire? It's lit with a spontaneity I can't configure. Its brilliance marks a fissure in the grain of the everlasting shrug[9] of evenings in this place. Though my reckoning with the world's fatal wounding has taught me that neglect is enough to stoke a flame, it remembers me, against a deluge of faceless others, to stay awake.[10]

▪

The biggest dare is that I allowed myself to suppose God as Filipino. I imagined Him smiling down at all our barbecues, at all the fire.[11]

▪

The silhouette of my neighbour's frame is stuttering. *Who watches?* The wind their singular audience. I know them like I know violation, their figure *painfully familiar in that very strange(r)ness.*[12] Pronouns fill their person with subjunctive possibility. Our subjects undifferentiated, their noiseless frame a flock of wings open-mouthed between sound and its capture. The poetics of a body unlanguaged are enacted at the frontier of this aberrant knowing:

I am them. They are me. They give me a history.

▪

Here, you hold it.

▪

Brown boy. After school. He is crying. A gang of his schoolmates have tied his hands behind his back and his mouth with a gag that cuts his cheeks into two sturdy, red tranches. The noises that escape him are thick and muted, the boys constellating his person a makeshift nimbus. I'm young enough to know not to use the landline without adult supervision. I finger my school dress. *Who do I call?*

The boy is hurting, his sobbing much like a wolf begging kin to approach. *Please.* His captors hold in place an injunction on decolonial longing: for the boy, now, hands recall the twisting of linen, the vicious boundedness of a tortured masculinity. They parade him across an open street where thresholds don't open to him, the inner life of houses a distant wilderness in which his brokenness is heard, distantly, as a nightbird, beautiful as empty elevators.[13] Nobody opens. Nobody comes in his misery to claim him. His body's defeat suggests that he has, or will be, beaten. That this is the arrival of the inevitable conclusion in a history of beatings wherein his body is transformed into a bright, expanding bruise.

I watch from my grandparents' window. My limbs fill with a stickiness that stitches my feet taut to the carpet. I can't move. I know the violence of boys. The closing of doors.

My history tells me that perhaps he will not be beaten at all. Maybe the violence is more like a settlement made from a place inside his captors to a place deep inside his person. Maybe his cries are intentional practice. He is rehearsing how to be filled.

▪

Before I start school, I begin swimming lessons. I'm a good swimmer. I hold my head underwater and count the seconds before I am pulled up by my shoulders. I like the way water transforms. I'm lighter, my person like a fish. My dad teaches me that submerged sound is more perceptible than sound in plain air, clicking the two plastic dice attached to my scrunchie by the side of the pool together to show what he means. The sound of each die's hard edge hitting its counterpart is sharp and reverberant. The clacks voyage beyond the pool's frontiers and, I imagine, echolocate beyond the suburb. They live in the water as cyclical matter, nature's riposte to object permanence.

▪

In memory, the boy is still a boy. I still am a stranger. He is me. He hasn't grown beyond time to inhabit the subjectivity of an agent of burning.

He starts no fires. Ruins no life that isn't his own. I finger the landline's worn grey rubber to save him. Stall.

Who would I call?

In memory, he is stitched to the background of a frieze that positions him as always-already too distant from me. His back is a mirror that reveals my witness as an ebbing ocean. I approach. Hold my isolation.

Who do I call?

▪

Do you feel like killing yourself? The man on the other end of the receiver asks. You tell him, I feel like I am already dead …

I am in death's position.[14]

He is my history: I mean to drown him.

▪

June. My neighbour is drowning. They clutch their throat with feral desperation, air a foreign body denying itself entry to their person. I pick up my phone. *Who do I call?* A diving plane. Gasping vacantly, they fling imaginary fish from their sleeves as itinerant cargo that thrash the floorboards with an insistence on life after the body, the wild gesticulation of their flailing limbs painfully familiar in that strange(r)ness. My neighbour clutches the window ledge like a buoy and tugs violently at its frame.

Open. A rush of plosive air. They contract with oxygen's decompression, craning their neck beyond the window's enclosure as if thirsting for the expanse of it. If I'd called an ambulance, I would have had to explain that the flow of air momentarily lapsed in its circuit through my neighbour's respiratory system, perhaps, indexing oxygen's citationality – how, in the wake of a disturbance, air deals itself out sparingly. Lungs overreact.

My neighbour breathes as if it's the last thing they've been entrusted to do in a history of things that now don't matter. The only mattering left is air. Tonight, oxygen is superlative. The wind won't always be as biting, as if the body barely hangs on by its outermost tendons. In this looking, I am seized.

∎

Does my attention not render me a haunting?[15]

Do I have permission to approach
a drowning man from behind?[16]

∎

A girl, I'm underwater. The unbreathing head of me is under water. I wonder when I'll be allowed to breathe. My arms wonder. They fling bright, brilliant fish from the open nakedness of me.

He is just a boy. I know him. He's no stranger. His hands hold my neck in a vice grip as if he doesn't already know that water is entrapment enough. My throat is aching. His laughter arrives at intervals, refracted by the enclosure of waves around my frame. He counts the seconds a human body might subsist unbreathing. He's made a mistake: it's not a human body but a child's within which history hasn't been allowed to harden like a sieve. I remember my lessons. I'm like flounder, a good swimmer. I breathe durationally. Feign lifelessness. If I'm alive, it is because I have learned that water is citational: it echoes with a history of use.

There is a water within me. It is mine: I house it.

∎

Boy. On occasion, he hits me. I don't keep the memory of the hitting but the expectation of its sharp arrival. He's rough. He trains me to flinch when he raises his hands. For many years after, elation and exasperation are collapsed into the same spectre of violence's mutability.

While young, disruption to the ordinary makes my stomach hurt. I make my body like a snail and hold my abdomen to suture a falling-apart. On occasion, it's not the hitting that raises my nervous attention but that his hands move with a comfort over the independence of my body, which hasn't yet determined its horizons. Inside, a fire is ignited, this burning a bright, expanding bruise. *I am it. It is me.*

▪

In a poem I write that winter, I assert *I am overextended.*

I am alive.

People exceed their epistemic positioning so, here, I hold.[17]

One does not need to feel weary to be worn, like a rag that has soaked up history's detritus. One wears it like saturated clothing. Return to the water to jettison weight.

> *Human blood is salty, and sodium [...] has a residence time of 260 million years. And what happens to the energy that is produced in the waters? It continues cycling like atoms.*[18]

▪

There is a water within me. It is mine: I house it.

Like water that does not answer to perlocution, it cycles
its own time in a crypt of tortured becomings.

It is drowning: I house it.

■

In Richard Matheson's *What Dreams May Come*, Hell is imagined not as a burning pyre but as a cold, barren wasteland. The protagonist enters death's doorstep to rescue his wife from the wreckage of eternal glaciation, her suicide having consigned her to an afterlife in a house become a site of demolition. Its innards bear the markings of water's ruination, thick sludge risen to the knees such that all movement is slowed by wading.

She has entered death's position.

To save her, he chooses submission to the conditions that govern her provenance in the no-place of trauma's wreckage. He chooses a life waterlogged.

It is a history: *water houses it.*

■

Girl. A house. Light's spectre anointing the room with colour, though in memory there's only a little of it, submerged by distance. The door is shut. Outside, the world voyages beyond the boundary of thresholds left behind, closed by hereafter's slow stride forward. The boy slides his hand under my skirt and beneath my underwear. *No* rings like an echolocated verb through the suburb, the city, the country of memory's colossal birthing. In that expansiveness, I'm not heard. My noise is thick and muted.

His fingers are hot and unwanted. I hold my legs tight together in the hope of suturing a flooding. I don't yet know that those in death's position are always already sunken. The deluge rings with no-sound, raising the walls of a history that clicks neatly shut upon recollection. He persists. *No* rings like an echolocated verb through the flesh, the bones, the veins of deep ocean stalling. If I had not made a noise, the fabric of remembrance would perhaps be left unpunctured by the birthing pains of departure from a girlhood soundless in its aftermath. My thighs are burning. Everything is wet.

Because I leave the house the way I came, I'm not granted the finality of an exit. I live the logic of that day over, and over. Time won't allow me the grace of duration to say goodbye.

■

There is a history that revisits me as a stranger. In its very strange(r)ness, memory's signifiers and signifieds course the veins of rivers running into a body of water of world-making.

I mount a declaration on the declivities of that vastness:

my memory is a submerged country.

It is mine: the ocean houses it.

Sitting like a tired leakiness in the sunken theatre of broken language where all manner of viscera swim unencumbered,

it has spilled its lexicon to fill my body with the grammars of ravaged beholdenness:

here, I hold it.

In its wake, the city moves as if perched by the urgency of remembering it.

Who is lighting that fire?

Who does it call?

■

'What were you before you met me?'
'I think I was drowning'
[...]
'And what are you now?'
[...]
'Water.'[19]

▪

In a photo taken in my lola's country, the tide rushes my child's feet. Ilocos. The air is more breathable here. Mountains hold the earth on their limitless, green shoulders. None of that weighted thickness. None of that burden of always-time.

The hills are lit with a fire that promises to subsume everything in its wake. *Who lights it?*

A sky outside history.

The horizon sets alight anything it beholds. *Because the sunset, like survival, exists only on the verge of its own disappearing.*[20]

Perhaps my biggest dare was to imagine memory as a stranger. Perhaps remembering is the incommensurability of the fire with water's ruination.

The subjection of water to the rhythms of the universe fills the earth with subjunctive possibility. There is a little sun here. It demands its own kind of holding.

Here, you hold it.

1 Belcourt, Billy-Ray, *A History of My Brief Body*, Two Dollar Radio, Columbus, 2020, p. 34.
2 Muñoz, José Esteban, *Cruising Utopia: The Then and There of Queer Futurity*, New York University Press, New York and London, 2009, p. 1.
3 Muñoz: 'Queerness is not yet here. Queerness is an ideality. Put another way, we are not yet queer, but we can feel it as the warm illumination of a horizon imbued with potentiality.' From *Cruising Utopia*, ibid.
4 Nguyen, Hieu Minh, *Not Here*: *Poems*, Coffee House Press, Minneapolis, 2018, p. 25.
5 Gilbert Caluya: 'For Alphonso Lingis, in facing another addresses me and in doing so stands over and before me [...] This distance, across which the face of the other appeals, is both the occasion of discourse and the condition for responsibility.' From 'The (Gay) Scene of Racism: Face, Shame and Gay Asian Males', *ACRAWSA e-journal*, vol. 2, no. 2, 2006, pp. 8–9.
6 Brand, Dionne, 'Thirsty', Poetry in Voice, https://www.poetryinvoice.com/poems/thirsty
7 Billy-Ray Belcourt: 'In the act of self-documentation or reflection, we don't think of ourselves as linear beings. Memories come to us suddenly and without explanation, and recollection is never clean or surgical.' From Neilson, Sarah, 'Read Me: Billy-Ray Belcourt Imagines a Decolonial Future', *them.*, 14 July 2020, https://them.us/story/read-me-billy-ray-belcourt-a-history-of-my-brief-body
8 Belcourt, *A History of My Brief Body*, p. 12.
9 Rankine, Claudia, *Don't Let Me Be Lonely: An American Lyric*, Graywolf Press, Minneapolis, 2004, p. 5.
10 Billy-Ray Belcourt: 'I think it is midnight / – the wall clock caught fire / from neglect a long time ago.' From *NDN Coping Mechanisms: Notes From the Field*, House of Anansi Press, Toronto, 2019, p. 13.
11 Gambito, Sarah, 'Sarah Gambito on "I Am Not from the Philippines"', Poetry Society of America, https://poetrysociety.org/features/in-their-own-words/sarah-gambito-on-i-am-not-from-the-philippines
12 Ahmed, Sara, *Strange Encounters: Embodied Others in Post-Coloniality*, Routledge, London and New York, 2000, p. 21.
13 Dionne Brand: 'This city is beauty / unbreakable and amorous as eyelids, / in the streets, pressed with fierce departures, / submerged landings, / I am innocent as thresholds / and smashed night birds, lovesick, / as empty elevators.' From 'Thirsty'.
14 Rankine, *Don't Let Me Be Lonely*, p. 7.
15 'Diana Khoi Nguyen: A Conversation', *The Poetics of Haunting in Asian American Poetry*, http://poeticsofhaunting.com/index.php/poets/diana-khoi-nguyen/
16 Nguyen, Diana Khoi, *Ghost Of*, Omnidawn, Oakland, 2018, p. 23.
17 Paraphrasing Butler, Belcourt asserts that 'the norms of gender and race fail to regulate us completely', although '[b]oth beget a sense of immobility'. From *A History of My Brief Body*, p. 13.
18 Sharpe, Christina, *In the Wake: On Blackness and Being*, Duke University Press, Durham and London, 2016, p. 41.
19 Vuong, Ocean, *On Earth We're Briefly Gorgeous*, Penguin, London, 2019, pp. 237–238.
20 Ibid., p. 238.

an ifugao speaks

grace ugamay dulawan

watch the ifugao do tribal dances and learn that he digs

As elsewhere in this book,
a gloss for an Ifugao term
helps identify a particular sense,
not all possible senses.

▪

I don't know exactly how old I was when I began to see my parents as separate from myself. It was as if I was standing at the bow of a boat that had started to move, the initial jolt in the knees followed by a bodily understanding – the eyes confirming that, yes, I had come away from land. From the new vantage point I could see the figures my parents cut – outlines of the youths they were before they brought me into the world. Yet I cannot place them nor see them clearly: my parents as children, my father as a son. It's his figure that draws me in most. As my mother says, *You are your father's daughter*. There is something in my gaze that goes beyond the surveyable land. I stalk their shadows, can't let them be. It is as if I want to make a map of their movements, directions of their words passed down: a way to navigate back.

▪

Similarly, a Latin binomial
following a local plant
name posits a close similarity
between the indicated
botanical and folk
taxa, but it does not necessarily
specify the range of that similarity
or imply exact equivalence.

▪

anthropometric measurements of fifty ifugao men and women

Hide your flat feet. Broad noses. Flared nostrils. The pupils of the eyes as close to black as you can get. Full lips: the top and bottom roughly the same – two segments of the same sliced-open fruit. Hair thick and strong and straight. It's the legs that are distinct. Calves sharply contoured, bulges on the verge of ripeness. A squat people with a low centre of gravity – close to the earth and of it.

Of the things I have inherited from my parents: my mother's long face and pointed chin, my father's glossy hair and dark skin. Beyond and before them, it's unclear what can be traced from either side going back in time. This is how genealogy works, a bag of tricks that skips, circles and jumps up again – somewhere, somewhen, someone else.

▪

a half-way sun: philippine pagans
common terms and phrases

American answered arms asked become believe better blanket blood body Bontok bring brother called carry ceremony chickens cock comes continually court customs dance death debt deceiver deities eagle enemy face fact father feel feet fields folk four full-fledged girl give gods half hand head headhunting hill home-region Ifugao judge Kalinga keep Kiangan killed leaves less lived looked marriage married monkalun mountain never night pagans party Philippine pigs pine pitch plate priest probably region rice rice-wine seemed sent shout side soon soul spear stand stone strong sure taken tell thou thought told took town tree tribe turned university usually vengeance village wife woman women young

■

lost soulstuff
when the loss is known there, all is terror, rage and confusion

if i had been alive then
  a half-way sun: the philippine pagans
    i might have been a priest
      rituals require a form of sacrifice
        a half-sun, way of the philippine pagans
          now though I am a dweller of words
            most rituals require a form of sacrifice
              dwelling and swelling the records
              now, though i am a dweller of words
            one travels between neighbouring hamlets
              dwelling and swelling the records
            often – exclusively – on foot
          one travels between neighbouring hamlets
        look around, back, away; look again, forward, at
      often – exclusively – on foot
look now, there, here, behind you – look. just look.

▪

hunting soulstuff

if attention is a form of love – how they adored us / an ecstasy born of the heart / that propelled them to / know the breadth and height / of our bodies / and the grammar and diction of our speech / the phonology and dialect as if exactitude / was a kiss // the words they wrote / and studies conducted / a kind of vow to keep us / to have and to hold / until death do us, do us— // a love that left us / no room to be, they / meant it literally: all-consuming / nothing left of us after / all that loving

▪

los infieles igorrotes

to be an infidel is to divine the soulstuff in a stone / to offer up animals under your care / to read in the split liver of chicken carcasses whether one is to proceed / a bird in the path says *go*, *don't go* / a tug in the pit of your stomach that says *here*, *upstream*, *downstream*, *skyworld*, *underworld* / the collapsing of time as in a line in a poem

▪

Before I was civilised	I was artless
Before I was civilised	everything had soulstuff
Before I was civilised	the world was animated by a warm whisper
Before I was civilised	: skyworld, underworld, downstream, upstream, here
Before I was civilised	vengeance exacted from memory
Before I was civilised	– my blood-kin all
Before I was civilised	body bent, lithe, inhabited
Before I was civilised	names of generations stored in the flicking muscle of my tongue

Before I was civilised	what the entrails of animals could tell me of the future
Before I was civilised	I knew myself, now no longer, one day once more, time reckoning
Before I was civilised	: what need of writing when memory served?

▪

One travels between
neighbouring hamlets
and districts mostly – often
exclusively – on foot. This map
indicates all principal routes
used in this manner.

Throughout my life, the life of my father comes to me like the slow drip of a leaking faucet – a pause between each drop, like a breath, a way to space time.

Father: The only thing I remember of my mother / and your uncle he yelled / my father was from a different / we used to play / one time I got so angry I / then when she died / a month later my father too / I screamed take me / your uncle saw me playing he / when I was ten I / they decided I could take a wife / I ran away to / they took me in / I always had my eye on your mum / she was from a rich family / I drank too much / your aunty she always had / in school the teachers didn't / the priests and church were the only ones who / at the cemetery I used to help / I was always so angry / on the basketball court I was / your uncle he stopped me from / and on it goes—

Daughter: Why do I switch between calling him / my father and my dad as if to dilate and foreclose the distance / whip-like, whiplash from the movement / Far: A figure I can describe / Close: A person to whom I am accountable / Far: The World Vision child / a dollar a day could give him clean drinking water / Success Migrant / Rags to riches / Rice to ROI / Carabao to Audi: both vehicles in the end—

I am the one who interviews my elders, who asks them questions, who is plagued by the mission to harvest this knowledge. I go back to the past like an animal on a hunt, the trail of a scent and nothing else to go on. I take notes, I transcribe, I record, I photograph. I become the record keeper as if I can overwrite what has been written, as if I can keep the thread going, as if it has not already been cut and worn in places, as if I cannot feel that this repetition is its own kind of violence.

▪

ritual incantations

These are the words I want to revive, to claim as my own even though my hands cannot give them spirit nor can the arch of my back give them shape. It's only with the voice that they are allowed, loud:

Weed Tread Mulch Sluice Plow Harrow Pick
Hoe Delve Pitch Ferment Plant Grain Crop Cultivate
Seasons Foliage Pollard Hamlets Woodlets Hulled Sheaf
Reap Harvest Bundle Hearth Swidden Midden
Bovine Floral Crop Domesticated Fields
Sacrifices Terrace Dwellers
Sow Panicle

Suddenly I am in a panicle: any loose, diversely branching flower cluster.

▪

primitive revelation

I am interested in the myth I've made of my father, the myth he has built and told us of our specific heritage as Ifugao, Mountain, Igorot people. Yes, I am interested in examining those tenderly – so as not to do them damage.

There are many ways I use the stories of my father / To shock, to entertain, to show off / When a friend talks about Filipino traditions / About the mano, I say rather haughtily / My dad says that was a colonial gesture / And he never made us do that to him growing up / We weren't made to take his hand and press it / Gently to the crown of our bowed heads / (Is this where I first learned to disrespect him?)

Have I built a cabinet and placed inside – unknowingly – my ancient heart, not meant for these eyes and these voices to discuss and appraise and, yes, why not, to patronise. What cruelty my curiosity wields and how wrongly I may have calculated. I have built a zoo peopled by these foreign injuries.

look around, back, away
look again, forward, at
look now, there, here, behind you
look. just look.

▪

first ifugao–english word book: four thousand roots

And of these roots is there, this word book I do not possess, the meaning to my middle name – the name my father gave to me – my father's mother's name? Better yet, to find or invent some word or phrase, not easily translatable into English, that specifically expresses the condition of looking but not finding: a kind of seeking in desperation that leads only to mirages, the straining to read in low light over a lifetime, a kind of sight that inflicts damage to the eyes in the process. And if I am straining to read these roots, is this lack of ease, this desperate effort, a way to say – stop this digging?

▪

in the light of the natural moral law

Increasingly, I suspect that what I am doing is less a gathering of histories and more a collection of objects for curation. It is as if I am making a museum of dried and pitiful sentences. Each scrapbook of my father's, the conversations I recall and mine for details, questions I put to him to check the facts I have against his experience: all of this done with a little thrill. I know I am infringing on lives that do not belong to me. A longing does not make belonging. The small tremble that goes through me. A hunter closing in. It is this same impulse I have when I take a photo, capturing a thing. When I release it later, on my own terms, how is the caught thing changed?

▪

repeatedly summoned forebears

I, as in pursuit of my father's story / as in love and fully present to the past / as my mother is with her lola Basilia / my mother's mother's mother / or the mother of my mother's mother / simply *grand.* // I've never understood the need to dredge up the old tales / about Lola Basilia *this* Lola Basilia *that* until I realise I am doing that too / all – look at my father. what he contains let me / hold it up to the light and refract story after story a continuous thread. // my lola Basilia as alive today – perhaps more so than / when my mother was a girl. this is / what myths do. keep us alive. keep us from dying out. // and like my lola Basilia's love and my father's life's beginnings / a lightly traced figure to be drawn and redrawn / the lives thickening with time and all its repetitions.

▪

on the concepts of tribe and tribal society

The closest analogue comes from plants. The stalk of a bud pinched at the root. I am a kind of pot plant, cut off from the rest of the network.

▪

the mythology of the ifugaos

I want to know all the uses of a myth: the ways it nourishes or starves you. Would it keep you warm in the highlands, let the heat seep out of you in the lowlands. And how does it sound its own name and in whose language. How is its gait weighted, equally or a little heavily on the left foot. What is the lifespan of a myth, or does it never die, then what shapes does it take on to survive. Naked, belly-sick and lonely, I wonder: Have I made it all up, distorted it, made of it a kind of garbled song, harshly sung, with only fools to listen.

I make my father say all kinds of things / Like, *My mother died when I was seven. A month later, my father died.* / In saying that line, he omits another / I don't make him say, *Financial security is freedom – / Grace, you should make your money work for you. / Don't work for your money.* / Which is the wisdom he imparts to me around the age of ten / when he gives me a copy of *Rich Dad Poor Dad* / I want to make him say, *I don't want you to be poor / because I was poor.* But he's never said that.

The myth of my father is a road map.
        Do this. Go there. Be better. Play. Jump. Read. Run. Learn.
        Earn. Stay safe.
The myth of my heritage and inheritance is less clear.
        Hold this. Cut that. Let this go. This is yours. That is not. You
                are with us. Yes, you. Not you.
                We aren't you. You aren't us.

▪

these common terms and phrases
one travels between neighbouring hamlets
they are hunting our soulstuff
often – exclusively – on foot

this primitive revelation
most rituals require a form of sacrifice
we are made from their eyes
if not so treated, illness and misfortune

traced, summoned forebears
sibling set by sibling set
generation by generation

▪

ifugao genealogies

pedigrees can be counted
back easily for eight to ten generations

I have spent most of my adult life trying to see my parents clearly. They are always a little out of focus; they blur their faces – turning away, tilting back. What I want is an impossibility, a simple narrative that fits neatly in my pocket. If I could make of them a portable thing, I would have a kind of talisman and map at once. It is the act of movement that has thrown everything off. Movement from my mother's ancestors from the lowlands to the highlands. Movement uncaptured by records on my father's side, from where to where – somewhere in the mountains. Movement of my parents to bring me and my brothers from one land to another. A body can only take so much movement before nausea settles in. Is it that, a kind of nausea, that is my inheritance?

The more I look at my father, the less clearly I see him. To look quickly at once has its merits. I have looked too long and too longingly to be able to see. I have looked at the portraits and looked at the records. I have looked at my family's history and looked at our names. A look takes you only as far as your sight goes.

Should I have spoken instead?

■

ifugaos 129,380
genial, docile, mystic. tendency to run amok.

Bibliography is Biography

as in decorative	as in oriental	as in superstitious
as in adornment	as in genial	as in quaint
as in embellishment	as in docile	as in stealthy
as in domesticated	as in mystic	as in small
as in wild	as in dainty	as in childlike
as in exotic	as in effeminate	as in simple
as in an Other	as in crude	as in bold
as in exquisite	as in aggressive	as in backward
as in evasive	as in timid	as in indigenous
as in frank	as in outspoken	as in—

as in such a quantity of words produced to reduce us to what we are seen to be, and still.

■

How did we see ourselves before they saw us? Can we shed their looking at us, to really look – get a real look. What I want is to see and be seen clearly. An impossibility: I have only these eyes, inherited the gaze I can't unsee. How to see ourselves as ourselves, without that damage of their sight. Site of so much— Other. Subject. Object. Naked allure. Contrast up. To know oneself by proximity or distance to an Other. To reclaim one another, or simply to tend to the wound.

What I want is to reclaim a costume but make of it home clothes, separate the rice from its husk. The futile search for authentic, awful, awry oration – grandstanding. I am a descendant of— I am a member of— I am the daughter of— How to count, to make it count, to be accountable for these performances, so easily drawn out.

■

spectacle of the century

I was formed by men who learned our ways, noted our CUSTOMS, stayed. They asked us questions – What, How, Why – like so many children. One of them took some of us on his arm to his country and put us not on a pedestal but our own arena in which we performed for a CAPTIVE audience. They had but a PRIMITIVE understanding of us and we, with such genteel CIVILITY, obliged twenty million visitors, their eyes SAVAGED us. An account of their RITUAL right to my MORES, and more. I want to say I'm not EXQUISITE but merely human?

To place word after word is to create a kind of boundary, an enclosure in which you invite people to look. And I have looked at myself, long and wide and deep. Is my gaze driven by the same lust as those twenty million who flocked to the St. Louis World Fair in the early light of the last century to gawk, slack-jawed, and point and look and look and look?

■

The rice is left to rot in flooded pond-fields. The mountains, carved and terraced long before leather boots stomped, vestal dress walked the mountain ridges. The carabao go wild, sweet potato vines reach, root, multiply. The livers of the sacrificed chickens go unchecked. No reading or sign to proceed. The land is unharvested. The gods unsacrificed to. Descendants summoned to richer earth elsewhere. To labour under other skies. To live with abandoning.

▪

everything has soulstuff – the question is, how much?

The Ifugao conceives every entity
as having a soul,
linauwa, and soulstuff, alimaduan.
His conception of the soul
is not much different
from the usual one, but soulstuff
needs elucidation.

Can we make of our songs a song? And not a picture to be taken away, a noisy crackling voice bodiless and somewhere else. Can we make of our songs a song? To be heard and not made exquisite or likened to some other thing by some other selves. Can we make of our song a song we sing for us? Sometimes forgetting the words or falling asleep, not aware of strained ears or shutter clicks or a pen's scratchy rhythm. Let us sing once for us – aloud and untranscribable.

▪

pagan basketry: 1–9

Behind glass you grow dusty; in storage, you don't see the light. Nothing touches you. You touch nothing. All around you – space. To go from a thing held by grubby fingers so the groove of the hand that holds you shows – worn in – as if you were made for this hand only (and whose hand made you?) to fall into gloved hands that, with care and precision, handle you now as a prize, a precious rarity, now uncommon – as metal replaces wood. Re-purposed. Re-assigned. Kept, filed, rotated in and out of display. The hands that hold you long gone and far away and for such a long while.

▪

I am trying to get back to the womb where I was cradled before I was civilised / before I was civilised I had a song sung freely / a song sung freely and without tremor / without tremor or the thought to be ashamed / to be ashamed of my clothless voice / my clothless voice we didn't know enough to not / enough to not be as we were: woundless / woundless we were in the womb / in the womb before we were civilised / now the wound is a kind of womb

▪

Look. Look. Look.
The verb starts to spook,
the *L* pulling down and across,
its corner a sharp insistence.
Each *O* a cartoon eye.
The *K* a kind of arrow that
points in all directions,
its limbs splayed.

▪

After I was native	I became better
After I was native	my hands soared, my shoulders broad
After I was native	nobody left me alone, no home anymore
After I was native	I was asked to do a show, to make sense, to give a taste of
After I was native	the stuff lost soul, bit by—
After I was native	I could not go back nor was there a track
After I was native	the load of inheritance became heavier, and my baskets were behind glass
After I was native	I was saddled with a weight I could not buck and that was not mine to bear

After I was native it was so lonely
After I was native I got pneumonia, or polio, or tuberculosis and—
After I was native I was pressed between pages, my figure committed to ink
After I was native I was translated, transported, transubstantiated generations beyond death
After I was native : my voice was caught, time stopped
After I was native I walked on

▪

At the end of the day and for the record: I am my mother's daughter, my father's daughter, I have my father's mother's name. It's not just that I am their daughter. It is that I descend from them. I do not speak for anyone. I speak to hear how we have been sounded out and to re-sound it and to make a claim, place a stake in the storyland and say: you do not know us as you think you do. Plainer than that, I don't know. I am me and come from we and us – well, we keep on changing.

▪

now the wound is
a kind of womb
before i was—
after i was—
i to you
you to i
to we
to us
—

Aftermath

Suneeta Peres da Costa

A few days before news began to break about the extent of India's second COVID-19 wave in April 2021, I was due to give an online interview to some Indian research students about my practice and the topic of Indian diasporic writing. I had asked for questions beforehand, but, as they had not come, I thought it might be alright to wing it, to extemporise. On the surface, the students' questions seemed innocuous enough: What is your idea of home? When you write fiction, do you self-identify? Indeed, I had been answering similar questions throughout a literary career that had begun several decades earlier. But, instead of feeling familiar with or confident of the terrain I was on, I felt unsteady, caught off-balance. Because of seismic shifts in the landscape of cultural discourse since the beginning of the pandemic (whose fissures and fault lines had no doubt emerged much further back), the questions felt slippery, like they might now trip me up or, worse, unearth something *in me* that couldn't be tamed or controlled.

One of my young interlocutors was in Delhi, the other in Mumbai, and I was giving the interview from my living room in Sydney, on Gadigal land. We had already begun when, with further consternation, I realised I had forgotten the Acknowledgement of Country.[1] Unsettled by this and the fact the students kept calling me 'Goan' and 'Indian', I almost stuttered as I answered. I wanted to break through my constitutional shyness and politeness, to interrupt, to qualify. At one moment, exasperated, I wanted to declare, *I am Australian and Portuguese too and my work critiques identity through the prism of colonialism and post-colonialism!*[2] I said 'colonised' when I meant 'converted', and that the film *The Mission* was set in Brazil (whereas it is actually set in Argentina). I later wondered whether I was uneasy because, in promoting my creative work – in particular, two books of fiction that placed Goan identity at their heart – I myself had trafficked in these descriptions of myself.

Perhaps *I* had created the Frankensteinian monster of essentialism that I was now coming face-to-face with? Or maybe I was discomforted that my image and words were being live-streamed on Facebook, to be recorded forever; that what I said would be taken as authoritative or definitive, whereas I often experience tremendous doubt and ambivalence as a writer. Rather than being an objective intellectual inquiry, I regarded the unconscious element, the not-knowing, as an expression of intimacy with others and the world, and my embodied relationship to writing as inescapably ontological. When asked what inherently 'Goan' things I do, I wanted to joke in Esperanto that *I don't break into song in Konkani (in fact, I am so deracinated that I understand very little Konkani, which was not even my mother's tongue), nor do I dance dekhni nor play gumott. I do eat fish curry rice,* but *I also eat unhulled tahini straight out of the jar, listen to Thelonious Monk and Rachmaninov, and read Tang poets in English translation.*[3]

But I was too tired to be clever or performative, too anxious that my dark humour might be misconstrued amid tyrannical climates of censorship and a clamorous 'cancel culture'. I was also more than just tangentially aware of the spectre of the neo-colonial Indian state that hung not simply as a mere backdrop to the conversation, but as something that touched it directly, complicating underlying Global North–South coordinates. For example, since corresponding with the interview organiser (a pleasant Mumbaikar who was a novelist herself) and agreeing to participate months earlier, I had uncovered a link between her organisation and BJP Maharashtra that troubled me. I sought the advice of my circumspect friend, V., in Goa. A left-leaning architecture scholar concerned with matters of social justice, cultural heritage and the restoration of historical monuments, V. engaged in realpolitik to ask: Which literary events or festivals in India are *not* funded by the government, in this case a BJP one? I trusted his judgement and he advised me not to get too hung up, to put any scruples I had aside, to be pragmatic and proceed.

Still, I do wonder whether to be wayward, to choose refusal or non-participation, might be a conscientious and courageous form of satyagraha and ahimsa, a necessary exercise of citizenship and sovereignty during such times.[4] Since 2015, a slew of Indian writers, referred to as the 'Award Wapsi Gang', have been doing just that – protesting communalism, attacks on freedom of speech, the imprisonment of journalists and intellectuals, and the erosion of Indian Muslims' and minorities' constitutional rights – by handing back their awards from the Sahitya Akademi, the nation's pre-eminent literary body, or resigning membership of its General Council. If literature and literary forms don't merely represent but arise from conditions, including historical ones, of the lifeworld, what moral responsibility attends claims of being an author of subcontinental or Goan heritage today? What is the jurisdiction of such responsibility? Should a diasporic cultural inheritance incline me to speaking out or to silence?[5]

In her searing memoir *Minor Feelings*, Cathy Park Hong documents not only how internalised racism produces psychological and visceral shame in the one who is made its object, but how it insidiously reproduces itself in the social body, such as when, performing her poetry, Hong finds herself creating a consumable Korean American identity for overwhelmingly white liberal audiences.[6] However, if I felt hypocritical, inauthentic, it was because, under the circumstances, I failed to register my distress about *Mollem National Park and the adjoining Bhagwan Mahavir Wildlife Sanctuary in Goa being cleared to make way for major coal-corridor infrastructure projects approved by the BJP Goa government.*[7] When the students asked me whether magic realism was a useful device for diasporic writers, I felt disingenuous not answering that, *if so, it was no more than for the Delhi Police who, in February 2021, had brought unbelievable but true charges of pro-Khalistan criminal conspiracy and sedition charges against several young people, including twenty-two-year-old college student Disha Ravi, for editing and sharing a Farmers' Protest Toolkit on Google Docs.*

The organisation that apparently created the notorious Farmers' Protest Toolkit was called the Poetic Justice Foundation. Is poetic justice more than a literary device? Speaking of the non-performative, cultural theorist Sara Ahmed's work on institutional racism questions the assumption that speech acts such as diversity statements name what they in fact do; indeed, how they may even become the virtue-signalling pretexts for bureaucratic procrastination and inaction about racism.[8] Perhaps my own non-performativity or refusal to rehearse being 'an Indian diasporic writer' in the instance of this interview reflected less a resistance to the semantic classification per se, than to prevailing cultural hegemonies that determine who is called on to undertake the work of being diverse or diasporic (or a migrant or culturally hyphenated) and – in any given historical moment – for which audience or whose benefit?[9] By agreeing to name or define myself within the rubric (or is it Rubik's cube?) of contemporary identity politics – to extend the material/metaphor Ahmed has used regarding the brick walls diversity work creates – wasn't I also allowing myself to be *walled in*, ghettoised?

I wanted to assert that *all non-Indigenous Australians are diasporic*, but with a mystifying, escapist air instead said that, had I been born in Goa or India, perhaps I would not have become a writer … I now see that the feelings the interview aroused were symptomatic of a malaise – emotional exhaustion and indifference – to which I had been succumbing for some time. Muddle-headed, I also had a presentiment of dread as the interviewers signed off with smiles, good humour and grace. I did not forecast that, only days later, my allegiance to one part of a body politic rather than another would seem less like a matter of cultural or intellectual irritation than a Brechtian struggle, a matter of life and death. As the second wave ravaged the lives of so many in India, I fell into a deep state of despair. I cried bitter, hopeless tears for those close and unknown to me suffering from the virus, but also for the sicker state of Indian democracy and the wanton negligence of the central government of Prime Minister Narendra Modi.

■

Communications had been suppressed, but international footage showed Indian hospitals overflowing, turning away patients, while desperate relatives faced oxygen tank shortages and black markets, and bodies overflowing crematoria were burnt in the street. Bodies began washing up on the Ganges and Yamuna rivers and being retrieved by stray dogs in a spectacle that journalist Rana Ayyub, in a 12 May 2021 tweet, characterised as 'the most haunting image of the devastation'. In Goa – India's smallest state, and my diasporic home or 'imaginary homeland' – the county's highest per-capita positivity rate of fifty-two per cent was recorded. Between 11 and 16 May, from 2 am to 6 am (the 'dark hours'), eighty-three people died at Goa Medical College & Hospital, not from logistical issues but from preventable oxygen supply shortages. Yet the Goa government's dereliction of its duty of care had occurred much earlier: for months, it had allowed wealthy Indian tourists from other states free rein to come for 'lockdown holidays' and to frequent Goa's numerous casinos.

So consumed was I by the images I had witnessed that, when meeting a friend at the Sydney Writers' Festival on 30 April, a mild autumn day, as I was stopped at the Carriageworks entrance to undertake a routine COVID-19 check – Had I been feeling unwell or run a temperature in the last few days? Had I been near any hotspots? – I was overcome by an uncanny sensation of impostor syndrome; I answered in the negative but nevertheless felt that I was dissembling, that I had been *in India*. That night, deploying powers under the *Biosecurity Act 2015*, the Australian Government announced an unprecedented ban with criminal penalties on Australians attempting to return between 1 and 15 May. Any sentimental gratitude I may have indulged during the pandemic about my parents having come to the so-called 'Lucky Country' turned quickly to impotent rage about Australians abandoned to their fates in India.[10] I felt vicarious trauma – 'There but for the grace of God', etc. – but also moral injury and survivor guilt. I sent emails, as indignant as they were probably futile, to the prime minister, the health minister and the minister for foreign affairs:

> My parents were immigrants to Australia from India in 1971 and 1972, just one year before Whitlam effectively ended the White Australia policy, yet this response smacks of the worst days of that racist policy.

Every Australian of Indian origin would come to know someone who died during India's second COVID-19 wave. When, a week into the ban, a Senate Committee hearing found that, of the 9500 Australians stranded in India, an estimated 950 were vulnerable and 173 were unaccompanied minors, I grew numb and took to my bed. The government's response to public backlash was not to overturn the ban but to announce that, from 15 May, Australians returning from India would be repatriated in double numbers to the Howard Springs 'Centre for National Resilience'.[11] It was like a bad episode of *Wakefield* merging with *Stateless*. One *Sydney Morning Herald* columnist called the Indian diaspora 'too magnificently welcome'. A gracious defence, but its well-meaningness rested on problematic 'model minority' ideals, about whose citizenship and diasporic identity are deemed acceptable and legitimate; under different conditions, as Australia's migration history had demonstrated, such 'multicultural tolerance' could become the basis for disqualification, demonisation and deportation.[12] On the other hand, being perceived as welcome was at least better than what the British colonists and settlers must have been when they arrived here, lying and calling Australia uninhabited while plundering Indigenous lands and engaging in genocidal practices, subsuming over 250 Indigenous languages and myriad nations while weaponising the juridical fiction of 'terra nullius'.

■

Of course, the narrative of an only-fairly-recent Indian presence in Australia is simply not historically factual. It's likely that people from the subcontinent landed on the Australian continent 4000 years before European settlement.[13] There were ethnic Indians on the First Fleet. Beyond artist Peter Drew's efforts to reclaim Monga Khan as a poster boy for Australia and mythologies surrounding 'Afghans', lascars, hawkers and cameleers, historian Samia Khatun's pioneering *Australianama*, among other accounts, recovers subjugated knowledges and migration stories of South Asians in Australia.[14] Khatun evidences how South Asian labourers engaged in key 'nation-building' industries from the 1860s onwards, working within the racist, draconian terms of the *Immigration Restriction Act 1901*; their journeys along traditional Indigenous trade routes, where they encountered Indigenous people, cultures and languages, also track alternative narratives of colonial enterprise, 'progress', and the epistemic and actual violence of traditional Anglophone histories of Australia and their Enlightenment biases.

Arguably, the settler-colonial 'Australia' project (and Britain's coterminous colonial ventures in Asia and Africa particularly) were economically enabled by the East India Company's fortunes. Of all its colonies, India was literally the Jewel in the British Crown because of the East India Company's crippling system of land taxation and tariffs; labour exploitation, including the indentured servitude of Indians in other parts of the British Empire; stranglehold over raw materials, trade and export goods; and outlawing of local Indian competition and industry.[15] Operating dual-currency economies, through depredations and the looting of India, especially from the mid-eighteenth to early twentieth centuries, the East India Company generated staggering wealth and investment for Great Britain, to the extent that British industrialisation was at the cost of India's. Some Australian colonial infrastructure, including streets like Sydney's Pitt (named for the Tory prime minister William Pitt the Younger), are linked directly to the inglorious genealogy of the East India Company.[16]

▪

About this time, I opened my inbox to find an invitation of solidarity from a colleague asking me to contribute a non-fiction piece to a series responding to the 'India situation' or 'the ban'. The request evoked a sense of déjà vu, stoking the turmoil and bewilderment I had not resolved regarding the interview. Except the ethical dilemma appeared to now concern the power to conceive of, identify, empathise, to be a native informant or cultural expert with a poetic licence to imagine and interpret both worlds – all while living safely in Australia. Again, I felt burdened with a heavy moral responsibility. I wobbled and wavered. Less than the question of form or genre, there were the ethics of representation itself – namely, of perspective, authenticity and legitimacy. How should I begin to choose among the voices of 1.3 billion or 9500? Or perhaps I should write from the point of view of the first Afghan camel? Or through the eyes of the first pariah dog that may have landed on the Australian continent 4000 years before colonisation!

I asked my colleague to find someone who might be more 'affected', as my experience, being vicarious, now seemed somehow less legitimate. I didn't admit that I was *wary of participating in a project in which irreducible differences, multiplicities of experience and expression of 'Indian identity' could be collapsed into, or might be seen to have relevance merely because of, an experience of collective trauma, discrimination or victimhood.*[17] I did not say that *I feared writing about the trauma of racism might limit the scope of experience and interiority while enlarging the influence of the white gaze or dominant cultural imaginary.*[18] In her poem 'Enlightenment', Natasha Trethewey subtly elucidates irreducible, but also ineluctable, differentials in the 'afterlife of slavery' as they mediate the poet's relationship with her father while they walk through former US president Thomas Jefferson's estate (now a private museum) on the erstwhile slave plantation Monticello.[19] When the guide says, '*Imagine stepping back into the past*,' the speaker whispers to her father:

This is where
we split up. I'll head around to the back.
When he laughs, I know he's grateful

I've made a joke of it, this history
that links us – white father, black daughter –
even as it renders us other to each other.[20]

When my colleague told me there was no-one to take my place, I decided to offer a poem-in-draft called 'In My Father's House'.[21] Set in a magic-realist pandemic-ridden Goa, I added a line – 'the virus has been among us now over a year' – that I thought might provide a timely, pragmatic resolution. Before it was published, I sent the poem to my friend V., but it was met, unusually, with hesitation. He said he liked the imagery of the poem, except … It was not the new line but another that had concerned him: 'Father is delirious from the fever he caught toddy-tapping'. Where had that come from? I tried to explain how I had imagined a man in Goa, in the middle of a monsoon, so desperate for alcohol that he takes it upon himself to climb a coconut tree and tap the toddy. The poem tackles the themes of patriarchy and environmental catastrophe and is written in the voice of the man's daughter. V. said the problem was that, in adopting this perspective, it might seem as though I was appropriating the perspective of a toddy-tapper's daughter.

I knew the toddy-tappers were a caste in Goa called Bhandari (Catholic toddy-tappers are known as Rendeir). Anthropological descriptions of the quaintness of toddy-tapping or upper-caste plaints about scarcity of labour or descendants' 'abandonment of the trade' are frequently silent on the perilous nature of the work involved in harvesting sap (sur) from the coconut flower, which is used in the preparation not only of urak and feni, but of jaggery, vinegar, pau and so many other Goan food staples. But I did not know that Bhandari/Rendeir are still fighting a historic battle to formally be recognised as a Scheduled Caste.[22] Did V. himself think that I was appropriating the perspective of a toddy-tapper's daughter? In all our discussions about social justice and casteism, it had never come up – but my friend now told me that he was from the Bhandari. This revelation was like a key, one I did not want to turn at first, for through the door of that house, if I walked into it, I would likely see evidence of the legacy of my own ancestors: Brahmin landowners (batcars) who, within Goa's feudal ganvcar agricultural system, exploited Bhandari/Rendeir labour.[23]

▪

Years ago at an Australian sandstone university, urged to understand James Joyce's mastery of style through the prism of irony, I got lost in a maze of formalism. I was told to look no further than wannabe artificer and aesthete Stephen Dedalus' declaration at the end of *A Portrait of the Artist as a Young Man*:

> I go to encounter for the millionth time the reality of experience and to forge in the smithy of my soul the uncreated conscience of my race.[24]

A young writer with much cultural baggage of my own, I could not help associating the irony of Stephen's lofty aesthetic ambition with the failure of his cultural mission to 'fly by [the] nets' of 'nationality, language, religion'.[25] When we encounter him again at the beginning of *Ulysses*, Stephen is grieving his mother (whose death has compelled his return to Ireland) and remains haunted by filial Catholic impiety, having refused her dying wish that he pray for her. Ambivalent about homecoming and Irish nationalism, he makes ends meet teaching history at a private boys' school where he suffers an acute awareness of his unequal status as a British colonial subject. Modifying his manifesto, he tells the bigoted, pro-British headmaster Mr Deasy that history 'is a nightmare from which [he is] trying to awake'.[26]

Of the connection between settler-colonial practices of dispossession and the appropriation of Aboriginal stories and voices, Waanyi writer Alexis Wright has said:

> The genius in every individual's story is lost forever when you lose the ability to tell your own story [...] What happens when people feel that they are not in charge of their stories either locally, or in a globalised world, is alienation.[27]

Speaking for myself, I've been reflecting on the koan 'Original Face' in Case 23 of the *Gateless Gate*, generally cast as, 'What is your original face before your mother and father were born?'.[28] For me, the koan provokes self-inquiry about connections between myth and ancestry, kinship and home, here and there, subject and object, appearance and reality, non-duality and non-self. Seeing and expressing things as they really are, beyond diasporic escape routes or performative traps, with self-awareness and authenticity, I don't find art/life/culture/history/language can really be separated, any more than issues of identification and representation – relationships of self and Other – can be unyoked from the ethics of storytelling. Because we are always already in-relation, as Édouard Glissant observed, '[s] ometimes, by taking up the problems of the Other, it is possible to find oneself'.[29] More questions arise: *Isn't imagination conditioned by this mind-body's sovereignty? Can I speak of freedom to imagine or write while another's life is still inscribed as a living palimpsest of racist, caste or other settler-colonial violence, and when intergenerational legacies of state-sanctioned trauma, such as the Stolen Generations, are perpetuated in ongoing policies or practices, such as 'deaths in custody'?*

In her poem 'Question Time', the late Meena Alexander poignantly recounts being startled by a peremptory question from the audience:

Hand raised in a crowded room –
What use is poetry?
[...]
Standing apart I looked at her and said –
We have poetry

So we do not die of history.
I had no idea what I meant.[30]

Alexander's poetics of fragmentation situate the diasporic literary imaginary in the very unevenness and deep fissures of history's terrain. In the rhetorical breach of the collective 'we', the consolation of poetry is given as a generous answer, despite the speaker's intimate awareness that, for some, being free of history is only a dream. When writing the earliest drafts of my novella *Saudade*, I remember my own quietly revolutionary epiphany, recognising how the protagonist Maria-Christina's journey evolved out of a series of narrative exceptions – imaginative leaps that, privileging one reality, simultaneously obscured multiple others. I realised, like a perfect lesson in deconstruction, that the aporias were all mine, and the paradox that the text's aesthetic quality, its craft, arose from what it made visible as much as what it elided.[31] In the end I changed the line in my poem to 'father is delirious from the fever he caught *chasing toddy*'.

This essay was supported by an Australian Government Research Training Program Scholarship at UNSW, Sydney.

1 Bundjalung poet Evelyn Araluen's 'Acknowledgement of Cuntery', published in her debut collection *Dropbear* (University of Queensland Press, St Lucia, 2021), deconstructs the self-congratulation and virtue-signalling of such pat settler-colonial phrases. As Timmah Ball states in an April 2021 *Mascara Literary Review* analysis of the book, Araluen simultaneously unsettles the poetics and politics of the 'incredulous construction of Australia'.

2 Portugal's Prime Minister, António Luís Santos da Costa, is a member of the Goan diaspora.

3 Born in what was then British India, my mother spoke English at home.

4 Satyagraha and ahimsa, whether in contemporary India or elsewhere, might be usefully compared to the politics of refusal *as* the exercise of sovereignty, as scholars such as Audra Simpson have elaborated. See, for example, Simpson, *Mohawk Interruptus: Political Life Across the Borders of Settler States*, Duke University Press, Durham and London, 2014.

5 It is worth noting that India does not permit dual citizenship, so those of the 721,050-strong Indian-born Australians who *are* citizens have, at the time of writing, become so by surrendering their Indian citizenship.

6 Hong, Cathy Park, *Minor Feelings: An Asian American Reckoning*, One World, New York, 2020. Hong speaks of han, a distinctly Korean concatenation of feelings: 'a combination of bitterness, wistfulness, shame, melancholy, and vengefulness' (p. 100). But she also scrutinises the myth of shame as racially interiorised rather than innately racial: 'Shame is often associated with Asianness and the Confucian system of honor alongside its incomprehensible rites of shame, but [...] my shame is not cultural but political' (p. 136). For relevant Japanese Australian critique and context, see Fukui, Masako, 'Embracing Ugly Feelings: Living with the Cold of the Soul', *Griffith Review*, no. 72, May 2021, pp. 132–138.

7 This protected area of the Western Ghats – named a world biodiversity 'hottest hotspot' by UNESCO, and which covers 240 square kilometres – is 'home to 128 endemic plants, birds, butterflies, reptiles and a variety of wild mammals including leopards, Bengal tigers and pangolins', plus unique species of ant and dragonfly. See 'Mollem: The Battle to Save a Biodiversity Hotspot in India's Goa', *BBC News*, 29 November 2020, https://www.bbc.com/news/world-asia-india-55082645

8 Ahmed, Sara, *On Being Included: Racism and Diversity in Institutional Life*, Duke University Press, Durham and London, 2012.

9 An incisive 2021 review by Mindy Gill examines the political problem of self-representation, audience and the reproduction of racist tropes in fiction by emerging Australian writers of colour: 'Preaching to the Converted: Burdening Literature with Moral Instruction', *Australian Book Review*, no. 433, July 2021, pp. 15–16.

10 *The Guardian* reported on 19 May 2021 that three men – one Australian citizen and two permanent residents – subsequently died of COVID-19 in India, at least one of whom while seeking to be repatriated.

11 Significantly, at the same time that the ban was enacted on the return of Australian citizens from the subcontinent, in May 2021 the Sri Lankan Tamil Nadesalingam family (who had been forcibly removed by the Australian Border Force from Biloela, Queensland, in 2019) were the sole inhabitants of Christmas Island – at the cost of an estimated A$6 million.

12 Megalogenis, George, 'The Race Card Just Doesn't Stack Up in Australia', *The Sydney Morning Herald*, 8 May 2021, https://www.smh.com.au/politics/federal/the-race-card-just-doesn-t-stack-up-in-australia-20210507-p57ps7.html

13 Kumud Merani has crafted an extensive two-part radio special on 'the links between India and Australia going back thousands of years' for SBS Hindi (first published in 2014, updated in 2019): https://www.sbs.com.au/language/english/audio/the-story-untold-the-links-between-australian-aboriginal-and-indian-tribes

14 Samia Khatun's *Australianama: The South Asian Odyssey in Australia* (University of Queensland Press, St Lucia, 2018) retraces the journey of a particular book of Sufi poetry, *Kasasol Ambia*,

written in Bengali, published in Kolkata and discovered in a Broken Hill mosque. See also Reichstein, Ben, 'Rethinking "Real Aussies": Our History of Migrant Labour', *Overland*, 10 August 2016, https://overland.org.au/2016/08/rethinking-real-aussies-and-our-history-of-migrant-labour/; and Tan, Cher, 'Seeking Welcome While Australian', *Overland*, 1 March 2017, https://overland.org.au/2017/03/seeking-welcome-while-australian/

15 I am drawing heavily on Shashi Tharoor's economic synthesis in *Inglorious Empire: What the British Did to India* (C. Hurst & Co., London, 2017). However, I do not agree with Tharoor's argument that reparations are impracticable or unnecessary, nor that members of higher castes in India should decide this on behalf of minorities or lower castes. The Indian indenture system, through which at least one million Indians were transported to labour in European colonies, sought to fill the vacuum that arose, particularly in the sugarcane industry, following the abolition of slavery in the British Empire from 1833.

16 Pitt's great-grandfather, an early merchant, amassed personal wealth by pilfering the Madras diamond and selling it on for a song; the diamond has been on display, as part of the French Royal Treasury, at The Louvre, since 1887.

17 Following the Atlanta spa killings that occurred on 16 March 2021, I was also wary of conflating my experiences of discrimination with those of other Asian women. The students were referencing an article I had published at the beginning of the pandemic on the topic of structural racism in Australia: 'Beyond the "Bamboo Ceiling"', *Sydney Review of Books*, 27 March 2020, https://sydneyreviewofbooks.com/essay/beyond-bamboo-ceiling/

18 There is insufficient space to cover the range of issues involved, but Black and Asian American fiction writers as various as Toni Morrison, Zadie Smith and Amy Tan have defended fiction from the insistence that authors should be representing 'their' race when writing. Hong, in *Minor Feelings*, has thus expressed her frustration about racism-trauma narratives (largely made for the benefit, she argues, of a dominant white publishing industry): 'Will there be a future where I, on the page, am simply I, on the page, and not I, proxy for a whole ethnicity, imploring you to believe we are human beings who feel pain? I don't think, therefore I am – I hurt, therefore I am. Therefore, my books are graded on a pain scale. If it's 2, maybe it's not worth telling my story. If it's 10, maybe my book will be a bestseller' (p. 91). Pertinent contrasting views in Australian literary criticism about the problem of racial appropriation in fiction include: Fernandes, Sujatha, 'The Great White Social Justice Novel', *Sydney Review of Books*, 25 May 2020, https://sydneyreviewofbooks.com/review/cummins-american-dirt-krien-act-of-grace/; Leane, Jeanine, 'No Longer Malleable Stuff', *Overland*, no. 241, Summer 2020, https://overland.org.au/previous-issues/issue-241/feature-no-longer-malleable-stuff/; and Leane, Jeanine, 'Other Peoples' Stories', *Overland*, no. 225, Summer 2016, https://overland.org.au/previous-issues/issue-225/feature-jeanine-leane/

19 The 'afterlife of slavery' is a term coined by Saidiya Hartman in *Lose Your Mother: A Journey Along the Atlantic Slave Route* (Farrar, Strauss and Giroux, New York, 2007) to speak of the 'racial calculus' and 'political arithmetic' of slavery in contemporary life, including 'skewed life chances, limited access to health and education, premature death, incarceration, and impoverishment' (p. 6).

20 Trethewey, Natasha, *Monument: Poems New and Selected*, Houghton Mifflin Harcourt, Boston, 2018, p. 160.

21 The piece can be read in full in *Island* magazine, https://islandmag.com/read/in-my-fathers-house-by-suneeta-peres-da-costa

22 State legislation relating to toddy-tapper welfare was enacted in 1984 and amended in 1993: https://www.legitquest.com/act/goa-toddy-tappers-welfare-fund-amendment-act-1993/6634

23 Like the agricultural labour of fishing and rice-paddy cultivation – industries that provide Goa's other food staples – coconut cultivation has also historically been assigned to the Shudras from whose ranks in the varna system of caste the Bhandari, a jati or sub-caste, come.

24 Joyce, James, *Portrait of the Artist as a Young Man*, Penguin Books Australia, Victoria, 1973, p. 253.

25 Ibid., p. 203.

26 Joyce, James, *Ulysses*, Penguin Books Australia, Victoria, 1992, p. 42.

27 Wright, Alexis, 'Telling the Untold Story', 2018 Stephen Murray-Smith Memorial Lecture, State Library of Victoria, 3 December 2018.

28 Yamada, Kōun, 'Think Neither Good nor Evil', *The Gateless Gate: The Classic Book of Zen Koans*, Wisdom Publications, Somerville, MA, 2004, pp. 111–117.

29 Glissant, Édouard, *Poetics of Relation*, trans. Betsy Wing, The University of Michigan Press, Ann Arbor, 1997, p. 18.

30 Alexander, Meena, *Birthplace with Buried Stones*, TriQuarterly Books, Chicago, 2013, p.89.

31 Peres da Costa, Suneeta, *Saudade*, Giramondo Publishing, Sydney, 2018. As Maria-Christina's communist history teacher tells her, 'History was written from the perspectives of the victors, but there were many other, hidden sides … if we looked closely enough, could we not see?' (p. 97).

'... billions of deteriorated or rebellious cells ...'[1]

Ouyang Yu

子曰：'予欲无言。'

∎

I came across a remark by E. M. Cioran, who said, and I quote:

> To deprecate your own kind, to vilify and pulverize them, to attack their foundations, to undermine your very basis, to destroy your point of departure, to punish your origins ..., to curse all those non-elect, lesser breeds, torn between imposture and elegy, whose sole mission is not to have one ...[2]

And I was reminded of *Songs of the Last Chinese Poet* (1997), in which I wrote,

> thinking of destroying everything
> thinking of destroying a civilization
> a civilization as long as the footwrappings of a feet-bound woman

we are a dying race
no longer can we live on our own
but must we metamorphose by losing our tongue
our beautiful sexy body
into something we would have been ashamed to see
something hairy something so self-centred
that only a T.V. set can match[3]

∎

I'm growing to like Evelyn Conlon's *Skin of Dreams*, and I underlined a remark by Maud in the book that goes, 'We're supposed to say yes these days, yes to everything. To say no is a perversity.'[4] Not long after, when I drove to Bundoora to post a few books to China, I wrote a poem that goes:

What I wrote while driving to Bundoora on Plenty Road

the sky over here
  is called
indifference
  every day
  is a
  no
that's 365
  nos
  for you
multiplied
  by 30
who wants to
  no this?
who cares?
  who gives a
  fake?

∎

Logged in to Facebook. Saw a famous writer's news about his new book. Only one 'like'. I clicked 'like' as a thought came to me: no number of literary awards can guarantee people will like you forever.

A couple of hours after, when I went to the loo, this expression came to me: 文人相轻 ('literary beings belittle each other'). One can write a whole book on that topic but the core of the truth remains: there is little mutual regard between men and women of letters or characters.

▪

2002, I think it was, when I went to San Francisco to attend an international conference on Chinese diasporic writings, I went on an outing with Hong Ying, a bus tour. My memory is fading. But I remember the moment the thought came to me because I paused and said to her, by the window: I've found the solution. She was bewildered and I explained that this was to do with my novel-in-progress. I didn't give her any other details. But, as soon as I returned to Melbourne, I gave the story a new twist. One of my characters left the army and became a wartime tourist, roaming the mountains in Yunnan.

My thought sequence should have been reversed because I thought of *that* after I had read this, again by Cioran, who writes:

> Faced with the Nile and the Pyramids, Flaubert thought of nothing but Normandy, according to one witness – nothing but the landscapes and manners of the future *Madame Bovary*. Nothing but that seemed to exist for him. To imagine is to limit oneself, to exclude: without an excessive capacity for rejection, no plan, no work, no way of *realizing* anything.[5]

The novel I wrote then is *The English Class* (2010), in which a male Chinese student majoring in English at a Wuhan-based university elopes with his teacher to Melbourne and ends up suffering schizophrenia.

▪

Before he launched my collection of prose poetry, *Living after Death* (2020), Kevin Brophy had a chat with me over the phone to check a few things. Among other things, I asked him not to use the tired adage 'the angry Chinese poet'. I have other qualities, such as humour and love.

Yesterday, when I picked up *Joseph Roth: A Life in Letters*, I came across 'a sort of poetic spleen'[6] and I thought: Oh, yes. That's perhaps what I have to do from time to time and everyone has to do from time to time. Why the label, and such an unfair one, too?

▪

When I came across this remark by E. M. Cioran that goes, 'Man makes history; in its turn history unmakes man',[7] I was sharply reminded of Nicolae Ceaușescu and Muammar Muhammad Abu Minyar al-Gaddafi, with their violent deaths, achieving a perfect balance in their lives of rise and fall.

▪

During the Second World War, John Curtin was known to have said that he wanted to 'hold this country and keep it as a citadel for the British-speaking race'.[8]

I have always thought that what I'm speaking apart from Mandarin Chinese is English until I came across that. If I had known it was that, I would not have decided to learn the language in the first place. Even when I went to university to study English literature, I never thought it was 'British', let alone Australian. Does anyone speak Australian in a country called 'Australia'?

▪

It was only yesterday that the thought came to me while I was having a walk outside in the park that the last straw on us is the arrival of fully robotic beings to replace us. What do we do if that happens? Lie in state alive? Then this, again from Cioran: 'Everything indicates that humanity is going downhill …'[9]

It's more downhell, in my opinion.

▪

E. M. Cioran and Cao Xueqin. How different are they? But when Cioran said, 'Harmony, universal or otherwise, has never existed and never will exist',[10] it sounds close to what Cao said in a poem in *The Dream of Red Mansions* that I'll approximate in my translation below:

Everyone knows that gods are good
But no-one can forgo achievements and fame
Where are the ancient generals and ministers?
All gone, leaving behind a grassy mound

Everyone knows that gods are good
But no-one can forgo silver and gold
They complain that they never stay together long enough
But, when it is long enough, their eyes are closed for good

Everyone knows that gods are good
But no-one can forgo his beautiful wife
When you are alive, she makes you feel good
But, when you die, she goes with someone else

Everyone knows that gods are good
But no-one can forgo his own kids and grandkids
There are so many loving parents since ancient times
But filial kids and grandkids are very few

If things are like that, where can one find harmony? Perhaps the only harmony one can find is *harmoney*, a word I wilfully coined.

▪

I think I've entered into a state of posthumousness. I didn't know what happened before I was born till years after I was born. I shall never know what will happen when I die. Now that I think I am already dead and I am living a dead man's life, in a country that is most suited for that purpose, I am literally futureless. Being futureless, in other words, is being deathful. Or being alive. Then it's fitting to quote Cioran again, near the end of *History and Utopia*, where he writes:

> No more past, no more future; the centuries collapse, matter abdicates, the shadows are exhausted; death turns to ridicule, and ridiculous too is life itself.[11]

As I said in a poem I did this morning while having a walk outside in the park, in this country everyone dies-lives, their hearts pieces of ice.

∎

In Martin Heidegger's *Being and Time*, '[i]t has been maintained that "Being" is the "most universal" concept'.[12] I just had to laugh at Heidegger for being so preposterous. For one thing, 'being' as a word is untranslatable into Chinese. For another, the closest thing it rhymes with in Chinese is 病 (bing), a 'disease' or 'condition'. That something so serious as 'being' is dissolved into ridiculousness in another cultural and linguistic context serves as a reminder that, unless the universe in that 'universal' contains the rest of the universe, it is not a complete one.

∎

'...the villages themselves – they want to be cities.'[13] This remark, by Joseph Roth, in his novel, or novella, *The Emperor's Tomb*, that I came across this morning, standing pissing in my loo, caused me to award it with an underline, with my red pen.

I recall a visit to the village of one of my postgraduate students. It's not a village. It's a town with tall buildings and wide streets, accessible by car. The only difference is that the village-city borders on the rice paddies and a hill not far away where there are orange trees for profit. The village has an enticing name: Houma – literally, 'back horse'. Or 'rear horse', if you like.

My village, the one I was sent down to for re-education in the early 1970s, had a path leading between two ponds across a creek, with forty households in a row, from east to west, or from north to south, overlooking the ponds. That's how it still remains in my memory. I have not been back since.

Then, this, where Roth says, 'My hearing is acute, so I pretend to be a little deaf',[14] which won another red underline from me. Please note that I have read so many books without even bothering underlining a single line. But this, in a matter of two pages.

It reminds me of this landlord's son in *my* village, who had a habit of not hearing anything unpleasant chucked his way although he was known to have acute hearing.

■

I grew increasingly interested as I read the account of John Sampson, who 'was active in a dispute with the mine-owners and formed the Australian Miners' Union' and 'was promptly dismissed and was never employed in a mine again'.[15] Why was I interested in this? Because it coincides with an Australian organisation for whom I have worked for over two decades not giving me any more work, for no reasons at all, very recently, at about the time when I read this. And I was not even in dispute with them; I had only sent queries. Working as a contractor, one is not in any way protected by anything. That's Australia for you, formerly known as 'The Workingman's Paradise'. Go and keep cheating the migrants with that.

■

Goethe is a practitioner of self-censorship. I worked this out from reading his poetry in Chinese, translated by Qian Chunqi. The poem in question, 《你为何赋予我们慧眼》 (roughly, 'Why Did You Bless Us with Intelligent Eyes?'),[16] has a footnote to the effect that Goethe wrote it about Charlotte von Stein, claiming that she and he were husband and wife in a previous life. But Goethe did not include the poem in his collected works.

I was interested in this because I have now entered into a period of massive self-censorship. One word that is typical of my life at this particular stage is 'cut'. Cut, cut, cut. Cut, cut, cut. It's the singing of a bird called self-censorship. One cuts oneself dead even before one dies. More so in an age of utter political correctness. How can one even breathe, being so squeezed by correctness? Does one stop shitting altogether because shit is bad and it pollutes the environment?

Although Kazuo Ishiguro has warned young writers against 'self-censorship', it's easier said than done. He doesn't have to, because he believes he is in 'a privileged and relatively protected position'.[17] What nonsense! Is he a god?

∎

Breakfast. A conversation between a husband and a wife.

H: Just came across the Queen's 'Never complain, never explain' rule.[18]

W: I heard you. I understand.

H: It's about always being positive. When I was a teenager, Mother got very worried when she heard me sigh a sigh. She said, in her Wuhan accent, 'But a boy like you shouldn't sigh. A young person should never sigh.'

W: Yeh, you do like complaining.

H: So do you. So do all Chinese people.

W: Australians do that all the time. In the shop I ran, Australian customers would complain all the time. That's what they liked doing most. They complain so much, never happy with anything.

Hours after, when I tried to find the same article, I found something different, with an additional message, that goes, 'Never Complain. Never Explain. Never Apologize!'[19] And I thought: how similar is that last line to the Chinese Communist Party claim about itself being always great, glorious and correct? Only when you are always correct, you will never apologise.

■

Kenneth Koch, whose exuberance I love, has a line in his poem 'The First Step' that goes, 'Nothing but Chinese absence soup'.[20] My immediate reaction to this is: 'There is no such soup', followed by a wonderment if that is a soup in which nothing Australian exists. Still, I like the soup and what diverse images it helps evoke.

■

I often wonder if our solitude – I mean my own solitude – is not a direct result of the total extermination of insects around me, such as flies, mosquitoes and tiny little insects, crawling or flying. When we are as clean as the detergent itself – when I, I mean – what hope is there for a living being alive with other living beings in a shared community of lives instead of a detergent living being alive till it is dead and purified in the fire, or purifired, in the incinerator?

This is the thought that came to me as I took my morning walk in the nearby park, bathed in the morning sun and accompanied by no-one, not even a fly, only singing birds in the far trees, as well as something I had read last night in bed.

Curiously, a rhyming couplet we were taught as children in China came back that goes, 庄稼一枝花，全靠粪当家 (Zhuangjia yizhi hua, quan kao fen dangjia) – 'Good crap, good crop'. Since when did they start replacing human excrement with chemical fertilisers?

■

Last night, I thought of something and put it down in two fragments: 'characterless tombstone' and her wish to 'remain unknown'. Now, night again and time to expand on them. Wu Zetian (624–705), China's first and only woman emperor, had a tombstone erected in her honour that had no inscriptions on it. Hence its name 'wu zi bei' ('characterless tombstone'), a tombstone with no inscriptions as she ordered, 'character' referring to the Chinese characters as compared with the English words.

I had intermittently wondered about the mystery of this and of Chinese women in general until last night when, perhaps for the hundredth time, I recalled again this woman's wish to remain unknown, not only for the rest of her life but also for the rest of her death, not wanting to keep any traces of her life on record or even wanting to be written about.

I know her. But I can't disclose any details about her except that there is a strong connection, I feel, between the woman emperor and her, a woman commoner, for reasons that are beyond me. To be honest, I found it quite touching, in a mysterious way.

▪

I went to the city by tram yesterday. Someone sat down next to me and started talking, to himself mainly. Everyone else looked the other way. I kept reading, lending one ear to what he was talking about. It was all gibberish until a young woman sat down opposite him when he started talking to her as if they had known each other for a long time. I heard him say to her, 'Were you born in Australia?' The answer was yes. Then he said, 'You look very young, only fourteen.' The answer was no, and wavering, hesitant, embarrassed. The man carried on for the entire length of the journey till the woman left. Then he stood up and went to the door, preparing to disembark. Then he changed his mind and went to another door as a string of expletives rolled off his tongue. People stared. I, about to disembark, stared, too. He didn't seem unhappy. He just talked and kept saying 'fuck you', his eyes raised skywards. No-one knew what he was talking about or whom he was angry with.

Just now, in one of my numerous visits to the loo, I picked up Cioran's *The Trouble with Being Born* and read:

> 'Life seems good only to the madman,' observed Hegesias, a Cyrenaic philosopher, some twenty-three centuries ago. These are almost the only words of his we have … Of all oeuvres to reinvent, his comes first on my list.[21]

'I must go and check him out,' I heard myself say, finding the coincidence so felicitous and thinking: perhaps we don't need philosophers in Australia as long as we've got them elsewhere?

▪

I took a photograph of the books I read per day, thirty-two in total, and added a caption: 'These are the books I read on a daily basis.' Before I posted it on Instagram, I had changed my mind and ditched the idea. Why bother? Then I started reading one of the books and found this that I had underlined and copied:

> In 1983 she [Helen Quach] became ill. Needing medical attention and total rest, she came back to Sydney and bought a house overlooking Sailor's Bay. Apart from treatment and rest, she also spent her time reading and studying operas, only occasionally conducting concerts. Although she had received a Western education, Quach inherited an interest in Chinese culture and thought. In recent years she has shown a tendency towards introspection, as evidenced by her study of the philosophy of Laozi and Zhuangzi, and her time spent in meditation.[22]

I continued to read, and to copy, what Leonard Bernstein had to say about her:

> Miss Quach runs the danger of being a pretty young woman, and thus conquering all hearts for non-musical reasons. But her performance as our assistant this season (1967–68) has given us reason to believe that she will succeed on musical grounds as well. Her rhythmic sense is sharp, her reflexes are quick, her address to the orchestra captivating. She seems to be at her best in works of large dimension (odd for so diminutive a creature), and if there is such a thing as a Maestra, Miss Quach could well be it.[23]

I hate to explain myself. But, if I have to, I like the reference to her inherited interest, something that is ever *so* slightly slighted in this country.

1 Cioran, E. M., *Drawn and Quartered*, Skyhorse Publishing, New York, 2012, p. 130.
2 Cioran, E. M., *The Trouble with Being Born*, Arcade Publishing, New York, 2012, p. 176.
3 Yu, Ouyang, *Songs of the Last Chinese Poet*, Wild Peony, Sydney, 1997, p. 2.
4 Conlon, Evelyn, *Skin of Dreams*, Brandon / Mount Eagle Publications, Dingle, Ireland, 2003, p. 100.
5 Cioran, *The Trouble with Being Born*, p. 187.
6 Roth, Joseph, *Joseph Roth: A Life in Letters*, trans. and ed. Michael Hofmann, Granta, London, 2013, p. 39.
7 Cioran, *Drawn and Quartered*, p. 37.
8 Curtin, John, quoted in Day, David, *Claiming a Continent: A New History of Australia*, HarperCollins, Sydney, 2005, pp. 267–268.
9 Cioran, *Drawn and Quartered*, p. 38.
10 Cioran, E. M., *History and Utopia*, Arcade Publishing, London, 2015, p. 116.
11 Ibid., p. 117.
12 Heidegger, Martin, *Being and Time*, trans. John Macquarrie and Edward Robinson, Blackwell, Oxford, 1962, p. 22.
13 Roth, Joseph, *The Emperor's Tomb*, trans. Michael Hofmann, Granta, London, 2013, p. 1.
14 Ibid., p. 2.
15 Sampson, John, quoted in Menzies, Robert, *Afternoon Light: Some Memories of Men and Events*, Penguin, Middlesex, 1970, p. 6. Sampson was Menzies' grandfather.
16 See 钱春绮, 《歌德名诗精选》, 太白文艺出版社, Xi'an, 1997, 第129页.
17 Ishiguro, Kazuo, quoted in Jones, Rebecca, 'Sir Kazuo Ishiguro Warns of Young Authors Self-Censoring out of "Fear"', *BBC News*, 1 March 2021, https://www.bbc.com/news/entertainment-arts-56208347
18 Shields, Bevan, 'How Meghan Blew Up the Queen's "Never Complain, Never Explain" Rule', *The Sydney Morning Herald*, 12 March 2021, https://www.smh.com.au/world/europe/how-meghan-blew-up-the-queen-s-never-complain-never-explain-rule-20210309-p5798k.html
19 Reston, James, 'Never Complain, Never Explain, Never Apologize!', *The New York Times*, 10 May 1970, p. 172.
20 Koch, Kenneth, *The Collected Poems of Kenneth Koch*, Alfred A. Knopf, New York, 2019, p. 468.
21 Cioran, *The Trouble with Being Born*, p. 191.
22 Lee, Lily Xiao Hong, *The Virtue of Yin: Studies on Chinese Women*, Wild Peony, Sydney, 1994, p. 91.
23 Bernstein, Leonard, quoted in ibid., p. 92.

when we blink

Hasib Hourani

at a writers' festival for young people a woman in her thirties talks to us about branding. she says 'you can only be three things', 'pick your three things carefully', 'don't write about dick and vagina', 'or do, it just means that you've used up two of your three things'.

my parents' internet stopped working and they couldn't leave the house so my dad took our childhood photos out of their albums and put them on the computer. for a week i scrolled the whatsapp dumpsite in the morning and in the evening. sometimes fifty pictures sometimes more. once i woke up and found 531. once my housemate walked their guest to the front door, passed my bedroom and said 'what are you doing' and i was in bed with wet eyes and i said 'looking at photos of my family', 'it's not as sad as it sounds', 'i promise', 'i'm happy about it'.

i am six months on testosterone. now i am eight months on testosterone. and when you read this i may be ten, or twelve, or more months on testosterone. at first my dosage was so low that my cells didn't know what to be, so i didn't get my period and instead i spotted indefinitely, and when i bought new underwear i made sure it was dark enough not to stain but it still discoloured because spotting is acidic and i was spotting non-stop, always on the cusp of something else.

when i was ten i burnt my hand on pyrex taking chicken out of the oven and the burn took more than a month to scab over. it was wet and infected. it was squishy and yellow and i leaked pus around the 1101 corniche apartment for weeks.

the pictures are spat all over the floor. pick one up place it in the scanner wait for it take it out flick it move on to the next one.

i can't be anything but palestinian without the word 'guilt' sinking down into me from the sky. it is made of cement and painted black.

my dad believes that heaven and hell are not places we go to. he believes that they're energies and when we die we either become positive or negative energy.

when i was nineteen and out of home i wanted to go back to every house i had ever lived in, ring the doorbell, get my camera ready, take a photo of the new tenants the second they opened the door, then say thank you and walk away. i would call the series *the replacements.*

when i was twenty-one i went back to the 1101 corniche apartment and rang the doorbell but the door never opened. i heard footsteps on the other side of the wood but i guess they didn't like the look of me through the peephole.

my parents are living with me now and my dad is helping me build shelves for a nook in the wall. he finds a photo in a gold frame. my siblings are smiling, i am in my favourite t-shirt, my hair is in two braids, i look like myself but also i am six years old. my dad says 'where did you get this' and i say 'i don't know i brought it with me when i moved' and he says 'good thing you have a scanner upstairs' but i don't want him to digitise this photo, i want my copy to remain the only one that exists.

i so often wake up pissed off because of dreams that go like this: i see a bird i have never seen before; i take a picture of it; i wake up before getting the chance to ID it; awake, i realise the bird does not exist. the first time i had a dream like this i was ten and using my family's digital camera to take pictures in our apartment zooming in on the details: the pile of a carpet the thick dark wood of a desk leg the metal handles of its drawers. i woke up and spent the next two days with my eyes closed, commemorating the photos.

last night i was in newcastle in my sleep and a cross between a baby penguin and a cattle egret flew onto the windowsill and entered through the closed window. the sea was purple, the sun was setting and the bird crawled into the hollow between my crossed legs and slept there while i held my breath and watched him.

i take an onion from the basket. i put it on the chopping board and when i look down it is like confetti. so many little pieces ready to be sprinkled and i am crying.

there is a four-panel comic that i love by bjenny montero where in each panel someone is asking 'what are you lookin' for?' and in each panel someone is replying 'i'm just lookin'': out a window, through a magnifying glass, on a walk, in bed and in love.

my friend hassan asks me about summer in mexico, what it was like when i was there. he needs it for a piece he's writing. i say 'stuff was so brutal i have a lot of memory loss around my time in mexico'. i say 'i went somewhere near the coast for a week where it rained the whole time, that was kind of beautiful', 'like a constant dusk sort of vibe', 'always on the cusp of daylight'. and then i say 'i shaved my face today but am keeping my moustache and pathetic little sideburns'.

my mum combs her hair with her hands. she does it with an aggression that makes my jaw tight like steak. sitting on the couch, clawing through clumps. i live one road over from the citylink but still i can hear each piece of hair as it rips, either off her scalp or somewhere in the middle, cut-offs falling softly onto her lap.

for some reason almost everyone from my high school is private on instagram and i don't follow them which means i have no idea what they're up to. every now and then i check who's viewed my story and i click on their profiles and the little padlock shows up on the screen. they are the replacements looking at me through the peephole.

i put this essay down for a month because things are escalating in palestine and i experience the most efficient burnout of my life where sometimes i sleep twelve hours a day but the other twelve are always spent thinking and speaking and writing and emailing. and i pick up seven commissions in two weeks, which is a big deal for me. my instagram followers double and i text my friend 'seeing my name and face everywhere', 'idk man i wana like seeing that', 'and i have not been able to', 'headshots everywhere i am like, oh boy this is not how i wana get famous' and then i ask them if they have an accountant.

i don't know how to be anything but palestinian right now and last saturday i got 1000 milligrams of reandron injected into my left buttock and i bruised for three days and i shaved my face with cream a brush and a razor blade, not because of ritual like before but because my peach fuzz has started growing thick and black like pubic hair, and that was the first time i ever shaved my face properly and still i do not care because i am one thing: palestinian. and my hands are literally changing shape, i look down at my fingernails, they were never this wide, my knuckles are like paperweights now and still i do not care, and my voice is cracking like it's slipping right out of my throat and still i do not care. i am just one thing: palestinian.

when i went back to ḥiṭṭīn, where my grandad is from, it had been demolished. i have written this landscape so many times, i don't have it in me to do it again. i just want to ask 'what do we leave behind when we leave?' ḥiṭṭīn looked like dust. it was not sand, it was rock flour. after leaving my fingers felt gritty. i wanted to step into a hot shower and scrub the backs of my ears.

dust bunnies and stray hairs loiter around the metal legs of my writing desk. on twitter today someone posted something like 'respect to the tboys who transitioned for no other reason than to be acceptably gross'. my skin gets terrible if i go one day without cleanser and i used to only wash my hair once a fortnight but now it greases over far too quickly for that to still be my routine.

i took a point-and-shoot and a DSLR and a polaroid with me on that long trip to mexico and only used one camera once for half a day and that's it. back in my bedroom a month later i blu-tacked the photos to my closet doors. in bed in the dark i would look into the 4 × 6 rectangles stuck on the closet and try to remember what each photo was of. i don't sleep with my curtains closed but still it is too dark to tell.

according to islam you can't sin in your sleep so anything you do while sleeping doesn't count which means that when i fall asleep i exist only in the dreamscape, my body doesn't exist. except once when i went to sleep with scissors on my bedside table and woke up with a thick bit of my hair missing.

i stole my dad's theory on heaven and hell and improved it. i believe that heaven and hell are not places we go to but we do go somewhere. when we die our spirit splits up into all the experiences we've ever had. and these little bits of spirit settle in the geographies they happened in. in bed in the dark i try to remember my life and where it will split up into after it's over.

my mum is upset with me today because 'you say you're anti-patriarchy but you and your sister only ever talk and write about being palestinian. what about lebanon? what about me?' and i say back 'we're palestinian right now because palestine needs us', 'and when the explosion happened last august i was from beirut and i was only writing about beirut', and even though what i say is true, still she is right and still i feel bad.

in her essay 'the terror of total dasein' hito steyerl talks about *junk-time* which is when you split the body up into proxy-bodies and exist on multiple planes at the same time. so me having twitter instagram and facebook profiles is me existing in junk-time. and me whatsapping my parents 'saba7o kifkoun?' is me existing in junk-time. and i think about what happens when i facetime my friend seneca in los angeles, and what happens is that my physical body becomes just an avatar and at that moment i exist only on the screen and nowhere else. and the same goes when i am on my couch scrolling twitter. or when i am asleep. or when i blink.

i'm googling 'junk-time' to fact-check this paragraph but i'm writing while the cloud company fastly is experiencing an outage so websites as big as amazon and cnn are down and i click the top result of my search and see '502 ERROR: The request could not be satisfied'.

my dad spends months building out our family tree on myheritage.com and does a good job at it, he's really proud of it, he's logged hundreds of us. he sends me and my siblings an email invite to collaborate on the project. my brother scrolls the email right down to the footer and sees 'myheritage ltd. (israel)', so the database my dad has been using to catalogue our dispersed bodies was created by the state that split us into pieces in the first place.

my body is in los angeles now on a facebook messenger video call with seneca in her westwood apartment. her lightbulbs look fluoro i hate fluoro bulbs. she is saying 'i'm not sure i believe in fate' and i am saying 'me neither' and we settle on the theory that fate is what happens in the world but it stops there. and what happens to you personally is not fate. and what you do with what happens to you personally is not fate.

i switch my T from gel to shots at the six-month mark and end up late to the palestine protest because my GP is always thirty minutes behind schedule and the tram that goes down commercial road is infrequent and inconsistent. i march three hours with a sore left side. i'm trying not to force my metaphors but this one feels too perfect.

i talk to my trans friend and he says 'has your writer's voice changed since you started transitioning?' and what i think is 'i want my readers to feel like they're on an unsuccessful dumpster dive' but what i say is 'yes it's dirtier'.

i am two drafts into this essay right now and reading back on every single line like 'this is too neat, why did i write it like this?'

once my dad is finished scanning all the pictures he puts them in the recycling bin.

on my third draft i go back and change every phrase like 'do not' and 'cannot' into a contraction because that feels dirtier. on the fourth draft i change some of the contractions back because i like the inconsistency.

my mum's telling me about a dream she had last night where she looks down and she's accidentally cut off like four inches from a chunk of her hair but it's not her hair it's actually the hair of a little girl who's two years old and she's saying 'it's okay', 'i don't really care', 'i didn't need it, did you?' losing hair and teeth in dreams is a bad thing according to islam according to my mum. she's sitting up in bed and telling me about this dream and plaiting her hair into two braids and when she's done she looks six years old.

broken glass. a bottle that dropped and shards everywhere. i make the person who dropped the bottle clean it up and they do a poor job of it. so i go back after them and pick up the large pieces of glass, collecting them onto a paper tray balanced on my palm conscious of how flimsy the paper is, and of the wind.

on new year's day at eight in the morning we're driving to the airport and i'm having a bad comedown on an empty stomach. i vomit onto the M1. my body is on the M1.

i walk into the bathroom one morning and look at my feet and scattered on the tiles are twenty or thirty scraggles of black hair, they are not mine, i leave them there.

i dream i'm holding a golden point-and-shoot camera above the water as waves slush at my neck. my feet sink into sand. i am not nervous about the camera i am nervous about the film getting wet and ruined before i have the chance to develop it.

i don't take my weekly transition selfies because i'm too tired in the morning, i forget during the day, and i don't like the light of the evening.

i got my period in jerusalem in the morning. bloody fingers and burning skin washing a silicone cup under a running faucet. a faucet i have set to the hottest it can be. my body is in jerusalem now because i bled there. when i die my spirit will go to the galilee because my ancestors bled there. when i die i want my body to go somewhere near the sea even though i don't like the wind.

my friend will goes to the grey cairns of camster in january, it is a tomb in scotland and none of the tourism websites say anything about it being haunted but will steps into the tomb and immediately gets a blood nose. and they turn to look back at the entryway and their partner is standing with the light behind her saying 'let's get out of here'. i don't have an anecdote of my own so i have to use this one. i have to write an example of our bodies never truly going away. and then they make other bodies bleed too.

when i was in texas my bedroom living room and kitchen all had white lightbulbs screwed into the ceiling so i bought three soft lamps and lots of tealights and used them for the year. the bathtub was disgusting it collected grot like a hobby. i once washed a red puffer jacket from an op-shop in that bathtub the water turned brown it smelled like piss. my partner wanted to get me yellow lightbulbs for christmas but didn't 'because you're only here for five more months' and they were right. when i packed up in may i tried to leave none of me behind. but i didn't scrub the bathtub or the toilet and i didn't mop the floors.

we're around the dinner table and my mum has made three vegetarian dishes all high in iron because my sister was just diagnosed anaemic and her blood is weak. my dad asks what to do about the family tree. he says 'but isn't it kind of cool that we're using their own software against them?' and my sister and i say 'no' because she doesn't want to give them our bodies i was never okay with him digitising our family because how many copies of us need to exist?

my parents leave in two weeks and i will live alone again. after i shower i comb my hair and it comes out in thickets. this is the full dose of testosterone. my sink takes longer to drain i need to stop tapping the fallout into the bowl.

after the palestine rally we sit in my brother's living room to look at ourselves through home movies. i am too scared to see myself but we are optimising family time before my parents start existing only in my iphone. the videos haven't started yet and already i am slamming down the stairs and closing the bathroom door behind me curling onto the white tiles and dribbling onto them crying breathy and violent and sore.

Island Bodies

Frankey Chung-Kok-Lun

Within you live the voices of stardust, the echoes of your body on the planet and the stories of which you are an intrinsic element. The same lenses through which you examine your memories shape your relationship with your environment; they trigger what only deep reflection can provide. It's all alive, from the trees to the voices to the rocks – all matter.

Claudia Rankine
Beth Loffreda

In the way that *white writers often begin from a place where transcendence is a given*, so too have *Homo sapiens* crafted a worldview in which they have the ability *to inhabit all, to address all*, without sufficient consideration as to why. It is evident in their invisible structures such as the prisons of race and class. The humanist means well; they speak of human rights, the importance of people whose lives are at stake. You see how factions of *Homo sapiens* have attempted to reconstruct the value of matter – of what 'matters' – for who could speak to the rights of extinct life forms, of trees, of rocks? Who could ever suggest that *Homo sapiens* find equals in *matter*?

engaging in knowledge is an unending journey as you become a *part of that nature which [you] seek to understand*

Karen Barad

In this quest for meaning, you turn to Claudia Rankine and Beth Loffreda. They speak of turning within – of writing to one's interior landscape. You encounter the limits of the imagination and take it upon yourself to expand those frontiers. Confronting the fallacy of *Homo sapiens* as centre, you expose modes of discrimination against non-human matter.

As you face the realities of our impact on this planet, you realise this path is not easy. You begin to see, with your eyes and mind, how our imaginations are not entirely our own, but rather carved by the structures of the collective *Homo sapiens*: far too white, far too centred, far too Othering. And so you decide not to restrict yourself to words, the language constructed by your species. You widen your horizons to take in the matter of your world – the animals and the rocks. You proceed, humbly.

Engaging in the difficulty

history is not an act of the imagination. [it] is the condition from which [you] start

Claudia Rankine
Beth Loffreda

From the introduction of your *Homo sapiens* body into this world, you were nourished by the currents of Springvale, Clayton, Beau Bassin, Roche Bois, Bambous and Port Louis. You bathed in your parents' Mauritian Creole, the establishment's Australian English, the bureaucracy's Mauritian French and your grandparents' Hakka Chinese. In this ocean, the words blended in their alphabet soup:

Baneing, ki kalite, sa? Drol, no?[1] Gerunds melted into African verbs.

A few million years before or after the first gorilla was born on Earth – the science is always shifting – Moris ('Mauritius' in English, 'Île Maurice' in French) erupted from the insides of this planet. Today, the fresh ground is eight to nine million years old; specks of the ocean floor inhabit the alveoli of your lungs, the recesses of your blood vessels, holding onto their stories. Before *Homo sapiens*, Moris lay beneath the stars with a blanket of forests, once inhabited by many.

In Moris, as your body stretched further and higher, you learned of the dodo (*Raphus cucullatus*), as embodied in a plush toy – cute, cuddly, mythical, something you took to bed each night. That toy reflected the European distortion of the bird: overfed, caricatured by taxidermy. You later learn it is a falsehood.

Number of dodos that ever lived: ?

What *Homo sapiens* today know about the dodo, including its appearance, is limited by a lack of reliable sources. Accounts speak of a greyish-brown plumage and yellowish feet. Our closest insight into the dodo's DNA is provided by Nicobar pigeons (*Caloenas nicobarica*), which live across islands thousands of kilometres to the east; their plumage appears to contain all the colours of the universe. Most of our deduced dodo knowledge stems from specimens collected at Mare aux Songes, a lagerstätte in the island's

---

1 Mauritian Creole. There is no direct English translation, especially with the words *kalite* and *drol*. The general vibe is: 'Bathing, what kind of nonsense is that? Strange, isn't it?' *Bane* is literally 'to bathe'; recast as a gerund, it implies the action 'bathing'. *Kalite* means 'quality'; *drol*, 'queer'. It is a common Mauritian reaction to question something that one admires; see also, 'Would you look at that!'

south. Today, the swamp is visible from a human hotel, albeit covered in agricultural land.

It had been made clear to you that the bird no longer existed, but, as to what it looked and felt like, you were taught that *il n'y a pas de hors-texte*. Every presentation matters. Your conception of the dodo was informed by cartoons and wooden souvenirs in tourist markets. Your grasp of the dodo's last days is clouded by the accounts of colonisers who pillaged Moris of its florae and faunae. The sanctuary of an island is not always sacrosanct.

Jacques Derrida

She drew her head down against her body,
fluffed her feathers for warmth,
squinted in patient misery [...]
She didn't know it,
nor did anyone else,
but she was the only dodo on Earth.

David Quammen

With its small wings, the dodo was flightless; it also had a keen sense of smell due to the large olfactory bulb in its pointed beak. The bird flourished in the dry coastal areas of Moris' once-abundant forests of *Sideroxylon* and *Pandanus*, of which, now, less than two per cent remain. It fed off fallen fruits, digested with the help of swallowed rocks held in its stomach.[2] Over its lifetime, a dodo would have grown as tall as a bamboo stalk grows in a day, around a metre from the soil. The dodo, you think, enjoyed a quiet life before humans. Like *Homo sapiens*, the dodo crafted its home on the earth. You picture one waddling through your concrete apartment. An adult *Raphus cucullatus* weighed as much as a *Homo sapiens* toddler, at seventeen kilograms. Despite being

---

2 You draw a string figure using the 'stone eaters' of N. K. Jemisin's *Broken Earth* trilogy.

a fast runner, it didn't feel the need to run from us before it was too late.

wiped from existence by human influence;
not seeking restoration but getting on together
there were dodos before; there are no dodos after

You were first taught the dodo went extinct because it was hunted by the Portuguese in the sixteenth century. You learned this the same way you were taught by the late Eric Carle that caterpillars turn into cocoons that turn into butterflies. You were told by the Catholic education system that there is a hierarchy in which all other life is at the mercy of *Homo sapiens* – the so-called *Scala Naturae*, the Great Chain of Being.

Then you learned that, perhaps, the dodo's extinction was a consequence of Dutch hunting in the seventeenth century. The truth is uncertain because few at the time paid attention to the bird's disappearance. It was not until the nineteenth century that those *Homo sapiens* asserting authority over what counts as 'truth' conceded to Georges Cuvier's notion of *extinction*. By then, the bird was recognised as lost within decades of its 'discovery', lost in time. You pause to mourn.

Volkert Evertsz

We drove them together into one place
in such a manner that we could catch them
with our hands, and when we held
one of them by its leg, and that upon
this it made a great noise, the others
all [of] a sudden came running as fast as they could
to its assistance, and by which they were
caught and made prisoners also.

You know that if you take a scientific approach, you'll get closer to your parents' land and to the true reason for the dodo's extinction: environmental change. Indeed, the story of *Homo sapiens*' excessive alterations to the climate began long before you were born. You no longer need to imagine the impacts of global warming. You learn that it was humans' destruction of the dodo's forest habitat and their introduction of agricultural and domesticated animals that forced the dodo to compete for natural resources. Moris shares this fate with Madagascar and New Zealand, locations that saw the extinction of endemic flightless birds following human settlement.

To attribute the crime against the dodo to hunting is mere romanticism; it suggests an unavoidable evil. The idea: to hunt without repercussion is to survive. It is an escape from responsibility, perpetuating the fallacy of *Homo sapiens* as the apex of an imagined food chain. How long before Mauritian Creole itself goes extinct in the face of ever-encroaching English? Does Moris exist without the dodo's eradication? Do civilisations exist without extinction?

Sugar cane builds colonies, after all, and domesticated animals must feed on the land to feed these colonies. Colonisation is zero-sum: when those who hold power divide land between spaces for 'nature' and spaces for cultivation, they deny *all* nature.

You lean on Donna J. Haraway's 'string figures' to see the interconnectedness of it all – except you have connected the dodo to stone eaters to colonisation to civilisation to capitalism to tourism to, now, the *scene of great relational complexity*. You're trying. Donna J. Haraway

the language of nature defines culture

In Mauritian Creole, *dodo* is both a noun and a verb. When you go to bed, you *dodo* – which is to say, you sleep like a dodo. You role-play the bird's extinction through slumber, armed with the privilege of rising from the imagined death; the dodo does not share such privilege. This adaptation of the word serves to colonise its meaning among locals, reframing it as Mauritian culture. It is an affectionate term.

In English, bestial degradation is imbued in the phrase 'dumb (or dead) as a dodo'. The dodo inhabits both worlds: the duality of wildness and domesticity, free and stupid. Seeing no reason to fear us, it readily cohabited without realising that it was being taken advantage of. More recently, scientific analyses of dodo remains show that its brain size was equivalent to that of pigeons, which you know, via Haraway, are *competent agents*. You take a moment to consider what it would have been like *becoming-with* dodos as you do with pigeons.

Donna J. Haraway

dodo (n.):	dodo (v.):
1. *Raphus cucullatus*	1. to sleep
2. extinction	
3. stupid	

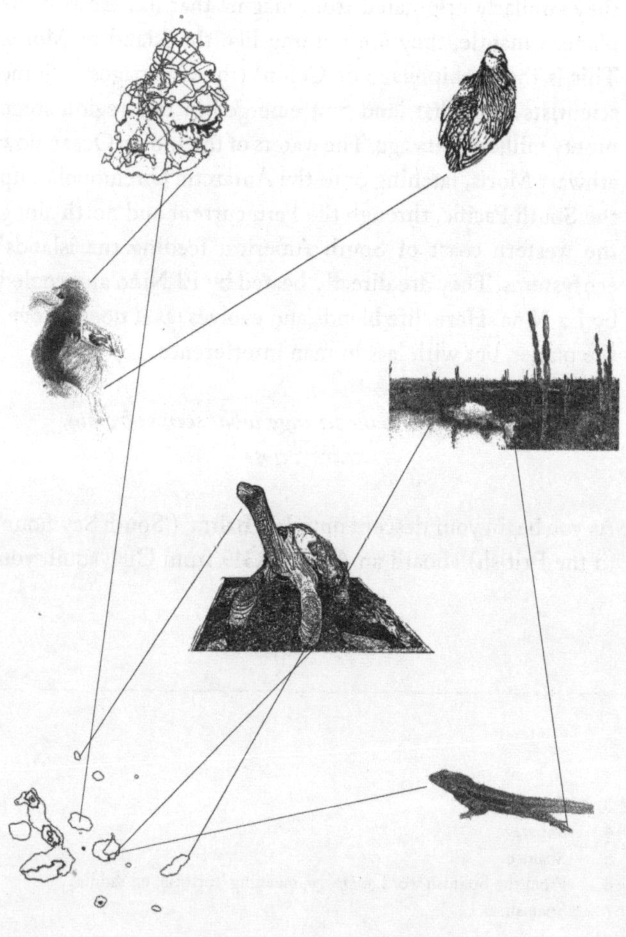

one ought to know to move past travelling to meet life;
sit with the web

becoming-with, not becoming, is the name of the game Donna J. Haraway

the eruption of a volcano
is a natural disaster
only if you name it so

Nine hundred and twenty-six kilometres west of Ikwayur[3]/ Ekuatur[4] ('Ecuador' in English), a chain of volcanic islands in the Pacific Ocean straddles Earth's equator. Although they similarly originated from magma that has escaped the planet's mantle, they are nothing like the island of Moris. This is the Archipiélago de Colón[5] (the Galápagos[6]). Some scientists posit that land first emerged in this region some ninety million years ago. The waters of the Indian Ocean flow athwart Moris, latching onto the Antarctic Circumpolar, up the South Pacific, through the Peru current and north along the western coast of South America, feeding the islands' ecosystems. They are directly heated by El Niño and cooled by La Niña. Here, life blends and evolves, as it does all over the planet, but with less human interference.

one might also make strange what seems obvious,
nearby, close Claudia Rankine
Beth Loffreda

As you begin your descent onto Isla Baltra[7] ('South Seymour' to the British) aboard an Airbus A319 from Guayaquil, you

---

3 Quechua.
4 Shuar.
5 Spanish.
6 From the Spanish word *galápago*, meaning 'tortoise' or 'saddle'.
7 Spanish.

catch the broken soil in a shade of red your eyes detect for the very first time. Here is where you have planned your epiphany. Here is where Peter Barry would say you attempt to *find yourself*. *Opuntia*, *Atriplex* and *Bursera graveolens* accent the arid landscape in sparse notes. These plants are prickly and sharp, afforded millennia to adapt to their surroundings.

our (*Homo sapiens*) proportional time
on this planet so far:
$\approx \frac{1}{20{,}000}$

Seated against the airport shuttle bus's window – made from fine grains of sand – you notice the water, a liminal shade between turquoise and teal. With increased gravity comes the slowing of time: you succumb to the pace of the tortoise. If the lifetime of this archipelago were represented as one rotation of Earth, the presence of *Homo sapiens* would be half a breath.

As you approach Isla Baltra, the bus's exhaust discharges toxic particles into the air. You alight. Your footsteps grind into the ancient rocks. You feel as if your trespass on these lands is absolved by virtue of the airport through which you have entered, but you are mistaken – there are no Jetstar Friday Fare Frenzy sales that will fly you here. Your participation as a tourist is complicit, so you had better make it worthwhile.

Serenella Iovino

always, one should be
adding new levels
to the place's mind

Walking along these islands, you role-play the emotions of early settlers in Moris – try to find the familiar in the strange. You are filled with the deepest awe. You trek through paths uncarved, untarred, unpaved. Volcanic boulders the size of igloos, yet untouched by *Homo sapiens*, offer waypoints and speak of the air that once was breathed by triceratopses and velociraptors.

You see the dodo in the Galápagos tortoises (*Chelonoidis*) and Galápagos sea lions (*Zalophus wollebaeki*) that approach you, not in fear, but in curiosity; they are fortunate enough not to have received designations of stupidity. You swim with adolescent sea lions amid vibrant coral reefs, for they are eager to play. The rainbow of fish dazzles. On long strolls, you tune in to the soundscape of quiet, spotted with the hint of rustling leaves as Galápagos lava lizards (*Microlophus albemarlensis*) scurry across your trajectory. The array of symbiotic lichen (*Usnea*), at first appearing stagnant, soon fill the landscape with colour.

nothing is stagnant, for
there is only the unfolding of life
form after life form, more or less
genealogically related, each
with a mix of characteristics

Greg Garrard

In an air-conditioned room within the Charles Darwin Research Station, built in Puerto Ayora on Isla Santa Cruz,[8] the taxidermied Galápagos tortoise Jorge (*Chelonoidis abingdonii*) is displayed in a humidity-controlled glass case. There aren't many visitors; right now, just you and Jorge inhabit the space. Scientists deduce that he was born in 1910 on Isla Pinta,[9] and he died on 24 June 2012 on Isla Santa Cruz. He is an *endling*, the last known member of his species.

In English, the tortoise is referred to as 'Lonesome George'. Much can be said of this moniker – a demonstration, of sorts, of the imbalance of power *Homo sapiens* holds in the construction of the world. It is the ultimate act of anthropomorphism, suggesting that Jorge exhibits the

---

8 Spanish.
9 Spanish.

human feeling of loneliness as the only survivor of his family. But he is lonesome for we have made him so.

John Berger

Jorge returns your gaze and, in that moment, you are aware of *both likeness and difference*. You, too, are lonesome on your journey through the Galápagos Islands: no travel companions, just the *Homo sapiens* you meet along the way, often in couples, families, tourist groups. You, too, in those moments, have searched for love, wandering through rocks in solitude, finding company in the trees and other-than-human life forms. Now, his agency has been taken from him one last time. Now, he *dodos* forever. Lifeless in a glass cage. Unlike false representations of dodos in museums, Jorge is re-presented for your enlightenment. Then again, he has seen many others like you, coming to stare at his filled corpse, day after day.

For some species of reptile, a hatchling's sex is determined by incubation conditions. This is known as temperature-dependent sex determination, and Galápagos tortoises exhibit this phenomenon. At higher temperatures, the eggs are more likely to hatch as females. At even higher temperatures, the embryos die during early development. As the global climate continues to warm, the existence of future Jorges becomes uncertain.

You sit with the weight of Jorge's demise. Just as the home of the dodo was decimated by introduced animals, so too was Jorge's diet of plant matter on Isla Pinta devastated by the introduction of goats. His kin were readily hunted (like Jorge, they moved at the pace of a rolling rock) – easy prey, as *Homo sapiens* prefers it. After realising our impact on his home's vegetation, modern humans quickly took Jorge into captivity to try to reverse the harm, to find him a mate to save his species. Their efforts were in vain. Was this privilege or misfortune?

held within the interior landscape of Lonesome George:
countless memories
a desire for love
a full life

You linger on Jorge's filled corpse, at his coarse reptilian skin. You catch your face reflected on the glass. Would it have mattered if he, too, could recognise himself in a reflection? You think of the sea turtles and sea lions you swam with just a few kilometres from this research station; who else have they swum with? Will they remember you?

but the epiphany never ends

you are always becoming

the disentangling and harnessing
of these things
is the writer's endless and unfinishable
but not fruitless task.

Claudia Rankine
Beth Loffreda

bringing close that which is so far away

You continue to develop your understanding of your relationship with your environments, illuminating new paths. In writing this essay, you have made your own truth. You realise that you are nature: you are the voices of stardust, the echoes of yourself on the planet. You are provoked to find equals in matter. You are the dodo; you are Jorge. You are Mauritius; you are the Galápagos Islands. You are nothing and you are everything. You continue until your *own sense of authority* is *undermined*. Your journey is just beginning.

Claudia Rankine
Beth Loffreda

Understand, and understand: and understand again.

Jordie Albiston

The 'string figure' image was inspired by Nasser Mufti's 'Multispecies Cat's Cradle' (2011) and uses manipulated personal photos and the following open-source images:

Friedel, Tom, 'Nicobar Pigeon', BirdPhotos.com, 16 October 2009, https://www.birdphotos.com/photos/index.php?q=gallery&g2_itemId=37265

Map of the Galápagos Islands, Google, accessed 28 May 2021, https://goo.gl/maps/xroJKsb2gLZ6xn419

Map of Mauritius, Google, accessed 28 May 2021, https://goo.gl/maps/XEcWJ4KapW3BN7LJ9

André Dao
is a writer working on unceded Wurundjeri Woi Wurrung land. His debut novel *Anam* will be published in 2023.

Barry Corr
is of Bundjalung descent living on Boorooberongal Country. As a student, he participated in the so-called Freedom Ride. Barry finished his teaching career specialising in Aboriginal education. Since his retirement, his writing has increasingly focused on the failure of settler societies to acknowledge and atone for the past.

Brandon K. Liew
is a doctoral researcher at the University of Melbourne with an interest in Malaysian literary history, cultural policy and the global novel. His recent publications include poetry in the anthology *Malaysian Millennial Voices* and the peer-reviewed article 'The Unquiet Dreams of Lesser Writers'.

Elizabeth Flux
is a freelance writer and editor-at-large for the UNESCO Melbourne City of Literature Office. Her nonfiction work includes essays, interviews and feature articles, and her fiction has been widely published, including in *New Australian Fiction 2020*, *Collisions*, *Best Australian Stories* and *The Big Issue Fiction Edition*.

Frankey Chung-Kok-Lun
is a writer with the privilege of calling Naarm (Melbourne) home. He holds Commerce and Law degrees from the University of Melbourne and is currently engaged in a Master of Creative Writing, Editing and Publishing. His writing pursuits include eco-focused literature, theatre and creative non-fiction.

grace ugamay dulawan
is a writer of Ifugao and Ilocano descent. She lives and works on unceded Gadigal land.

Hannah Wu
is a writer and musician from Aotearoa, studying on unceded Wurundjeri Woi Wurrung land. Her work has been published or is forthcoming with *Cordite*, *un Magazine*, *Island Island* for Bus Projects, SEVENTH Gallery, *Liminal*, *Yale Art History Journal*, Enjoy Contemporary Art Space, *Disclaimer* and others.

Hasib Hourani
lives and works on unceded Wurundjeri Woi Wurrung Country. He is a 2020 Wheeler Centre Next Chapter recipient and is completing his debut book of poetry on suffocation and the occupation of Palestine. You can find his work in *Meanjin*, *Overland* and *Going Down Swinging*, among others.

Hassan Abul
is an interdisciplinary artist, writer and editor living in Naarm (Melbourne) on unceded Boon Wurrung and Wurundjeri Woi Wurrung lands. In 2021, he won the inaugural *Liminal* & Pantera Press Nonfiction Prize. His areas of interest are desire, automythologies, how we construct others and how we relate to them, and investigations into 'culture'. His work has been published by *The Lifted Brow*, *Liminal* and *Subbed In / Ibis House*, among others.

Jon Tjhia
is a radio maker, musician, artist and writer from Naarm (Melbourne). His writing has been published by *un Magazine*, *Liminal*, *Going Down Swinging*, *The Lifted Brow*, the Barbican Centre and the Institute of Modern Art.

Kasumi Borczyk
is a writer whose work has appeared widely both in print and online. Find out more at https://kasumiborczyk.com

Lou Garcia-Dolnik
is a poet of Ilocano descent working on unceded Gadigal land, and an alumnus of the Banff Centre's Emerging Writers Intensive. Their writing has been awarded second prize in *Overland*'s Judith Wright Poetry Prize and an Academy of American Poets University Prize, and has been shortlisted for the Blake Poetry Prize and Val Vallis Award.

Lucia Tường Vy Nguyễn
is a Vietnamese Australian writer exploring the intersection of South-East Asian folklore, ludic violence and global technoculture. She is invigorated by the opportunity to play and dream within, around or even outside capitalist structures of 'work'.

Lur Alghurabi
is an Iraqi and Australian writer, poet and playwright. She is a winner of the AM Heath Prize for Prose and the Scribe Nonfiction Prize, and a shortlistee for the Deborah Cass Prize. Lur holds a Master's in Creative Writing from Oxford University and is currently working on her first book of personal essays.

Mykaela Saunders
is a Koori/Goori and Lebanese writer, teacher, community researcher and the editor of *This All Come Back Now* (UQP), the world's first anthology of blackfella speculative fiction. Mykaela is a 2021 Wheeler Centre Next Chapter recipient, and has won prizes for fiction, poetry, life writing and research.

Ouyang Yu

came to Australia in 1991 and has since published 139 books of poetry, fiction, non-fiction, literary translation and criticism in English and Chinese, including his award-winning novels, *The Eastern Slope Chronicle* (2002) and *The English Class* (2010); his collection of poetry, *Songs of the Last Chinese Poet* (1997); and his poetry book *Terminally Poetic* (2020), which won the 2021 Judith Wright Calanthe Award. He was shortlisted for the 2021 Melbourne Prize for Literature – Writer's Prize.

Ruby-Rose Pivet-Marsh

is a writer, producer and arts worker living and creating on unceded Wurundjeri Woi Wurrung land. Ruby is currently the artistic director and co-CEO of Emerging Writers' Festival and is a co-founder of the Latinx arts collective Yo Soy.

Ryan Gustafsson

is a writer, researcher and podcaster living and working on Wurundjeri Woi Wurrung land. Their writing explores themes including knowledge, embodiment and loss, and has appeared in *Island* magazine, *Bent Street* and *Peril* magazine. Their research focuses on phenomenological approaches to Korean overseas adoption, diaspora and trans studies.

Suneeta Peres da Costa

is based on unceded Gadigal Country and writes fiction, non-fiction, plays and poetry. Her latest book, *Saudade*, about colonial legacies and the Goan diaspora in Portuguese Angola, was shortlisted for the 2019 Prime Minister's Literary Awards, the 2020 Adelaide Festival Awards for Literature, and a finalist in the 2020 Tournament of Books (USA).

Veronica Gorrie

is a proud Gunai/Kurnai woman, a writer and the author of the award-winning memoir *Black and Blue* (2021). She is passionate about and skilled in non-fiction memoir, and is extending her writing practice to film and theatre.

Leah Jing McIntosh
is *Liminal*'s founding editor. She is a literary critic and essayist, currently completing her PhD at the University of Melbourne. She researches possibilities of diasporic self-representation, and the fracturing of literary form.

Adolfo Aranjuez
is an editor, writer, speaker and dancer, and *Liminal*'s publication editor. He has worked across periodical and book publishing for fifteen years, with past tenures as editor-in-chief of *Metro* and *Archer*, and his essays, criticism and poetry have been published widely, including in *Meanjin*, *Right Now*, *Screen Education*, *The Manila Review* and *Cordite*. http://adolfoaranjuez.com

Annie Luo
is a multi-disciplinary designer and art director based in Naarm (Melbourne), with a predominant focus on visual identity, digital design and print media.

About *Liminal*

Liminal is an anti-racist literary project, publishing critically acclaimed art, writing, criticism and conversations. *Liminal*'s print and digital projects comprise brilliant and expansive work by minoritised artists, inviting new conceptions of excellence while intervening in the structures of white supremacy. Envisioning a more equitable arts sector, *Liminal* creates thrilling new spaces and opportunities for First Nations writers and writers of colour, running national literary prizes, international writing workshops, editorial mentorships, writing fellowships and literary events. Founded by Leah Jing McIntosh in late 2016, *Liminal* is made by a dedicated team located around the continent.

Find art, writing, conversations and more at www.liminalmag.com

Thank You

To this collection's writers, we are immensely grateful for your work – this book would not exist without you. To Brian Castro, Maddee Clark and Shakira Hussein, for your passion and sensitivity in judging the inaugural *Liminal* & Pantera Press Nonfiction Prize. To Lex Hirst, Alison Green, Kate Cuthbert and the team at Pantera Press, as well as Lucy Hamilton and the team at Writers Victoria, for supporting us tremendously in bringing this prize-turned-book into the world. And to the *Liminal* editorial team – Cher Tan, Adalya Nash Hussein and Danny Silva Soberano – for helping us to create another stellar publication.

Liminal is able to do the work we do in no small part because of our community, and we hope that this collection goes some way towards reciprocating that generosity.

